CD-ROSA 887

Fair Value for
Financial Reporting

Fair Value for Financial Reporting

Meeting the New FASB Requirements

ALFRED M. KING

WILEY

John Wiley & Sons, Inc.

657.3
K52f

This book is printed on acid-free paper. ∞

Copyright © 2006 by John Wiley & Sons. All rights reserved.

Published by John Wiley & Sons, Inc., Hoboken, New Jersey.

Published simultaneously in Canada.

No part of this publication may be reproduced, stored in a retrieval system, or
transmitted in any form or by any means, electronic, mechanical, photocopying,
recording, scanning, or otherwise, except as permitted under Section 107 or
108 of the 1976 United States Copyright Act, without either the prior written
permission of the Publisher, or authorization through payment of the appropriate
per-copy fee to the Copyright Clearance Center, Inc., 222 Rosewood Drive, Danvers,
MA 01923, 978-750-8400, fax 978-646-8600, or on the web at www.copyright.com.
Requests to the Publisher for permission should be addressed to the Permissions
Department, John Wiley & Sons, Inc., 111 River Street, Hoboken, NJ 07030,
201-748-6011, fax 201-748-6008, or online at http://www.wiley.com/go/permissions.

Limit of Liability/Disclaimer of Warranty: While the publisher and author have
used their best efforts in preparing this book, they make no representations or
warranties with respect to the accuracy or completeness of the contents of this book
and specifically disclaim any implied warranties of merchantability or fitness for a
particular purpose. No warranty may be created or extended by sales representatives
or written sales materials. The advice and strategies contained herein may not be
suitable for your situation. You should consult with a professional where appropriate.
Neither the publisher nor author shall be liable for any loss of profit or any other
commercial damages, including but not limited to special, incidental, consequential,
or other damages.

For general information on our other products and services, or technical support,
please contact our Customer Care Department within the United States at
800-762-2974, outside the United States at 317-572-3993 or fax 317-572-4002.

Wiley also publishes its books in a variety of electronic formats. Some content that
appears in print may not be available in electronic books.

For more information about Wiley products, visit our Web site at http://www.wiley.com.

Library of Congress Cataloging-in-Publication Data:

King, Alfred M.
  Fair value for financial reporting : meeting the new FASB requirements /
Alfred M. King.
     p.   cm.
  Includes index.
  ISBN-13: 978-0-471-77184-5 (cloth)
  ISBN-10: 0-471-77184-8 (cloth)
     1. Financial statements.   2. Fair value—Accounting.   3. Financial
  Accounting Standards Board.   I. Title.
  HF5681.B2K475   2006
  657'.3—dc22

                                                                        2005032777

Printed in the United States of America

10 9 8 7 6 5 4 3 2 1

To

MARY JANE KING

Thanks for your total support.

FINANCIAL REPORTING COMMITTEE
INSTITUTE OF MANAGEMENT ACCOUNTANTS

I hope I have contributed as much as I have received.

APPRAISAL ISSUES TASK FORCE

AITF members are the valuation profession's leadership.

University Libraries
Carnegie Mellon University
Pittsburgh, PA 15213-3890

Contents

Preface

We are in the midst of the greatest revolution in accounting and financial reporting since Pacioli wrote his treatise on double-entry bookkeeping in 1494. Until recently, accounting was based on the *cost* of assets acquired, and *income* was the difference between the cost and selling price of items exchanged or sold.

Over the past 30 years, the Financial Accounting Standards Board (FASB) in the United States and the International Accounting Standards Board (IASB) have been moving away from historical cost accounting and going toward Fair Value (FV) accounting. Although we have not yet arrived at 100% FV accounting, the trend is in that direction; it is only a matter of time until we will have to go to history books to read about historical cost accounting because it will no longer be taught to students.

In as few words as possible, FV accounting can be characterized by saying it involves having companies prepare their balance sheet on the basis of what assets are worth today, not what the assets cost when they were acquired. Thus, land that was bought at $1,000 per acre in 1970 would still show as $1,000 on a 2006 balance sheet under historical cost accounting. But if comparable land were worth $12,000 per acre today, if the land could be sold for that amount, then under FV accounting the balance sheet would show the higher figure. The difference between $1,000 and $12,000 ($11,000) would somehow be reflected as "Income" on the Profit and Loss statement, even if there was no transaction to validate the change in value.

For the past 110 years or so, there have been appraisers, valuation specialists whose professional ability revolves around being able to tell others what something is worth. What something is worth is usually the same as what someone would pay for the asset, what it could be sold for in a real-world transaction. But no matter how good the appraiser or the appraisal report, only when an asset is sold can its true value be determined. Nonetheless, it is impossible for all assets to be sold every year, so if the FASB and IASB want companies to disclose the FV of their

xiii

assets, valuation specialists must be called in to provide the required information.

This book is aimed at corporate financial managers who are responsible to shareholders and creditors for presenting accurately and fairly the financial information about their business. To the extent that Generally Accepted Accounting Principles (GAAP) incorporate FV information—and that is the trend we see—it is and will continue to be necessary to utilize appraisal services. But once a company has prepared its financial statements, including the use of FV information, one further step must still be completed. The statements must be reviewed and in effect approved by independent auditors.

So this book is written for both financial managers as well as auditors; both groups are having to accept ever-greater responsibility for determining and reporting Fair Value. Our audience is not other appraisers, who already know most of what is written here. Likewise, this is not a do-it-yourself book. We do not expect a corporate controller to be able to read this book and then determine his own FV disclosures.

What we hope to accomplish is an understanding by corporate financial officers and, by extension, independent auditors, of what a valuation specialist does and how it is done. The requirements for FV disclosures are substantial, and growing. Although we cannot cover every single GAAP Fair Value reporting requirement, we do provide information about how appraisers actually do their work, the types of information they need, and the assumptions they have to make.

The primary focus is on the FV requirements of business combinations, mergers and acquisitions (M&A), because this is where the FASB and IASB have put into place the most stringent FV reporting. Just as a single example, companies are now required to develop a value for liabilities assumed when they buy another company. If that target company has outstanding lawsuits against it, the buyer must determine the FV of the potential liability if the lawsuit were to be lost. This involves an estimate of the probability of loss and an estimate of the magnitude of the potential loss. Right now, this is only required for M&A transactions, but the IASB is proposing to extend the concept to *all* contingent liabilities irrespective of whether a business combination is likely or not. Changes of this magnitude led me to state at the beginning of this Preface that we are in the midst of an accounting and reporting revolution.

The reader will probably conclude that appraisers may benefit financially from this revolution, but we are not necessarily in favor of it. Our professional experience teaches us that a lot of assumptions go into any valuation. These assumptions deal with the future. Neither appraisers nor accountants have any particular expertise in forecasting the future, but neither does anyone else.

In order to prepare a valuation, we may have to make assumptions about future exchange rates, future taxes, the outlook for energy and raw material costs, changes in technology, as well as changes in consumer sentiment and taste. How accurate can *anyone* be with that assignment? It is easy to see why appraisers are most skeptical about FV accounting—even as we perform the work for our clients.

The one thing we can be sure of is that after the fact, many of the values we have developed for FV accounting and reporting will turn out to be in error. After all, changes in tax rates affect cash flows, as do changes in energy availability, or any of the other variables. What must be kept in mind is that as long as an appraiser approaches his work objectively, does not "put his thumb on the scale," the valuation answers are correct for that time and place. Telling a client that the FV of land is $12,000 and it later is sold for only $10,000 does not invalidate the original valuation report. All it means is that either circumstances have changed (environmental problems were later discovered) or some of the good faith assumptions about the future of the economy (e.g., interest rates) turned out to be incorrect.

It is common for appraisers to state that "valuation is an art, not a science." What this means is that professional judgment is inherent in every valuation assignment. One cannot use a black box, inputting certain variables and having a determinate answer appear. Different appraisers will arrive at different answers for the same valuation assignment, although with comparable assumptions two different appraisers should come within 10% of each other, but not closer.

Using the previous answer, if I value the land at $12,000 and another appraiser says it is worth $11,000, it is difficult to say either is incorrect. By the same token, if one comes in at $12,000 and another at $16,000, it behooves the reader (or a judge if it is in court) to verify the assumptions each appraiser made about the future. What the reader of the two valuation reports will find is that the appraisers made different assumptions about economic conditions. Again, one set of assumptions is not correct and the other incorrect. At the end of the day, one must read an appraisal report and draw your own conclusions about the reasonableness of the assumptions, and hence the indication of value.

There are three basic purposes for which appraisers are hired. They usually involve:

1. Taxes, including income, gift and estate, and property

2. Buying and selling of assets, including M&A transactions, buy and sell agreements in a partnership, sale and leasebacks

3. Financial reporting

This book deals with only the last of these purposes. Although we comment tangentially on tax issues and business issues, the major thrust is complying with financial reporting requirements set forth by the FASB and the Securities and Exchange Commission (SEC), as reviewed by auditors and the Public Company Accounting Oversight Board (PCAOB). Even within this narrower framework, this book essentially disregards two major areas of interest to certain companies. We did not include a chapter on valuing financial instruments and derivatives. The accounting literature alone for SFAS 133 is approaching 1,000 pages, and virtually every page of that literature involves FV in one way or another. An entire book, albeit more narrowly focused, could be written on just the subject of the FV of financial instruments and derivatives. This is not that book.

Also, because the IASB is ahead of U.S. GAAP in moving to FV, and because of space limitations, we have concentrated on companies that have to comply with U.S. financial reporting requirements. The next edition of the book will give greater space to the international aspects of FV reporting, particularly as the IASB and FASB converge in the development of financial reporting requirements.

In addition to thanking my wife, who has supported me throughout the gestation of this book, I want to give full recognition to two groups of individuals who have provided invaluable background and information. For some 25 years, I have been a member of the Financial Reporting Committee of the Institute of Management Accountants (IMA). The IMA is unique in having members from academe, public accounting, and the preparer community. The Committee, for the entire time I have been associated with it, has diligently responded to every proposal from the FASB, most SEC pronouncements, and many IASB proposals.

Twenty-five years ago my knowledge of valuation was of little use to the Committee. Now, virtually every issue discussed has a valuation aspect. Sometimes I have persuaded my colleagues to adopt my position, sometimes they persuaded me to adjust my thinking, and at times we have had to agree to disagree. Nonetheless, the members of the IMA Committee have invariably been hard working and totally dedicated to the improvement of financial reporting. As a Committee, we have not always persuaded the FASB, SEC, or IASB of the correctness of our position, but when they have not listened to us, we feel that time is on our side as to the wisdom of our positions. Having input from such a diverse group of Committee members has given the IMA a degree of credibility that few other organizations achieve. I want to sincerely thank my fellow Committee members for the knowledge they have shared with me over the years.

Five years ago, as FV reporting took hold, there was significant disagreement among valuation practitioners, auditors, and the SEC as to how to develop appropriate FV answers. Just as one example, the valuation of customer relationships has proven controversial, as is discussed in Chapter 6. I approached the then Chief Accountant of the SEC and asked that if a group of appraisers could get together and mutually agree on certain procedures and assumptions, would the SEC go along with our recommendations?

We formed the Appraisal Issues Task Force (AITF) and modeled it after the FASB's Emerging Issues Task Force. The AITF meets quarterly, and currently some 40 valuation organizations are members. Meetings are attended by observers from the FASB, SEC, and PCAOB. The meetings allow an exchange of views with regulators, and among practitioners, discussions about best practice.

Unfortunately, certain circles commonly believe that appraisers will give you any answer you want. While the savings and loan scandal in the 1990s seemed to lend credence to that assumption, I can state categorically that appraisers from the major firms today are completely professional in their approach. We do not always see things the same way, and in fact there are different ways of arriving at FV, but I am not aware of any appraisers today who do not provide their best professional judgment. In today's litigious society, it would simply be too costly not to be independent, so we must be perceived as strictly independent. The AITF, and it members, fully live up to this standard.

April 2006   ALFRED M. KING
Spotsylvania, Virginia   Vice Chairman
                                                    Marshall & Stevens, Inc.
                                                    aking@marshall-stevens.com

CHAPTER 1

Impact of Fair Value on Earnings per Share

"**W**ill this transaction be accretive to earnings?" This is the first question appraisers are asked by financial and operating executives of companies undertaking a merger or business combination. That the question is important goes without saying. Many companies act as though they will live or die based on reported earnings, as calculated under current Generally Accepted Accounting Principles (GAAP). Most corporate executives have heard that virtually every academic finance specialist argues that reported earnings are irrelevant, and that it is cash flow that counts. For some reason, most of our clients are stubborn and continue to remain interested in earnings per share (EPS).

In this chapter we discuss this number-one priority of practicing corporate executives. This book was written to help companies that face increasingly complex financial reporting requirements and want to present the best possible picture to the investing public.

In later chapters we discuss how Fair Value (FV) is developed. We make an effort to help financial executives and auditors understand the many new Financial Accounting Standards Board (FASB) pronouncements that involve Fair Value. In this chapter we highlight how companies, their auditors, and appraisers can estimate in advance the impact of a specific transaction on future EPS. The *goal* is always to be accretive to earnings; this goal, however, is often not attainable. Factors affecting future earnings include both the price paid for the target company as well as the nature of the specific assets and liabilities of the acquired firm.

The FASB, at the time this book is being written, is contemplating rather substantial revisions to the accounting required for business combinations. The thrust of most of these changes to required GAAP is to increase the use, and therefore impact, of Fair Value.

FUNDAMENTALS OF SFAS 141R

Statement of Financial Accounting Standards (SFAS) 141, issued in 2001, provided the GAAP framework for business combinations. We assume a basic familiarity with those requirements, which called for the buyer to develop the Fair Values of each asset acquired, both tangible and intangible. Any difference between the sum of the identifiable assets and the purchase price plus assumed liabilities was called goodwill. Under SFAS 141—for reasons described in Chapters 5 and 6—goodwill did not have to be amortized, although it was subject to impairment testing. All other things being equal, corporate financial officers prefer more dollars of an acquisition to be assigned to goodwill and fewer dollars to assets that have to be depreciated or amortized.

This preference is perfectly understandable inasmuch as the lack of amortization of goodwill puts it in the same category as land, with no impact on current or future EPS. All other assets acquired do affect profit and loss (P&L), albeit the actual impact is a function of the amount assigned and the future life over which the depreciation or amortization is to be carried out.

For purposes of this chapter, we assume the simplest capital structure on the part of the acquiring company, so that changes in Net Income affect EPS on a direct basis; that is, a 10% reduction in reported earnings equals a 10% reduction in EPS. This way we do not worry about dilutive securities, options, convertible bonds, and so forth. Also, we assume that the consideration paid is in the acquirer's stock. At the end of the day, an all-cash payment probably has the same ultimate EPS impact, but cash payments involve either drawing down existing cash balances, or incurring debt, or both. The impact of foregone interest income, or future interest expense, only makes our analysis more complex —and the real topic is how FV is calculated and how subsequent amortization, if any, of the acquired assets affects reported earnings and EPS.

How does a business combination, or acquisition of another company, affect future earnings? In exchange for the shares issued to the sellers, the buyer now obtains additional assets. The value assigned to the acquired assets will equal the value given up through the issuance of the additional stock. In other words, the asset values must equal the additional net worth paid out.

The role of an appraiser is to take the purchase price paid and to allocate it to the FV of all the acquired assets. In case the FV of the assets is less than the purchase price of the company, the difference required to balance the equation is assigned to goodwill. In the rare case when the assets are worth more than the price paid for the business (referred to as a "bargain purchase"), the FASB is mandating that the excess be a credit to income in the next P&L.

The fundamental assumption of most acquirers is that a new acquisition will enhance EPS, either immediately or in the near future. Conceptually, there is little point to buying a company and having future EPS go down. Existing shareholders would be better off with the status quo than with a dilutive acquisition. Many consultants and academics argue that, after the fact, more than 50% of business combinations end up not meeting anticipated results. This may well be true, but we have never seen an acquisition that was planned, on day 1, to reduce EPS. Future plans sometimes do not work out, but nobody plans a business combination in the expectation of incurring a loss.

What managers want, and need, to know is quite specific. "If we go ahead with this transaction, and our operating performance is as planned, what will our EPS look like?" The need for this information is obvious, but the problems in arriving at the answer may not be so clear. In the next section, we go over the balance sheet section by section, showing how new Fair Values for the acquired assets are derived. We then show how those new (presumably higher) values flow through to net earnings and then EPS.

DEVELOPING FAIR VALUE IN A BUSINESS COMBINATION

Cash is virtually never the subject of valuation by appraisers. Auditors confirm bank balances and review any foreign currency translation adjustments, so there is no work for an appraiser.

Marketable securities presumably were being carried at FV on the books of the target, so no real change should be required. It is beyond the scope of this book to deal with the rare situations where a large block of securities might be illiquid or have a control premium.

Accounts receivable historically were simply carried forward to the buyer's books at the amounts recorded on the seller's General Ledger.

Most companies show all receivables on the General Ledger at the amount(s) billed to the customer, with an "allowance for uncollectible accounts" set aside, in one gross amount, to cover the inevitable shortfalls in future payments on the existing accounts. To review, companies then charge off specific uncollectible accounts as they occur. At the end of the period, the company then increases back up to a level the overall reserve by a charge to expense; they do this periodically by a single line entry to bad debt expense and a credit to the reserve.

Under the new GAAP promulgated in SFAS 141R, there will be a total change. The buyer, or more usually the appraisal specialist, will effectively have to value each significant receivable for specific collectability. Unlike previous practice, the independent auditors can no longer evaluate the receivables, because under independence rules they cannot audit their own work. So auditors will only review the receivable analysis, not participate in any way in performing the analysis. Inasmuch as auditors tend to look skeptically at a client doing its own valuation, if the receivables are at all material, it will probably be necessary to have an appraiser do the work.

As noted previously, after the valuation is completed, there will no longer be a reserve for uncollectible accounts. Rather, each receivable will be shown at its estimated FV, which essentially is going to be the best judgment as to the specific amount to be received from that specific receivable.

Inventories have historically been carried on a company's books at "the *lower* of cost or market" (locom). Because cost is almost always lower than market, this has meant that in an acquisition, most buyers simply carried forward the seller's cost. This required virtually no work, no review, and no impact on either the balance sheet or future income statement.

A careful review of prior rules on accounting for merger and acquisition (M&A) transactions would show that buyers were *supposed* to value acquired inventory at FV. In practice, this was rarely done, and as mentioned, book values were usually just carried forward.

Now, in SFAS 141R, the rules have been made explicit and auditors and the SEC are going to make sure that acquired inventories are valued at FV, not the seller's cost. Because inventory cost accounting varies widely among companies, just understanding the seller's cost accounting system is a serious issue that many buyers simply passed over.

The assumption was, "if the cost system was good enough for them, it is good enough for us." No longer is this assumption appropriate. Now buyers, or more likely their valuation specialists, will have to make an explicit determination of the FV of each inventory category (i.e., raw materials, work-in-process [WIP], and finished goods). We discuss the entire subject of the FV of inventories in Chapter 11.

For purposes of this chapter, FV of inventories is essentially the same as "net realizable value," which has been a standard for inventory valuation in certain circumstances. The book *Wiley GAAP 2005* has the following definition of Net Realizable Value (NRV): "The estimated selling price in the ordinary course of business less estimated costs of completion, holding and disposal."[1] The key point at this stage of the discussion is that NRV of inventory is almost always going to be *higher* than the seller's cost. Put a different way, SFAS 141R will require a step-up in the value of inventory placed on the buyer's books. The consequences of this is a short-term reduction in operating profit.

Property, Plant, and Equipment (PP&E) are a major asset for most manufacturing firms. For distribution and transportation firms, they are significant, whereas for retail and service businesses, they usually are not so important. Nonetheless, GAAP requires a revaluation of all PP&E for every transaction. Chapter 9 is devoted to this topic. The essential point is that the revaluation will effectively discard the existing book value, which is the resultant of original cost less depreciation to date. In addition to the new values assigned to the PP&E, the appraiser will also recommend new remaining lives.

This aspect of a valuation is perhaps the most difficult for a company to perform itself, and certainly one where auditors can only review the work of others. In a nutshell, appraisers perform two tests in valuing a piece of used production equipment. The first is to see what a comparable asset could be acquired for in the used equipment market. This is referred to as the market comparable approach to value and involves knowledge of dealers and auctions of production equipment. The second approach is to look at the cost of a new asset, of comparable productivity, and then depreciate that cost to allow for physical depreciation, reduce it further for functional obsolescence, and finally, if applicable, apply a penalty for economic problems. This is known as the cost approach to value. We discuss these approaches in much greater detail in Chapter 4. Only rarely do the two approaches provide identical answers,

so the role of the appraiser is to apply professional judgment in correlating the two approaches into one final determination of FV, as defined
by GAAP and the Internal Revenue Service (IRS).

By the way, because the courts have opined on "Fair Market Value"
almost without limit, there is general agreement as to the appropriate
standard of value for tax purposes. The FASB, however, consciously
chose to use a different term, "Fair Value," so as not to get caught up in
any legal wrangling. At the end of the day, however, Fair Value and Fair
Market Value are going to lead to the same answer except in some very
unusual situations.

Intangible assets with a definite life are a major focus of M&A deal
makers, auditors, and the SEC, as well as the Public Company Accounting Oversight Board (PCAOB). Valuing PP&E is quite straightforward.
You can go out on the shop floor, see the asset, and "kick the tires."
You can call a dealer who will tell you what he would pay to buy the
asset, and a different (higher) price that he would sell one to you. You
can get a quote from the manufacturer, and while the determination of
depreciation from all causes requires judgment, and cannot be obtained
on the Internet or in a book, nonetheless the possible range—from
top to bottom—is fairly narrow. In short, auditors can feel comfortable
reviewing an appraiser's working papers on the FV of PP&E.

This is not so with intangible assets. For GAAP there are two classes
of intangible assets: those with a definite life and those with an indefinite life. The distinction is critical for calculation of EPS.

Definite life intangible assets must be written off or amortized over
the remaining life, so if a covenant not to compete has a three-year life,
the buyer must write off one-third of the value each year for that three-
year period. Depending on the amount at which the covenant is valued,
this write-off each year is going to have an adverse effect on reported
earnings and hence EPS. So, all other things being equal, which they
seldom are, most corporate financial managers prefer that as much as
possible of the purchase price be assigned to intangible assets with an
indefinite life.

The major intangible assets with a definite life that we find in most
acquisitions are as follows, and we briefly describe the valuation procedures for each later in this chapter in its own respective section:

- Patents and technology
- In-process R&D

- Customer relationships
- Software

Indefinite lived intangible assets, for reasons that appeared valid to FASB, do *not* get written off or amortized each year. As with land, they stay on the books indefinitely. The "no free lunch" principle works here, and buyers are required to test any such indefinite lived assets for impairment at least once a year. The theory, which is sound, says that if you are not amortizing a value down to a nominal amount, or even to zero, then you must assure yourself, and others, that it still has at least as much value as it had on day 1 when you bought it.

There are two major examples of indefinite life intangible assets that often crop up:

1. Trade names, such as P&G's Tide®
2. Government-granted licenses such as for a radio or TV station

The lack of amortization of either of these items makes sense. Taking trade names first, using P&G's Tide detergent as an example, as long as P&G keeps advertising Tide, the brand is going to retain its value and probably increase over time. Although companies cannot write up any such increase, by the same token they are not required to amortize a brand value that has every expectation of being continued in use. Similarly, history suggests that virtually all TV licenses are renewed at the end of the current agreement. Thus it would not make sense to write down their value of the asset if it will continue in use and probably increase in value.

Contingent liabilities, defined as something that could happen in the future, but has not happened yet, represent a new and previously untried attempt by the FASB to enlarge the role of Fair Value accounting. Until now, SFAS 5, dealing with uncertainties, effectively required companies to book a liability only when there was a greater than 50% chance of the event occurring. In other words, if someone sued you and your attorney said it was more likely than not that you would prevail (i.e., not lose), then your only duty was to disclose the event in the footnotes to the financial statements. There was no obligation to—and in fact you could not—set up a liability for some such potential future problem.

The SEC, in practice, has gone after companies for setting up liability reserves in advance, and then drawing them down at some point in the future, allegedly to enhance reported income. This technique has even been given a name, cookie-jar accounting; the principle is that in good times companies hide income in reserves, and then when they need something to meet a predetermined goal, they dip into the cookie jar.

Under the new accounting rules in SFAS 141R, the tables will be totally reversed. Now acquirers will have to value *all* liabilities, whether they are likely to require a future cash flow or not. As will be discussed in Chapter 7, a billion-dollar lawsuit filed as a class action may have only a 1% chance of being successful, but the buyer will have to recognize even the remote possibility of paying out $10 million by setting up a liability on the balance sheet for that amount. Disregarding the difficulty of even trying to estimate the probability of a future loss, perhaps by getting the General Counsel to hazard a guess and provide such a probability, the subsequent accounting is going to cause problems.

Under the new rules, assuming the foregoing fact pattern, if the lawsuit is settled with no payment to the plaintiffs, the company (at the date of settlement) will reverse the liability accrual and recognize $10 million in income. Conversely, assuming the worst outcome, if the plaintiffs succeed and the suit is settled for, say, $100 million, the company must charge an additional $90 million, which when added to the previously accrued $10 million equals the amount of the payment.

It does not take a Warren Buffet to realize that companies, in the case of contingent liabilities, are going to ask the appraisal specialist to support the *largest* possible amount going on the balance sheet. The offset, on day 1, is going to be to nondepreciable goodwill, so there is no adverse effect on EPS in having a large liability shown. Then, as and when the contingency is resolved, there will be a very real likelihood of a pickup in income, not a charge to expense. Meanwhile, barring some untoward event, the goodwill will continue to sit on the asset side of the balance sheet with no impact on reported earnings or EPS, irrespective of the outcome of the contingency.

As many observers have pointed out before, if something is too good to be true, it probably is. The FASB was totally aware of the possibility of abuse in its new contingency accounting. The response they give— and it is likely correct—is that companies have to try and do things correctly, and that the independent auditor is going to review the accrual calculation extremely closely. Finally, for public companies, the SEC will use the benefit of hindsight, in case of a large pickup in income, to question the original accrual calculations; in turn, this puts pressure on the auditors, who are largely responsive to SEC pressures. So companies will not have a blank check to produce future reported income, but certainly there will be great pressure to support a conservative position going in, always assuming that the worst can happen.

One more point about this accrual for future contingencies: Many observers have pointed out that if a company has one large lawsuit, and puts a large reserve on its books, that this may be a roadmap for the plaintiff, essentially conceding that there will be a loss. In turn this may strengthen the resolve of the plaintiff not to settle. The only answer to this conundrum is that most companies have many lawsuits in the normal course of business, and as a buyer they only put up a single number for lawsuit contingencies, thus disguising the impact of any one case. That, at least, is the theory.

Goodwill is the residual amount that results from adding up the FV of all the other assets (i.e., working capital, PP&E, and intangible assets) and subtracting that total from the purchase price of the target company plus assumed liabilities. Under current GAAP goodwill, like indefinite lived intangible assets, is *not* amortized. A moment's thought is all it takes to realize that if one wants to maximize the accretive value of a business combination, the way to do this is to put as much as possible of the purchase price into goodwill.

The drafters of current GAAP were totally aware of this potential, as have been the SEC and auditing firms. The SEC hates to see a lot of goodwill result from an acquisition. The SEC, and the accounting firms that are responsive to SEC wishes, probe relentlessly to ensure that companies have allocated the maximum amounts to amortizable assets and the minimum to indefinite lived assets and goodwill. In short, in virtually every transaction, there is tension between the CFO and the company on one side and the SEC and the auditing firm on the other. In the middle is the valuation firm.

As appraisers we want to be responsive to our clients, who are the companies, but at the same time our valuation report has to withstand detailed scrutiny by the auditors, and at times by the SEC. In Chapter 13 we discuss the review of valuations by auditors. Suffice it to say, for the purpose of trying to maximize EPS, companies and their auditors are often in opposition to each other on this vital point.

HOW AN APPRAISER LOOKS AT INTANGIBLES

The key to estimating the impact of an acquisition on EPS usually lies in the intangible asset analysis. Step 1 is to identify *all* of the relevant intangible assets that the target company may have. In SFAS 141, the FASB provided a list of some 29 identifiable intangibles ranging from the obscure, such as "newspaper masthead," to the common, such as patents and trademarks. Because the FASB allowed "immaterial" items to be excluded from analysis, we rarely identify more than five to seven separate items that are large enough that they must be analyzed.

In the final analysis, intangibles derive their value from the ability of the asset to generate future revenue and cash flows. So the analytical process consists of separating the components of future income into the various assets that, together, generate the income. In one sense, then, appraisers simply translate one overall future income stream into a series of smaller streams. A simple example will suffice.

A major consumer goods company acquired a well-known food company. The target had several very well-known brands. Those brands commanded shelf space on virtually every grocery store in the United States. The company had a specialized sales/delivery force that directly placed its products on the grocery store shelves, thus assuring continued shelf space. Finally, the products were carefully controlled in terms of the ingredients to replicate the taste(s) that consumers liked and therefore bought. In this case there were four interrelated identifiable assets, but only one income stream from the sales of those products to grocery stores, and then on to consumers.

The issue here was whether four separately identifiable intangible assets had to be valued separately. In theory we could have assigned dollars individually to the:

1. Recipe or formula
2. Shelf space on grocery stores
3. Trade name
4. Store delivery system

Upon reflection we assigned all the value to the trade name. The formula or recipe could change depending on the relative prices of the raw material ingredients, but the taste would be identical and the consumer could not tell the recipe had been modified. The shelf space in any one store, or chain for that matter, was a function of that retailer staying in business. Although rare, and taking a long time, the fact is that grocery chains do come and go. Putting a value on the specific customer relationship(s) would not recognize the fact that virtually 100% of all stores carried the brands. So if one chain went out, some other company would take its place—at least as long as people buy and eat food. Finally, one could argue that the store delivery system was a form of unpatented technology; the brands were strong enough that even going through other physical channels to reach the store shelves, the products would continue to be sold.

We finally agreed, with both the client and its independent auditor, that the values should be assigned to the individual trade names. The trade names in some cases were more than 75 years old, and sales were increasing each year. We supported the assignment of indefinite lives to the trade names, thus the client was able to avoid amortizing those values in subsequent years. The price paid was that each brand had to be valued every year thereafter, and if one of the brands was dropped, or sold, an impairment charge would be necessary.

In another case we had a casino client. It was permitted to operate in a locality only if it had a license, and the state sharply limited the number of licenses issued for the entire state. Obviously, the license had value, as long as the casino had customers who gambled there, thus providing an income stream to the casino owner. The customers without the license were of no value, and the license without the customers effectively could only be sold to someone else, who in turn would require a customer base.

In this case we determined that the customer base could be valued based on the dollars of revenue each customer generated (number of times they came to the casino times the average win per visit). The casino kept meticulous records on each customer who had "registered," and those individuals then received offers of complimentary food and rooms if they returned to the casino. Thus the customer records were excellent and we could estimate, actuarially, how long the existing customer base should last. The valuation was then a discounted cash flow analysis of expected future revenue (less direct expenses, including marketing costs) over the life of the customer base at the date of acquisition. We then valued the license as a residual of all future income, less anticipated returns to all of the other assets employed. This procedure is described and discussed in Chapter 6. So while there was one income stream, we did split it into two, one with a short amortizable life and the other an indefinite life that did not have to be amortized.

Briefly, we discuss the four most common types of intangibles that appraisers deal with:

1. Patents and technology
2. In-process R&D
3. Software
4. Customer relationships

Patents and Technology

Valuing both patents and technology is straightforward. In the case of patents, the valuation is based on anticipated royalty streams that the patent generates, if it is licensed to a third party. In the case of patents that were developed internally and only used internally, we apply a concept called "Relief from Royalty," which assumes that one would have to pay someone else for the right to use the patent. Depending on how much the patent generates, either in terms of increased sales or reduced production cost, we can assign a theoretical income stream, and that becomes the basis of the value assigned to the patent. In the case of a large patent portfolio, we do not analyze each patent separately, because experience suggests that the "80/20" rule applies, and we value the 20% of the portfolio that is generating 80+% of the benefits.

In many companies, so-called unpatented technology can be extremely valuable. This asset is sometimes called a trade secret or know-how. Some firms in an industry are simply more efficient than others, and that efficiency, no matter how derived, leads to lower costs and higher margins. Appraisers value this asset in the same manner as patents, effectively singling out the benefit stream and capitalizing it over its estimated remaining life.

In-Process R&D

We have devoted Chapter 10 to this subject, so only the barest highlight is discussed here. For 30 years, GAAP has required companies to charge off to expense immediately all expenditures on Research and

Development (R&D). The logic was that while no company rationally would spend resources on R&D unless it expected a future benefit, there was no good technique for determining the *value* of the R&D expenditures, as contrasted with the *cost incurred* for the R&D. Put a different way, if a company capitalized the cost of R&D, it would either be way overstating assets, in the case of failed projects, or way understating assets, because the value of successful R&D is likely vastly greater than the cost (think of a successful pharmaceutical project).

In 1973 the then members of the FASB said it was better to charge everything off to expense rather than try to value each R&D project, or even all R&D in total. But over the remaining years since 1973, valuation techniques have improved, and in the last five years companies have had to value R&D that was in process, that is, not complete. Such accumulated value then had to be written off immediately to expense. Without going into the details, many observers believed that this immediate expensing of in-process R&D led to serious abuse, as companies charged sometimes 80% of the purchase price of a company to in-process R&D (IPR&D), thus minimizing all other assets, with a P&L impact on future years.

In SFAS 141R, the Board dealt with this perceived abuse by now requiring capitalization of all acquired IPR&D, with future expensing if the project was a failure. The accounting for subsequent R&D, even on the same project, will continue to be expensed. This may sound confusing, and it is. The bottom line, however, is that whereas before SFAS 141R, many companies wanted to maximize IPR&D, there will now be pressure to minimize IPR&D.

Software

In the case of software, we determine essentially what it would cost today to replicate the existing systems for self-developed software. For purchased software (e.g., SAP or Oracle), we value it based on current selling prices. We do put in an allowance for installation and integration, because these major enterprise resource planning (ERP) systems sometimes require more resources to implement than to buy. For self-developed software, we estimate the number of man-hours required to replicate the existing software, usually allowing for some efficiencies if the task was to be completed a second time.

Customer Relationships

The subject of customer relationships has caused more trouble in valuing intangible assets than all of the remaining 28 in the FASB's list of 29 identifiable intangible assets put together.

In one sense, any buyer of a company is essentially looking for just a few assets in the acquired firm. The target should have:

- Products—that customers are buying
- People—employees who are motivated and trained and focused on service
- Customers—who are satisfied with the existing marketing efforts
- Suppliers—with competitive prices and delivery
- New products or services under development—to produce future growth

It is difficult to say which of the first three assets is most important, because in practice they are totally interactive. For a manufacturing firm, the products being produced are not an intangible asset, although the designs and technology may be, but many firms produce competitive products or services where there is no technology. They just do a good job of satisfying their customers—in terms of prices, delivery, credit, and so forth.

With regard to people, employees, right or wrong the FASB explicitly precludes companies from placing a value on the "assembled workforce." That employees are an asset is the mantra of virtually every CEO in the annual report, but in its wisdom the Board said that no value could be ascribed in financial statements to this asset.

So, if products are not an intangible, and if people cannot be recognized as an intangible, then a lot of the value of most acquired companies has to lie in its customer base. In fact, virtually every merger transaction must be approved by the Federal Trade Commission or Department of Justice. Both organizations look primarily at the customer base of the target in relation to the buyer's market position. Only in straightforward financial transactions, where the buyer has no relationship to the existing industry, does the government give a pass to the buyer.

The buyer's management is interested in the customer base of the target just as much as the government. Without customers, no business survives for long. What we have said is a fundamental principle discussed in the first week of any college-level course in management.

Why then is it so difficult to arrive at satisfactory agreement with buyers, and their auditors, as to the value of the customer base? How do you separate the customer relationship(s) from the products themselves? Appraisers have developed an approach that works, even if it may not be 100% pure in a conceptual sense.

Under current and proposed GAAP, for that matter, the value assigned to the customer relationship must be written off quickly to expense. Thus companies prefer, other things being equal, to show the minimum value for customer relationships of the acquired company.

Now, in one sense, you can argue that a company has an indefinite life (not an infinite life, but one that cannot be determined) and that as long as it stays in business, it is going to have customers. Put a different way, customers in total have the same indefinite life as does the company. No company in history has survived without customers. A customer base and the company have identical lives.

Now we get to the heart of the matter in valuing the FASB's customer base intangible: what customers, and what products should be included? History tells us that over time, customers turn over. Colgate is not selling to the same grocery chains it did 25 years ago. In fact, the famous *Fortune 500* list has had more than a 50% turnover since it began. Grocery chains come and go. Convenience stores and warehouse stores are rising while department stores are diminishing. It is a certainty that a relatively low percentage of today's Colgate sales are to customers of 25 years ago, but during all that time Colgate has continued to expand. So what is Colgate's customer base? Just as customers change, so do products sold to those customers. Colgate still sells toothpaste and detergents as it did 25 years ago, but while some of the trade names are the same, undoubtedly the formulations are totally different.

So, if the customer base turns over, and the individual products have a life cycle of their own, how do you measure the FASB's intangible of customer relationships? If we as appraisers were allowed to assign an indefinite life to this intangible, the problem would be solved. Remember that indefinite lived intangibles are not amortized each year; they are merely tested for impairment in case they diminish in value. Taking the Colgate example, the overall customer base undoubtedly has increased markedly over the past 25 years.

However, the SEC will not permit the customer base intangible to be treated as having an indefinite life. They argue, with some justification, that the specific customers on the closing date of the transaction do not go on indefinitely, and they would point to the secular decline in the number of grocery chains to support their point. If you cannot take into consideration the development of new products for new customers in measuring the value of the customer relationship, then you are forced back on a very narrow definition.

The author believes, although there is not universal agreement, that one should take a strict construction perspective in valuing the customer relationship intangible. Just as the Supreme Court has strict constructionists among its adherents, so should appraisers and accountants. It is our position that the valuation of a customer list or customer relationship intangible should focus solely on the existing customers and the existing products sold to those customers. It is clear that selling efforts commenced before the acquisition may result in new customers being added subsequently, but by the same token, some existing customers may already have decided to do business with a competitor. So, taking only the customers who are active on the date of closing fulfills both the letter and the spirit of SFAS 141.

The second issue is somewhat more controversial. We believe that the financial analysis of the customer relationship should be strictly limited to the existing products being sold. This means that as and when new products or services are introduced, the potential profit from those future products and services should not be incorporated into the profit potential. Put a different way, the analysis of the value of customer relationships on the date of acquisition will normally show a rather steep drop-off as the target company, along with most companies, introduces new products and services.

The logic behind this position is that one can count on existing customers remaining loyal for current products being sold at current prices, and with current service levels (i.e., delivery, quality, and so forth). Presumably, competitors have already done their best to erode the customer base, so in effect a status quo has been established.

As soon as *new* products or services are introduced, we believe that all bets are off. The acquired company will then have to compete all over again to obtain its customers' business. Competitors will take advantage of new product offerings to try and take customers away. The introduction of new products permits sellers to vary selling prices and other terms and conditions of sale, in effect providing a fresh start in the competitive arena.

For the acquired company to retain its customer base means that it will have to renew (and perhaps even improve) its sales and marketing efforts in order to ensure that it maintains its existing market share for the new products. A good example is an auto parts company selling Original Equipment Manufacturing (OEM) parts to a major automobile firm. Typically, the auto company will provide the supplier with assurance that its product(s) have been accepted for specific platforms, which usually have a four- to five-year life. When a new model platform is developed, the supplier must once again compete, and acceptance is far from automatic.

This logic says the value of the customer base on day 1 is limited to existing customers and existing products and services. All companies must continually market and sell both existing and new services. Experience suggests, however, that it is easier to maintain existing product relationships than it is to fight a new battle against competitors for new products and services. In the real world, there is obviously a complete spectrum: ranging from where every sale is totally competitive based on price, with no customer loyalty, to long-standing intercompany relationships, where the incumbent is virtually assured all future business volume.

Nonetheless, we must have some sort of distinct definition of how to measure customer relationships, and the methodology and assumptions spelled out seem to work and have been accepted by those who look at it. But since it does involve professional judgment, and different valuation specialists will bring different perspectives, this area requires close consultation among the company, the auditors, and the appraisers.

To sum up this section, then, appraisers have techniques that allow the valuation of virtually any type of intangible asset. The critical aspect, from the company's perspective, is the value assigned *and* the expected life, because these two variables directly affect future charges to income and a reduction of the potential earnings accretion. The subject of the estimated life will be discussed in more detail in the "Estimated Life of Assets" section later in this chapter.

INTENDED USE OF INTANGIBLE ASSETS:
"MARKET PARTICIPANTS"

One of the most troubling aspects of the FASB's recent pronouncement on valuing assets acquired in a business combination relates to their use of the term "market participants." The FASB's concept is that the best indication of value is the market, defined as what real people are willing to pay for an asset when money is changing hands. So, under that approach, you determine value simply by looking at transactions.

The problem quickly arises that for many assets there is no ready market, if in fact the assets are even bought and sold. Certainly there is no buying and selling of intangible customer relationships separate from the business itself. You cannot go to today's *Wall Street Journal* to determine yesterday's closing price for the value of an auto parts manufacturer's customer base. In the absence of an actual market, the FASB has specified that appraisers should determine the amount that market participants would pay for the asset. In effect it is up to the appraiser to estimate what the asset(s) would be worth to others than the actual buyer.

The problem quickly arises because, in a specific M&A transaction, the winning bidder—the ultimate buyer if there has been any competition—has paid more than anyone else was willing to do. In turn, this willingness to pay more is usually a function of synergies, the ability of the buyer to achieve savings by combining the two companies. So who then are the market participants, particularly if the transaction was conducted as an auction? By definition, at the final selling price, no other market participants were willing to pay the winning price!

The previous case was theoretical. Now we will look at a practical example. Taking our OEM auto parts supplier, suppose it is bought by another competitor. The buyer already sells to all ten car manufacturers. In fact, there are a total of only ten customers in the world for new auto parts. The seller sold to those ten companies, and the buyer already sells to them. In that situation, most observers would feel that the customer relationships had little if any incremental value because the buyer already had entrée into the purchasing departments of Daimler, Toyota, Ford, and so forth.

The winning bidder in any sort of competitive situation is always the individual or organization that is willing to pay more than anyone else. Why would someone pay more than everyone else? Simply because the asset(s) are worth more to the successful buyer than to anyone else. The question then becomes: How could assets be worth more to one group than another? The answer is that the buyer believes it can do more with the asset(s) and/or will have greater savings from synergies. Now it is a principle of valuation that Fair Value, the proverbial bargain between a willing buyer and a willing seller, should *not* include synergies to a specific buyer, but rather what everyone could achieve. For example, if a company is so poorly run that *any* buyer would fire existing management, then savings to be achieved by replacing the management can be encompassed within FV, but if a specific buyer has unique management talent that allows it to pay more, then appraisers are supposed to disregard this fact in determining true FV.

The FASB has wrestled with this conundrum, which assumes that the final buyer will probably have unique circumstances but that those same unique aspects supposedly should not influence the development and use of FV in the subsequent accounting. The FASB addressed this issue in requiring appraisers, in developing the FV of specific intangible assets, to consider these market participants. In the auto parts example, if the only market participants, prospective buyers, would be other OEM suppliers, then one could reasonably assume little or no value for the customer relationships, but what if a potential buyer is a financial buyer, not a strategic buyer? A financial buyer (e.g., a buyout firm) would need to utilize the seller's existing relationships with its automobile company customers. This is obvious because the buyer is not in the auto business at all, but rather in the business of buying and selling companies, which must continue to be run as they were before.

The impact of this conundrum is clear if one assumes that the choice comes down to the difference between assigning substantial amounts to customer relationships, which must be amortized, as against those same dollars remaining in goodwill and not affecting future EPS.

A really good example of this was the purchase of PeopleSoft by Oracle. The principal of Oracle, Larry Ellison, publicly stated he was going to acquire PeopleSoft for its customer base. He was going to migrate those customers to his own Oracle programs, thus achieving substantial savings by spreading the overhead to maintain the Oracle software over a much bigger customer base. Ellison stated that he had no use for either the PeopleSoft software or the PeopleSoft trade name—because he did not propose to maintain either one.

In this situation Oracle was the only prospective buyer of People-Soft (other than perhaps SAP) that could accomplish the benefits of the business combination with PeopleSoft and yet not use the product or name. In this situation, who are the FASB's market participants? If the answer is Oracle and SAP, then the appraiser should assign no value to the software and trade name. If the market participants, however, are the two or three largest private equity firms, then to those buyers the software and trade name are equally—if not more—critical than the customer list.

At the time this book is being written, there appears to be no definitive answer as to who are the relevant market participants. It probably comes down to the professional judgment of the appraiser, responding to appropriate questions from the auditors, and eventually the SEC and PCAOB. So, as in much tax work, it will be the facts and circumstances that control.

ESTIMATED LIFE OF ASSETS

In determining the impact of a prospective, or actual, acquisition upon the buyer's EPS, we have seen how important are the determination of which intangible assets are recognized and the value(s) assigned to them. CFOs would like everything in goodwill (not amortizable), while the SEC, as represented by the auditors, presses for low goodwill and high amounts in amortizable accounts.

The discussion so far has focused on *what* intangible assets must be recognized and how they should be valued. One more variable is critical in determining whether a business combination can end up being accretive to EPS. For identifiable assets that are going to be amortized, the *life* over which the asset will be amortized certainly affects annual earnings, albeit with no impact on cash flow. Keep in mind that *all* intangible assets for tax purposes (IRC Section 197) are written off over 15 years, irrespective of their accounting treatment. Thus a three-year noncompete agreement and goodwill are similarly given 15-year tax lives, while the first is written off over three years for books and the latter is never written off unless impaired.

Many corporate accountants are concerned that the financial accounting treatment for intangibles will somehow affect taxes payable, hence cash flow and possibly even reported EPS. Invariably, they give a big sigh of relief upon learning those fears are ungrounded. That for an intangible asset the life assigned for financial reporting purposes does affect reported earnings is incontrovertible. More time is usually spent by management and appraisers on the valuation, and less time is usually devoted to the useful life. This relative assessment of time and resources devoted to the two issues may in fact be counterproductive. Just for an example, if it would cost $1 million to replicate a sophisticated reporting system's software, it makes a large difference in current reported earnings whether this is given a three-year life as contrasted to an eight-year life.

There can be no rules of thumb for assigning lives to assets. The correct answer, in every case, is a function of specific facts and circumstances. If the company has definitive plans to migrate the new company over to existing software, a three-year life might even be aggressive. However, if there are no plans to change the basic business game plan, the software's life is going to be a function of when the existing system has to be rewritten or upgraded.

Few intangible assets have an infinite useful life; hence the FASB used the term "indefinite" to reflect when a specific useful life could not be determined. But the SEC's direction is to reduce significantly the number of intangible assets that are assigned the *indefinite* determination, which means that for practical purposes, virtually all such intangible assets must be given a useful life, and then amortized.

At this point we bring the reader's attention to an issue that splits the valuation profession: Should valuation specialists even be involved in determination of the useful life? One school of thought states that an appraiser is responsible for determining the value of an asset. The assignment of a useful life, and the calculation of subsequent periodic depreciation or amortization charges, are considered the responsibility of the client and its accountants. In other words, those appraisers taking this position will not express an opinion on remaining useful life, if that determination is used by the client in the financial statements. Whether this concern stems from fear of legal liability, or a feeling that the appraiser is not qualified, is difficult to determine. Suffice it to say that some appraisers turn over the values to the client and the auditor and consider their job done. In Chapter 13 we deal with the auditing of valuation reports.

We feel that appraisers do have a responsibility to provide our best professional opinion on the remaining useful life of the assets that we have valued. It is a fundamental principle of valuation that while we provide our best professional estimates, in the final analysis all financial reports are the responsibility of the client, not the appraiser. Clients do not have to use our values. In fact, companies do not have to use outside valuation specialists at all. In 35 years, we have had less than a handful of cases where we provided our best professional estimate and the clients deliberately chose not to use our work, but that is their prerogative and their choice, as long as we receive payment for the work we do.

No professional appraiser will accept a valuation assignment, by the way, that makes payment for services dependent on arriving at a predetermined answer. Undoubtedly, in the history of U.S. business, such situations have occurred (e.g., when in the 1980s the Savings and Loan scandal unfolded, one of the chief culprits was appraisers who did provide values to the clients' specifications). Any appraiser or appraisal firm subject to the Uniform Standards of Professional Appraisal Practice (USPAP) is precluded from doing anything other than providing its best professional judgment on a totally independent basis.

In the case of providing clients with our professional estimate of remaining useful lives, we feel that we have had more experience and greater knowledge than the client. That is why they hired us in the first place. As a generalization, in the case of hard assets, machinery and equipment, the longer the assigned remaining useful life, the lower will be the depreciation charges, because the value of the asset today, based on either the current cost or on the used equipment market, is pretty much independent of the anticipated life. Of course, a machine that has only one year of use left, because it is all but broken down, will have a lower value than identical equipment in good condition, but this situation is rare, and the useful life of assets is usually determined by physical inspection, with due consideration for physical depreciation, functional obsolescence, and occasionally economic obsolescence. These concepts are covered in detail in Chapter 9 on hard assets.

In the case of intangible assets, the value of the asset is often a function of its useful life. If we are valuing a patent with two years until expiration, the value will be much less than if the identical patent had been issued just three years ago. If we are valuing a trade name that because of new competition has only a few good years left, it will be worth a lot less than a similar trade name that has little competition. A nonrenewable franchise license with three remaining years is worth far less than a renewable agreement with a history that virtually all agreements are renewed.

The key point here is that an appraiser probably can value hard assets without considering the life, but for intangibles a greater degree of knowledge and understanding is required. In many instances, and customer relationships are one example, the value of the intangible increases almost proportionately to the increased life.

If a customer base is worth 5% of revenues to those customers, then the total value is going to be a function of how long the existing customer base for that product line continues. If the product life cycle has only two years to go, the value will be low, but it will all have to be written off over two years. However, if one can reasonably project a declining life over ten years, the amount will be much larger, but the amortization period will similarly increase.

Although not a rule of thumb, the annual amortization charge for an intangible asset may be quite close for a short life and a long life—it is just that the longer life charge will go on for more years. The impact on any one year's EPS, however, may not fluctuate that much. This is the reason that appraisers can often estimate the FV of hard assets with a degree of precision without spending too much time. We are talking about estimates for planning purposes, not the final report, which will be audited. Although often reluctant to hazard a guess, a competent valuation specialist can usually provide pretty good estimates of FV with relatively little work.

When it comes to intangible assets, however, and the interaction between useful life and total FV, it takes more digging on the appraiser's part. Effectively, the appraiser must develop an understanding of the nature of the acquired business and what the buyer plans to do with it. Granted, this understanding of the buyer's plans in theory should not affect the values very much—if one is using a standard of market participants in developing the values—but even to understand what *other* buyers might do involves research and discussions.

IMPACT ON EARNINGS PER SHARE
OF FAIR VALUE CALCULATIONS

"Will this transaction be accretive to earnings?" That was the question we started with in this chapter. The answer has to be "It all depends." There really are two separate issues, however. The first is simply to predict, or project, what the impact of an acquisition will be, whether favorable or unfavorable, in the short run. The second question revolves around the issue as to whether a company can influence the allocation in such a way as to enhance the EPS.

Forecasting the EPS impact can be done with a relatively high degree of precision by an appraisal firm that has had substantial experience in the allocation of purchase price. Certain patterns recur, both for PP&E and intangible assets. The appraiser will want to look at the target's *Fixed Asset* register, and likely wish to discuss the situation with knowledgeable managers either of the acquirer or the target. Absent any highly specialized equipment or very old equipment, an experienced Machinery and Equipment valuation specialist can estimate the FV with a high degree of precision without performing a detailed inspection. If the opportunity arises to actually visit one or more sites, then this will provide added assurance to the preliminary estimates.

In many instances, the FV of PP&E is relatively close to book value. This results often from two countervailing forces. Typically, PP&E is depreciated for financial reporting purposes at a rate greater than the physical decline in useful value. Offsetting this is often the situation that industry technology has improved but has not necessarily been adopted throughout the target organization. Finally, we often find fully depreciated assets still in use, which have some value, offset by assets on the books, which cannot be located in a physical inventory. These latter factors can only be determined through a detailed appraisal, which provides a fully supportable new fixed asset register, but for initial planning it is rare to find significant differences between the initial preliminary estimate and the final appraisal report.

The determination of the nature of *identifiable intangible assets,* and an estimation of their value and remaining useful life, requires access to the financial statements of the target, the acquirer's preliminary plans for integration, and discussion with managements of both sides. With financial data available, and with access to both managements, an experienced financial valuation specialist can hone in on the FV of intangibles within a day or two.

Two questions we frequently receive can be approached here. First, in valuing a target company for a business combination in accordance with SFAS 141R, we disregard all intangible assets on the target's books. Certainly the amount of goodwill—the residual between purchase price and the FV of all identifiable assets—is based solely on the acquirer's own purchase. What the target had previously done is now consigned to the dustbin of history, and we start with a clean slate. With regard to other intangibles (e.g., patents, technology, and customer-related assets), we have to view these from the perspective of the buyer, not the target. Typically, intangibles on a target's balance sheet arose from acquisitions it had made and are only a fraction of the total intangibles for the target company as a whole.

Determining the FV of the intangibles requires a lot of experience if a reliable preliminary estimate is to be made. What really is required, in addition to historical results of the target, is the projections the buyer has made with regard to future plans and integration. It is rare that such projections have not been made, albeit they are sometimes less than detailed. Nonetheless, virtually nobody buys someone else's business without having an idea what they are going to do. This can range from leaving the new company totally alone with its existing management, to a quick and complete integration into the existing business with old management paid off.

It makes little difference to the valuation specialist what the plans are, so long as those plans are communicated. It should be remembered that despite the number of questions that appraisers typically ask in the course of their work, their expertise is not in operations but in financial analysis. We are sometimes asked, particularly by owner-operators, "How can you value my business in a few days when I have spent my lifetime running it?" The answer is that an appraiser is *not* trying to run the business, only trying to understand *how* it is being run.

Finally, we come to the question of whether a buyer can influence the amounts, classifications, or lives of the acquired assets. For PP&E the answer is probably not, because good market information is usually available independent of the transaction. If a buyer plans to sell or otherwise dispose of a plant, product line, or even technology, then the appraiser should be notified, because the definition of FV differs for assets that will continue in use from those that will be disposed of. Typically, the FV of an asset to be sold will be less than for continued use. So if it is likely that dispositions will be made, it is important that this information be incorporated into the preliminary valuation. That way the disposal, when it occurs, will not incur a reported loss, and there is a greater chance that nondepreciable goodwill will have been correctly assessed.

With regard to intangible assets, the thrust of the SEC and FASB pronouncements has been to reduce the scope for application of professional judgment. Because they do not like nonamortizable goodwill, or even indefinite lived intangibles that do not get amortized, more and more intangible assets are being given definite lives. The one possible area where judgment can be applied, with the effect of possibly reducing amortization charges, is in the area of products or services where trade names, customer relationships, and product formulas are important. In such situations, there is usually one cash flow stream, and it is a matter of professional judgment as to how it is split up among the various categories of intangible assets that the FASB has defined.

In most cases, the final area for impacting amortization charges, and hence the impact on EPS, is in the assignment of remaining useful lives. As we have seen at times, the longer the life, the higher the value, but in other cases one can often support a long life, as we did with a renewable casino license. Theoretically, we could have supported an indefinite life because casino licenses are virtually always renewed, but they can decrease in value if, say, an Indian casino opens next door. In this case the client did not want an indefinite life, and we were able to support a life in excess of 35 years—based on historical experience. Such a long life had a minimal impact on EPS.

To sum up this topic, experienced appraisers can provide detailed estimates of the EPS impact of a proposed acquisition, before the closing of the transaction. In fact, many companies want to obtain a preliminary valuation estimate even before the final negotiations. This can assure management and the Board of Directors that there will be no unpleasant surprises. An accurate projection is highly desirable. Even better would be assurance as to how to reduce the EPS impact. Most valuation specialists are highly competent, as well as professional, but they are not magicians. We may be able to marginally influence subsequent valuations, but by and large, what will be, will be.

One final point should be made in terms of estimating the EPS impact before the announcement of a transaction. Appraisers are used to dealing with highly confidential information, but many companies—and we support this request—want the appraiser to sign a *confidentiality agreement*. These are very common when an appraiser is asked to estimate the EPS impact of an acquisition before it is closed, and often before it has even been announced. Most appraisers and appraisal firms are willing to sign such documents. We recommend that any buyer have its legal department develop a standard form. It makes little sense to have two sets of attorneys spend time negotiating the details of any such agreement. Any reputable appraisal firm has already performed many confidential assignments for other clients. If there were even a hint of a leak, that firm would essentially be out of business. Appraisal firms, and their staff, therefore have no difficulty dealing with confidential information, and the confidentiality agreement is more of a formality than anything else. However, buyers, and their legal departments, are far more comfortable getting something in writing, and there is absolutely no reason for an appraisal firm to demur or decline to sign such an agreement.

CONCLUSION

Finally, the best advice we can give prospective buyers who are interested in whether an acquisition is going to be accretive is to give the appraisal firm as much time as possible to perform the required inquiries. An appraiser can benefit from the buyer's due diligence efforts, so the EPS calculations should wait until due diligence is completed, but at that point it makes sense to call in the valuation specialists as soon as possible.

If there are any unusual circumstances or situations, these can be fully discussed and understood by everyone *before* the deal is closed and announced. The degree of precision of the EPS estimate is going to be a function of the detail with which the preliminary analysis is conducted. Although some issues are always going to turn up only after the business has been sold, good staff work in advance will keep these surprises to a minimum.

No financial officer wants to report to management, "We forgot about . . ." It is our strong recommendation that as part of any due diligence effort for any potential acquisition, that the company discuss the proposed deal with experienced valuation specialists. Appraisers can really be of most value before the deal is consummated. If one waits until the purchase price has been paid, it will be too late to make adjustments. If one knows that, for example, contingent liabilities are going to impact financial results, these can then be negotiated for in advance while there is still time. To restate an old bromide, "It is better to be safe than sorry."

ENDNOTE

1. Patrick R. Delaney, Barry J. Epstein, and Ralph Nach. *Wiley GAAP 2005.* Hoboken, NJ: John Wiley & Sons, 2004, p. 305.

CHAPTER 2

What Is Fair Value?

For more than 100 years, appraisers have used the term Fair Market Value (FMV). The following definition, one of many similar definitions, is used by the Internal Revenue Service (IRS), and we used it in our valuation practice for many years:

Fair Market Value is defined as the price for which property would exchange between a willing buyer and a willing seller, each having reasonable knowledge of all relevant facts, neither under compulsion to buy or sell, and with equity to both.

Compare this with the Financial Accounting Standards Board's (FASB's) definition shown at the start of Chapter 3:

Fair Value is the price that would be received for an asset, or paid to transfer a liability, in a current transaction between marketplace participants in the reference market for the asset or liability.[1]

On the surface these definitions are similar, and while many appraisers have attempted to differentiate the two, in our opinion that is a futile exercise. The one substantive difference is that the FASB talks about "asset or liability," while FMV only mentions "property." In theory one person's liability is someone else's property, so the IRS definition can probably be stretched to encompass liabilities.

At this point we want to discuss the underlying concepts in the definitions as they have been developed over many years. First, nobody pays an appraiser to determine value if the information is readily available elsewhere at low or no cost. This seems so obvious that readers are probably wondering why we even mention this point. Appraisal reports are requested when one or both parties want to know the price or value *if* a transaction were to take place. The appraiser's judgment is sought in lieu of an actual negotiation or transaction between the parties. In short, appraisers are paid to determine value on a what-if basis.

To determine the results of a hypothetical transaction, one that has not taken place and may never take place, requires that the appraiser ask certain questions and make certain assumptions. To the extent the assumptions are reasonable, the answer should be reasonable and supportable. To the extent the assumptions are unreasonable and cannot be supported, the appraiser's valuation will have little credibility.

PURPOSE OF AN APPRAISAL

The simplest example of an appraisal is the current value of your personal residence. You may be interested in moving and want to know what your home would sell for. Although this approach is not recommended, you *could* place a For Sale ad in the paper, or list the house with a broker and see what price is offered. Most people would prefer to obtain an objective opinion, within a reasonable range, before they make a decision on whether to sell or not.

In this case, the homeowners want to know the market price of their house, but suppose the owners, instead, believe their property tax is too high. The local assessor will require that the homeowners demonstrate that the assessed value is too high. This can only be done by comparing the present house with the assessed values, and recent sales, of other similar homes in the neighborhood. In this case, rather than obtain the highest possible value (i.e., for possible sale), the owner wants the lowest supportable value. Many people would ask if the answer for the assessment issue should not be the same as for the potential sale. The answers will be, and should be, different.

The reason is simple and straightforward. Unless the local assessor is keeping every single property unit revalued at current FMV, which never happens, for assessment purposes you are only interested in *relative* values, not the absolute value of your home. For challenging an assessed value, the appraiser will look at the assessed values of nearby homes, and point out where the subject property is less desirable than the comparable homes. For example, your house needs to be repainted and does not have a swimming pool; although you do have a wood-burning fireplace, your basement is not finished. Meanwhile, the appraiser would look at current sales of similar properties and compare them to the assessed values of those properties, hoping to find that current sales are below assessed value.

Without getting too technical at this point, readers should remember that assessments can be at, say, 60% of FMV, and the corresponding tax *rate* would be proportionately higher. If a $300,000 house is assessed at FMV and the tax rate is $2.00 per hundred dollars of assessed value, the tax bill will be $6,000. If the local assessor values homes at 60% of FMV, but the tax rate is $3.33 per hundred, the financial impact is identical, but when properties are assessed at some percentage below FMV, the chance of error can creep in quickly. So, for the hypothetical example discussed here, the appraiser would look to see how 60% of the selling price of homes in the neighborhood compared with the then-current assessed values of those homes.

In this situation the appraiser would prepare a valuation report that summarized findings on the pluses and minuses of the subject house compared with its neighbors, and would evaluate current market transactions relative to *assessed value*. The appraiser, in effect, would have performed the work that the assessor should have done, recognizing that no assessor's office ever has the staff or resources to perform this type of detailed analysis for every single property.

A final determination of value for your residence involves insurance. Insurance companies such as Allstate and State Farm, from experience, understand that relatively few losses are total (e.g., the house burns down completely). Much more common are partial losses where, with repairs, the house can be made habitable again. The problem, from the insurance company's perspective, is that if the homeowner underinsures the property, say, by 20%, then in anything less than a total loss, the face amount of the policy will be greater than the actual cash loss, but if the house were insured for less than its total value, the premiums, based on value, would have been too low to cover all of the company's expected losses. This is why insurance companies are always pushing for insuring at full value—the premium is higher.

So, the question then is at what value the home should be insured. The answer the insurance company wants is the *replacement cost*. The value of the house for insurance purposes should be what it would cost to rebuild it in case of a total loss. How does an appraiser determine this value? By going through essentially the same thought process that a contractor would if it was bidding to build the same house today.

Keep in mind that for insurance purposes, the value of the land and the foundation are *not* included in the insurable value. Land cannot burn down, and usually the foundation, even in cases of a total loss, will be saved. Therefore, in dealing with the superstructure, the appraiser and contractor can use one of two methods. It is simpler to go to one of the building cost guides produced by Boeckh or Marshall & Swift. These volumes provide current costs on a square-foot basis at many locations throughout the country. Material and labor rates differ depending on location, with just one example being the use of union versus nonunion labor. Additionally, these books show the incremental costs for features like adding a fireplace or an extra bath.

The second, and more detailed, method of determining replacement cost is essentially to develop a detailed bill of materials for every portion of the house (e.g., framing, electrical, plumbing, sheetrock) and price out the required volume by current rates charged by each trade at that location. This second method is far more accurate, but for insurance placement and proof of loss is probably more detailed than necessary. Pricing out a building through one of the cost services will provide a sufficient degree of accuracy, at far less cost and time.

THREE DIFFERENT VALUES DO NOT DISPROVE APPRAISER INTEGRITY

At this point we have three different values: (1) value for possible sale, (2) value for property tax assessment, and (3) value for insurance placement and proof of loss. We could come up with still different amounts, on a supportable basis, were we as appraisers asked to determine the value of the property for purposes of an estate tax valuation or for a possible gift to a charitable institution.

In one case the owner would want the highest supportable value and in the other the lowest supportable value. For estate tax filings, most executors are looking for the lowest supportable value, whereas when giving a gift the donor and tax advisor usually want the highest supportable value.

Can *all* of these values be correct? Contrary to the belief of many people, even the conventional wisdom of financial executives, appraisers will *not* sell you any answer you want. Appraisers do not sell answers. The professional designation of Real Estate Appraisers is often abbreviated as MAI (Member of the Appraisal Institute) and is jokingly referred to by certain financial officers and lawyers as standing for "Made as Instructed."

How can buyers of appraisal service feel that the providers, appraisers, can be bought to provide any answer requested, while appraisers themselves absolutely believe in their own integrity, and that of other valuation professionals? Is this mismatch of perceptions real or imagined?

Thirty-five years ago, when the author was just starting in the appraisal business, the senior appraiser, who himself had more than 30 years' experience at that time, provided a few words of wisdom that have proven to be exceedingly perceptive ever since:

"Whenever you are asked to provide a value, you first must ask two questions,

1. To whom is the value information going to be given?
2. For what purpose will the value information be used?"

Let us look at each of these points, because they get to the heart of any misunderstanding about the integrity of appraisals and appraisers. A good example to use for this analysis would be a simple diamond engagement ring, sold by Tiffany, holding a one-carat D-Flawless stone. All of the following information assumes that the individual discussed the valuation with a professional appraiser. If the woman who owned the ring wanted to insure it, the appraiser would call Tiffany and ask what a comparable ring would be sold for at retail prices today. The valuation premise is cost of replacement, and for a standardized object like a diamond, there would be no question about depreciation from age, use, or technology.

Assume that because of financial problems at home, the woman needs to borrow money and goes to a pawnbroker. What will the pawnbroker offer? If the retail price of the ring is $10,000, the pawnbroker might lend $4,500. If the borrower defaults on the loan, and many borrowers do, in effect the pawnbroker has bought the ring. In the retail jewelry business there is usually a 50% gross profit, or a 100% markup on cost. This seemingly high profit margin recognizes that the turnover for any specific piece of jewelry is likely to be slow, and the seller needs to recover the cost of capital tied up in inventory. So if the pawnbroker is now the owner of the ring, he can do one of two things: (1) he can try to sell it himself, perhaps for $9,000, or (2) he can sell it to a more prestigious jewelry store at its wholesale value of $5,000.

Why would the pawnbroker have to sell the ring for $9,000 if it is worth $10,000 at Tiffany? Simply because a pawnbroker's retail location does not have the ambience of a Tiffany store. People who patronize pawnbrokers as their source for jewelry simply will not pay the same price as they would at Tiffany. Then the question could be, why would the appraiser obtain the replacement price from Tiffany rather than the pawnbroker? After all, if the ring were lost and the insurance company had to pay for a replacement, they would go to the pawnbroker rather than Tiffany, right?

Unlike the stock market, the market for diamond rings is not nearly as liquid. Although Tiffany undoubtedly would have another one-carat D-Flawless gem and could set it in a ring, how would the insurance company adjuster find that ring at a particular pawnbroker? Supposing the pawnbroker had a .95-carat diamond ring that graded F vvs. Would you or I be able to tell the two apart with the naked eye? Probably not. But the owner of the original Tiffany ring, having paid insurance premiums on a $10,000 ring, would not be satisfied with a slightly smaller, slightly less valuable diamond set into the ring. The easiest source—and the adjuster has only limited time available to canvas the diamond ring market—is for the insurance company to go to Tiffany, and they would quote $10,000.

Buyers who go into a pawnshop to purchase jewelry expect to look at whatever happens to be available at that point in time; they do not go in expecting to buy a specific piece. Furthermore, when shopping at a pawnbroker, nobody expects to pay full retail price. In short, there are at least two retail markets here that are quite separate and discrete.

Now at this point we have four different values for the same ring:

Value to the pawnbroker for a loan:	$ 4,500
Value to the pawnbroker for sale, wholesale:	$ 5,000
Value to the pawnbroker for sale, retail:	$ 9,000
Value to the owner for insurance:	$10,000

Now let us take this back further to previous levels in the diamond trade. Tiffany buys diamonds in the wholesale market in very large volumes, so it would be reasonable that they could buy the diamond for perhaps $3,000 and the ring setting, if platinum, for $300. Then they have labor to assemble the ring, so their cost would be $4,000, and that amount would be on their balance sheet. Carrying this example back through DeBeers to the people in Israel who grind and polish the rough stone and finally to the mine, we would have at least three different values for the same lump of carbon. At the mine the rough stone might be worth only $1,000, with increases up to $10,000 at each successive production step.

Now let us recap my guru's recommendation: "To whom, and for what purpose?" How could we have valued that diamond ring without knowing who wanted the value and what they were going to do with it?

A further example could be derived from purchase of a new automobile. A car with a manufacturer's suggested retail price (MSRP) of $30,000 might be bought from a dealer, after incentives and rebates, for $27,000. However, the very next day, the buyer could sell the car to a used-car dealer for only $25,000. Is the car any different? No. Why the decline? We are dealing with a different buyer in a different market. For the new 2006 Chrysler, if we were asked to value it, the first thing we have to know is who needs the value: the new-car dealer, the customer, or the used-car dealer? And then we need to know why the valuation is needed: Is it for financing, insurance, or sale? For each level of commerce, and each purpose for which the value information will be used, the answer is different.

If there is one point we want to make in this chapter, it is that there is no such thing as a single value for an asset. It is not merely an excuse for an appraiser to answer the question, "What is the value of this asset?" by replying, "It all depends."

WHY TWO APPRAISERS PROVIDE DIFFERENT RESULTS

We are fully aware of the respect, or lack of respect, in which appraisers are held. That there may be some substance to these perceptions is understandable, but the fact that some appraisers may shade their work to favor their client is not an indication that all appraisers sell predetermined answers. Let us see how outside observers may have arrived at these unfavorable opinions.

In a bitter divorce case, the wife was suing for 50% of the closely held business she jointly owned with her husband and that the husband ran on a day-to-day basis. Needless to say, negotiation and mediation had not worked, and the divorce was now in court. The judge was being asked to determine the value of the business, and presumably the husband would buy out the wife's interest and pay her cash or notes payable over time. In return he would end up with 100% of the company. The judge then suggested that an independent third-party appraisal might resolve the dispute, but rather than both parties agreeing on one appraiser and agreeing to abide by this valuation, each party hired its own appraiser. Now, anyone who has ever watched Jerry Springer or Oprah can imagine what happened next.

The husband's appraiser turned in a professional valuation of the business. Unfortunately for the wife, it appeared that the business was in deep trouble, had strong competition, might not be able to compete in the future, and at most might be worth $1.5 million. The husband therefore was willing to buy the wife's 50% share for $750,000.

The wife, feeling that she could not trust her husband or her husband's appraiser, hired her own valuation expert. Some weeks later this report was ready and turned in to the court. This separate analysis showed that the company was doing well, was on the verge of a breakout, and that at a minimum was worth $10 million! She was willing to sell her half for $5 million.

Now put yourself in the position of the judge. He has two separate valuation reports, each prepared by supposedly reputable valuation specialists, but one appears to be from Mars and the other from Venus. How can the same company be worth $1.5 million from one perspective and $10 million from another?

IMPORTANCE OF ASSUMPTIONS

We will discuss in much greater detail in Chapter 4 how appraisers go about valuing a business enterprise. There is no magic or black box that appraisers use. The principles and practices are straightforward and well understood by everyone in the profession.

The fundamental principle underlying all valuation is that an asset is worth today what it can produce in the way of income in the future. Future income from gold results from the expectation that gold can be sold at any time for immediate cash, albeit it does not generate current income by itself. An automobile has value because it produces transportation services. A house has value because it provides shelter. Without owning a car or a house, one would have to rent a car (or walk) and rent living quarters. Thus the car and the house provide income in the shape of foregone expenses. Gold provides income in the expectation of being able to sell in the future at a higher price than one paid.

By investing in a business enterprise, one expects positive cash flow from the profits, and as with gold, an expectation that if the business is profitable, it can be sold to another investor. Take the Empire State Building as an example. Over the last 50 years, at least a half dozen owners have bought it, generated cash flow for themselves, and subsequently each owner sold it to another investor.

Put in very simple terms, the value of an asset today is the Present Value (PV) of future cash flows. Those cash flows consist of both income from the property generated each year *plus* the cash to be received upon ultimate disposition of the business.

Now let us go back to the Divorce Court judge presented with two appraisal reports, one saying the business is worth $1.5 million and the other that it is worth $10 million. It is obvious that the two appraisers had disparate assumptions about the income the company could generate and/or what the business could be sold for at some point in the future. One was assuming low growth of the business, possibly even declining sales and income. The other appraiser obviously had a lot more confidence in the future and had to be assuming significant growth potential.

Sitting as the judge, which one is correct? Or should the judge simply split the difference and rule that $5.75 million is the value? The trouble with the split the difference approach is twofold. There is no supportable basis for that exact amount—it is simply a compromise result, not the real value of the business. Second, when a judge splits the difference between two competing answers, it only encourages attorneys (and appraisers) in subsequent cases to go even further in each direction. Attorneys will encourage their appraisers to go as high (or low) as possible. They will anticipate that if the judge does split the difference, then by having the highest (lowest) conceivable answer, their client will gain.

Our experience, in many lawsuits, is that some judges will read the two valuation reports and try to come to an independent conclusion of value, utilizing the two appraisal reports as the basis of their determination. In that instance the better reasoned report, with the more realistic assumptions, is going to carry the day.

Now let us see how in this $1.5 million and $10 million experience, two equally competent appraisers could have such diametrically opposite conclusions of value. In valuing a business, as will be shown in greater detail in Chapter 4, it is necessary to try to determine what the business will do in the future. If the outlook is promising, sales and profit potential high, then the PV of the business will be substantial. To the contrary, if the outlook for sales and profit is minimal, or even negative, the PV of the business will be low.

Thus in the previous situation, the wife's appraiser, knowing she wanted a high value, simply assumed that the company would grow, perhaps at even a faster rate than in the past. Profits, as a percentage of sales, would also grow. Perhaps optimistic assumptions were made about competition, new product development, taxes, and expenses. All together this set of favorable expectations can lead to what would appear to be a very desirable company, an investment for which numerous investors would pay a lot of money. Hence we can see how the wife's appraiser arrived at the high value in the report submitted to the court. In fact, with that scenario there is only one possible answer: The PV of the business is definitely high.

Now let us look at the husband's appraiser. He knows his client wants the lowest possible value that could conceivably be supported, thus minimizing any payments to the estranged wife. In this outlook, sales were going to be stagnant, gross profit margins eroded, competition heating up, new product developments mostly failures, taxes higher, and selling general and administrative expenses increased. Under this pessimistic scenario, there is only one possible answer: The PV of the business is definitely low.

EVALUATING AN APPRAISAL REPORT

How could the judge make sense of the two appraisal reports, not being an appraiser? How can you, the reader, evaluate an appraisal report? Step 1 is to stand back and apply the smell test. Does the value indicated in the report make sense? In our experience, most clients have a pretty good idea as to what values should be, even before we, as appraisers, have developed and supported our answer.

When there is a difference, when our preliminary valuation is a surprise, at least half the time we find out some facts we did not know about. "We forgot to tell you" or "You didn't ask about that" are the explanations as to why our values differ from their expectation. It is true that about half the time we have to explain why the client's anticipation was incorrect. The reasons a client can be wrong include having unrealistic expectations regarding the strength of the market and the strength of the business.

For the most part, when appraisers are asked to provide a supportable valuation report, the final answer is within the client's expectation. When a *conflict* exists between the parties, and each is looking for personal advantage rather than the true value, then the situation described previously occurs.

Nobody knows what the future will hold. Will there be war or peace? Will taxes go up or down? Will the dollar strengthen or weaken? Will the economy grow or shrink? Will oil prices rise or fall? Any one of those factors can affect future growth and profitability, and all together make predicting the future accurately an exercise in futility. All one has to do is review in December the predictions the nation's leading economists made at the beginning of the year. Of the 50 predictions, one will be closest to final results, but we did not know the winner in January. How did the 49 other eminent economists get things so wrong? The truth is that nobody knows, and all 50 economists in effect made their best guesses, and if you array 50 guesses, one of them is bound to be closest to the final answer.

The same holds true for an appraiser trying to evaluate growth prospects for a company. You do the best you can, evaluating past behavior and management's stated plans for the future. History tells us that for most companies, past trends are generally likely to continue relatively unchanged into the future. And, even more important, no company keeps growing forever. If you go back 25 years and look at the then-current *Fortune 500* list, you will find that at least one-third of the companies no longer have a separate existence; essentially they were acquired by other stronger firms. The fastest growing companies today might not even have been on the list 25 years ago.

So a safe set of assumptions for a company involves continued growth at about the same rate as in the past, with an ultimate slowing down to a level consistent with the economy as a whole, maybe 3% to 4% a year. Now we have the basis for putting ourselves in the judge's chair. Having received two almost diametrically opposite reports, the judge must evaluate them in order to arrive at a judicial decision. Step 1 is to look at the historical results and see what trends are present in terms of revenues, gross profit, SG&A, and taxes.

Any change in any of these trends in the projections should be explained in terms of what might be causing the change, and if negative, what if anything management could do to overcome the negatives. It is usually easier to project reduced sales and profits for a company than to project above-trend increases, because by doing nothing, competitors, customers, and suppliers will be increasing their productivity at the expense of the subject firm. Put another way, it requires serious management effort to keep up with competitors, and even extra energy to gain ground on them. One can support the position, even if unpalatable, that the company does not have the resources (including management and capital) to grow at an above-average rate.

On the other side, projections showing significant above-average growth *must* be supported by evidence as to what specifically will cause the improvements inherent in the favorable forecast. A lawsuit involving a major appraisal company demonstrates this point:

> The appraiser was hired to provide a "solvency opinion." This is a professional opinion stating that the subject firm is solvent; that is, it can pay its debts. These solvency opinions are often required in a buy-out situation where a lot of debt is being taken on. The lenders want assurance that they can be repaid and the sellers do not want to be accused subsequently of fraudulent conveyance.
>
> In the particular instance, unfortunately, the company went into bankruptcy in less than a year. The appraisal company, among others, was sued for professional negligence. Now of course the appraisal company can not be held responsible for management incompetence after the valuation date, but that does not stop plaintiffs' lawyers from suing everyone in sight, including the appraisal company.
>
> When the appraiser got on the stand, the attorney for the plaintiffs asked him how he had developed his projections, projections

which showed solid financial performance could be expected. The appraiser responded that he had been presented with three projections: (1) optimistic; (2) realistic; and (3) conservative. He had chosen the conservative projection so as not to overstate the value and cash flow of the business.

The attorney then asked if the projections had been made by management. It turned out that the projections had actually been prepared by the investment banking firm as part of their "book" to sell the deal to prospective investors, and that management had not actually signed off on the projections.

Finally, the attorney asked the appraiser, who must have been sweating at this point, how he could explain that the conservative forecast prepared by the investment banker and which he had used in his valuation, was substantially better than *any* previous year in the company's history.

It turned out that the company's actual results were more in line with previous experience, and not in line with any of the investment banker's projections. It should have been no surprise that the company became insolvent, despite the appraisal firm's professional opinion that the company was solvent at the time of the closing.

There are two morals to be drawn from this experience. First, appraisers should check very closely any projections given to them. Sometimes management and investment bankers are trying to put an optimistic face on things, and the projections are not realistic. The appraiser always has a responsibility to review any projections for reasonableness, and at the end of the day implicitly or explicitly accepts the projections that show up in a report.

The second moral of the story is that the *readers* of any report prepared by a valuation firm have a responsibility to review the total report, in detail. Although the appraiser cannot *prove* that assumptions are 100% reasonable, neither can the reader *disprove* the assumptions. Nonetheless, if a reader questions the assumptions, he can, and should, go back to the appraisal firm and ask what the results would be if some of the key assumptions were changed. Most appraisers do *not* put sensitivity analyses into their report, but do perform such sensitivity analyses while performing the work, primarily in order to provide a sanity check on the output. If an investor is going to make a multimillion-dollar investment solely on the basis of a solvency opinion, without doing its own homework, perhaps it deserves to lose. Even so, there will be a lot of trouble and expense for all parties involved.

If there is one take-away point from this chapter, it is this: *Read carefully any appraisal report you are given.* The appraiser will have laid out in detail the assumptions. You may agree, or you may disagree, with those assumptions. If you disagree, in any material sense, you owe it to yourself, and to the appraiser, to ask some tough questions.

ACCURACY OF APPRAISAL REPORTS

As discussed earlier, most appraisal reports have a false sense of precision about them. Answers are usually carried out to three and even four significant digits (e.g., $4,560,000 or $17,390,000). Yet these seemingly precise values actually cover a much broader range than is implied by the single value shown.

For many years, the author has told clients that valuations are probably accurate to within ±10%—but no more. In more than 35 years of experience, nothing has indicated that any appraiser, or appraisal firm, can come any closer than this variation. Essentially, an appraisal report represents the professional's best estimate of the amount at which a transaction would actually take place.

Now look at the world of actual transactions familiar to all readers. Selling or buying your house, and selling or buying a new car with an old car as trade-in are two of the most familiar scenarios. Those who have sold a house will have experienced low-ball offers from prospective buyers, hoping to get a bargain purchase. Other luckier sellers will have had several prospective buyers lined up offering above the listed price. Deciding when to accept what offer, or whether to hold out for a higher offer, is part of the uncertainty in any real estate transaction.

Very few sellers of real estate can predict with perfect accuracy what the house will actually sell for, despite the promises and protestations of real estate salespeople claiming that *they* will get a certain (high) price. For homes in established neighborhoods, a seller would be lucky to get a final price within ±5% of the amount originally estimated.

For automobiles, much the same holds true. Look in any Sunday newspaper at the used-car ads. For popular models with many offers, the range of price from top to bottom will easily be 20% or more. Of course, some of the differences relate to mileage and condition; even allowing for that difference, sellers each have their own ideas about what their cars are worth. Some sellers put a high price in the ad, hoping to negotiate down from that. Others put in a lower price, hoping to sell immediately without delay. A quick perusal on the Internet of used-car prices at Kelley Blue Book *(www.kbb.com)* shows a range of ±14% from the midpoint. The high price (on the date this is written), taking a 2002 Corvette convertible as an example, was $38,740, which is the retail price to be paid at a dealer; the low price of $30,675 is the amount a dealer would allow on a trade-in; and Kelley Blue Book suggests that private-party transactions, were the car to be sold privately, might be arranged at $34,605. Therefore, at a specific point in time, trying to estimate the real value of the 2002 Corvette still requires choice among a range of values depending on the assumptions.

Consider how much uncertainty there is regarding the value of a house or an automobile. It should be expected that for less readily salable assets, such as a business enterprise, estimating the final price, the appraiser's FMV, is an exercise in judgment, not precision. This is why we tell clients that our values are accurate only within that 10% range, up or down.

This brings us to a delicate subject, but one we must address. As was seen with the divorce valuation discussed earlier, clients sometimes want the appraiser's answer to come out at a predetermined amount, usually expressed as, "We really would like as *high* a value as you can support" or "We really would like as *low* a value as you can support." As also stated earlier, reputable and responsible appraisers do not sell answers. Valuation is a profession, and every professional has a responsibility to utilize his best professional judgment. Therefore we cannot, and do not, commit to providing any predetermined answer before accepting an engagement. Neither does any other responsible appraiser or appraisal firm.

Having said that, once we have completed our preliminary investigation, we will arrive at a value indication that we can discuss with the client. Often the client, recognizing the professional aspect of our work, will discuss, perhaps hypothetically, why our value is not either higher or lower, as the case may be. It rapidly becomes obvious, if it was not clear before, which way the client would like our answer to go.

Valuation is a professional service, and to be successful one must have satisfied clients, who come back on a repeat basis. So there is a built-in conflict: Maintaining professional standards on the one hand and being responsive to client desires on the other hand. What do we do when our preliminary indication of value is higher, or lower, than our client desires? Although we cannot speak for others, our policy has been to start by asking the clients to read our draft report and tell us where they think our assumptions might be wrong. We then consider their point of view and may or may not change the basic assumptions. If they point out an error, of course, we will correct it. If it is a matter of judgment, sometimes we will accept their assumptions, usually stating in the report that this particular assumption (e.g., sales growth, profitability, competitive position) was derived directly from the client.

The second thing we do is to discuss with clients the normal range inherent in any appraisal (i.e., the plus or minus 10% or so discussed previously). Certainly we can not go to the very top (bottom) of the range because readers of the report might be misled. However, it is possible to adjust, say, the discount rate from 13% to 14% (if we believe a slightly lower value is supportable) or from 13% to 12% (if we believe a slightly higher value is supportable). Because there is no way of proving that the 12%, 13%, or 14% discount rate is absolutely or precisely correct, this range is within our tolerance and within the normal variability of actual markets.

Put a different way, we can lean in a direction desired by our client where the facts can support such an approach, but essentially that upper (lower) boundary of 10% represents the outer limit, as far as we can go. Given the imprecision inherent in the valuation process, we feel we are maintaining our professional credibility, and at the same time trying to show our clients we are responsive to their needs and desires. Although not a perfect solution for purists, this approach has worked well for us, and based on discussions with many other appraisers, this is the way they also react to client pressure. At the end of the day, an appraiser must be able to support a conclusion of value to a skeptical observer. If you cannot persuasively defend your position, then maybe the answer is incorrect.

CONCLUSION

Fair Value, the concept being applied by the FASB to financial reports and discussed in the next chapter, has long been the subject of professional expertise by appraisers. The appraisal profession started more than 100 years ago, because of a need for impartial and objective determination of insurable values. The valuation business started with insurance valuations, but over the last 40 years, the range of services offered has expanded to include taxes and financial reporting, as well as settling disputes between parties over what an asset such as a share of stock in a closely held company is worth.

Consequently, the growing requirements for the use of FV in financial reporting represents nothing new for appraisers. What has changed is the use made of valuation information, not the information itself. Fair Value, or what appraisers have traditionally referred to as Fair Market Value, is an informed judgment by a professional appraiser as to what, in his judgment, an asset might sell for *if* it were placed on the market. Because for many purposes businesspeople want to know an asset's value, *without* trying to sell it, obtaining a good estimate from an appraiser appears efficient.

What many users of appraisal reports intuitively understand, even though they do not usually enunciate it this way, is that every valuation by an appraiser represents a judgment, and judgments can never be precise. Thus valuations, no matter how carefully prepared, and no matter how clear and supportable the assumptions, are never going to be accurate to much better than ±10%. If two appraisers are individually given the assignment, and work independently, their answers should come out within 10% of each other, but will hardly ever be identical. This variability is in fact the strength of the valuation process, not a weakness.

If values could be determined definitively, in effect without human intervention, then the appraisal profession would never have developed. If FV were simply a matter of plugging in variables to a formula, then there would be no questions, and no disputes, between parties. Taxpayers and the IRS would agree. Partners in a dissolving partnership would agree. Homeowners would agree with the assessor, and insurance companies could charge the correct premium with no disputes. The fact that value is a matter of opinion, subject to actual and potential disputes, requires objective and independent determination, the service provided by professional appraisers. With virtually no exceptions, appraisers can determine the value of any asset (or liability), but every determination of value is subject to a reasonable range.

This range of reliability does not mean that clients can dictate prescribed answers. Appraisals are *not* "Made as Instructed." Yes, appraisers invariably work for a client, and wish to be responsive to that client's needs and requirements, but if in the course of a bitter dispute each side comes up with an appraisal that supports the respective position, but they are several orders of magnitude apart, it means that the appraisers used unrealistic assumptions. Now what is realistic and what is not realistic cannot be specified in advance, but the dictum of the Supreme Court Justice who said, "I cannot define pornography, but I know it when I see it" could equally well have referred to valuation reports that stretch the imagination.

If a reader of this book ever receives an appraisal report that common sense tells you is wrong, the chances are that it is wrong, but just because some appraiser puts something down on paper that is not supportable to an outside observer does not disqualify all appraisers and all appraisal reports. You do not have to be a composer to critique a concert; you do not have to be a photographer to critique a portrait. Similarly, you do not have to be an appraiser to critique a valuation report. Read a valuation report carefully and critically, and the chances are that you will end up agreeing with the conclusions of value as long as the appraiser's assumptions make sense. If the assumptions do not make sense, go back and ask the appraiser to test out different assumptions and draw your own conclusions.

My colleagues in the valuation profession may not like the advice just given, but almost 40 years of experience supports my judgment. As President Reagan said in relation to Russia, "Trust, but verify." With regard to determinations of Fair Value by an appraiser, "Trust, but verify."

ENDNOTE

1. FASB Exposure Draft on Fair Value Measurements, ¶4.

CHAPTER 3

What Is Fair Value Reporting?

Fair Value is the price that would be received for an asset, or paid to transfer a liability, in a current transaction between marketplace participants in the reference market for the asset or liability.[1]

The use of Fair Value (FV) information in financial reporting is highly controversial. The financial accounting and reporting model that most financial executives and auditors have grown up with has been based on historical cost. Assets are acquired and put on the balance sheet at their cost. When they are sold, or collected, the credit to the balance sheet is that original cost. In the case of long-lived assets, Property, Plant, and Equipment (PP&E), the original cost stays fixed, and annual charges for depreciation are taken until the asset is fully depreciated, at least to salvage value.

At the date of acquisition, the historical cost and FV of the asset are usually considered to be the same; by stretching the usage, one could claim that we have been using FV information all along. But in reality FV financial reporting, as most observers understand, is that *changes* in the current value of assets (and liabilities for that matter) are recognized and flow through the income statement or equity section of the balance sheet each period. Obviously, today's accounting model, with few exceptions, prohibits changes in current value from being recognized. In fact, only financial instruments with active markets are shown at current FV on a balance sheet.

This situation is about to change dramatically. The Financial Accounting Standards Board (FASB) has publicly stated, in numerous places, that it believes FV information is of greater utility to users of financial

statements. The FASB's primary audience is *users*, as contrasted to preparers, of financial statements. Therefore, if users say they want (or
need) FV information, the FASB has felt obligated to require preparers
to develop and disclose these current values. It may be only a slight
exaggeration to say that the accounting world as we know it will change
forever if the FASB has its way with FV accounting.

FASB LEADS THE WAY

In 2004, before issuance of a final Standard, the FASB issued an Exposure Draft (ED) on FV. The final Standard prescribes how companies
reporting FV should develop the information. In practice, appraisers
and appraisal firms must understand and incorporate the FASB's new
approach. It must be stated, and the FASB has been emphatic that issuance of the new Standard does not in any way move us closer to FV
financial reporting.

The new Standard does, however, prescribe what information has
to be disclosed. It presents a three-stage hierarchy with what the FASB
considers the most reliable FV information as Level 1 and the least reliable FV information as Level 3. The proposals in the FASB's proposed
Standard on FV are incorporated into this book, but as will be seen,
numerous problems are yet to be resolved.

BALANCE SHEET VERSUS INCOME STATEMENT

Shortly after it began in business in 1973, the then members of the FASB
made a decision with far-reaching consequences, yet a decision whose
significance was missed by virtually every observer of financial reporting. Most accountants, and students of accounting, have grown up with
at least two basic principles: (1) the principle of conservatism and (2) the
principle of matching revenues and expenses.

The principle of conservatism is easy to understand and support,
because at least conceptually one does not want to recognize income
before it is earned. Optimistic thinking about reported results can
quickly lead to abuse. In fact, the reason for having outside auditors,
now mandated for publicly traded companies by the SEC, is to prevent
reporting abuses by management. The financial history of the 1920s
and early 1930s led Congress to mandate strict review of published

financial statements by independent auditors. To the extent auditors take their responsibilities seriously, they act as a check on the natural optimism of corporate officers and entrepreneurs.

The principle of conservatism has proven its worth over the years, and there have been few voices, until recently, arguing for a change. Even now, critics of conservatism argue that conservative financial statements help one group of investors at the expense of another.

The second principle, of matching revenues and expenses to determine net income, seems intuitively obvious, if not totally self-evident. Investors are interested in income because that is the basis on which securities are evaluated. Management within a company is interested in income because that is a measure of performance and ultimately compensation. Matching current revenues with the appropriate expense items will produce a report of operations—a report that highlights performance —which is useful for every reader of the financial statements.

Most readers of this book will probably nod to themselves, "that's right, so what?" Well, to the seven members of the FASB, at least, the system was broken. Having the matching principle as the primary criterion for deciding accounting issues led to some unusual results. Two examples explain the anomalies faced by the FASB.

Example 1: Oil and Gas accounting relies on matching the cost of finding the oil with the revenues derived from sale of that oil. Everyone knows that oil prospectors do not strike oil on every well that is driven into the ground. In fact, perhaps only one well out of ten yields oil. Yet the petroleum company must spend money on nine dry holes to get to the tenth gusher.

The question is, what should we do with the cost of the nine dry holes? Two alternatives appear reasonable. First, we can capitalize the cost of the nine dry holes and write them off against the revenue from the tenth. This is reasonable because it simply takes the cost of nine dry holes to obtain the revenue from the tenth. In short, the matching principle says, capitalize the dry holes, and readers of the financial statements will have a good picture of the profitability of the oil exploration business.

The second alternative is to expense the dry holes as they are incurred. This will probably show big losses up front, followed (when the gusher is drilled) by very large income from the oil revenues, off-set only by the cost of drilling the one last well. Proponents of the first approach argue that you cannot get the gusher without the dry holes, and therefore the matching principle requires capitalization of the dry holes, not expensing.

It is easy to imagine the contentiousness of this issue, particularly for executives of petroleum companies whose bonuses depend on reported income. In fact, the issue became so contentious when the FASB tried to mandate expensing of dry holes that the industry went to Washington, D.C. and persuaded Congress to allow the continued capitalization of dry holes.

Note: This explanation is not to be relied on for detailed accounting guidance for oil and gas exploration. It merely highlights the issue in a broad sense.

The way the FASB analyzed the issue, and the reason they wanted mandatory expensing of dry wells, was *because they were looking at the balance sheet as the primary financial statement.* They asked the question, "If you rely on the balance sheet to tell you a company's financial position, what kind of an asset is a dry hole?" Even the most ardent supporter of matching will admit that, standing on its own, an asset consisting of costs expended that proved worthless probably does not meet the test of an asset, which the FASB in its Concept Statement 6 (CON 6) defines as something that will "provide probable future economic benefit that enables it to provide future net cash inflows." It really is difficult to argue that a dry hole is going to provide future positive cash flows, because by definition there is no oil to pump out and sell.

Thus, taking a balance sheet perspective, and arguing that it trumped the matching principle, the FASB argued for expensing of all dry holes. A theoretical argument as to which is more important, the balance sheet or the income statement, ends up having practical consequences.

Example 2: Restructuring expenses occur when a company plans to shut down or sell a plant. In the process of ceasing production, there will be payments to workers to be laid off, rent payments on assets that will not be used, and taxes owed. The decision to shut a facility is never taken lightly, but once taken, companies like to get the bad news behind them. Thus in many instances, firms would estimate all costs associated with the shutdown, including future losses, and set up a liability on the books. The charge to expense, often a material amount, would be reported as a nonrecurring cost.

Financial analysts often disregard such one-time charges in evaluating a company. The effect is that the company gets a free ride on the costs associated with the restructuring. Analysts do not consider the charge, and in calculating future earnings, cash flows, and price/earnings multiples, it is as though the charges had never occurred. So the evaluation of management performance is usually not adversely affected currently, and future reported results will appear improved.

It is no wonder that the popularity of restructuring charges shot up. As is often the case, when something is too good to be true, maybe it is. In any event, based in part from pressure from the Securities and Exchange Commission (SEC), the FASB put out a ruling in SFAS 146 that companies may not accrue expected future losses associated with operating an asset scheduled for disposal while it is held for sale. In other words, firms were prohibited from accruing future losses even though they were known to be likely to occur.

The FASB's reasoning on the definition of a liability, again in CON 6, was that future losses did not represent an actual liability until "the event that obligated the entity has occurred." While a plan to sell a plant would seem to imply that anticipated losses will be incurred, until the plant is actually sold there is no liability for future losses. Once again, the FASB showed that the balance sheet was primary and the income statement secondary.

CHANGES IN BALANCE SHEETS MEASURE INCOME

By putting primacy on the balance sheet, the FASB now focuses on assets and liabilities, rather than revenue and expenses. This means that a two-step process must be adhered to in accounting: (1) What is an asset or a liability? and (2) What is the appropriate *value* of each of the assets and liabilities? As an example, a dry hole is not an asset, and future losses are not a liability. So far, this is easy to understand even if not necessarily easy to apply in practice.

The real crunch comes in the second point, the *value* of the balance sheet items. Borrowing a concept from Economics 101, the FASB believes that income for a period is the *difference* between *net* assets (total assets less total liabilities) at the beginning of the period and the end of the period. A good analogy is personal net worth.

A retired individual has current cash income from investments and Social Security of $100,000 per year, which he spends on current living expenses; he had a beginning-of-year portfolio of $1 million. If at the end of the year the portfolio had increased in market value to $1.1 million, this economic concept of income would say the individual actually had $200,000 of income, spent $100,000, and his net worth increased by $100,000. If, however, the portfolio had gone down to $900,000, then the individual would have had zero net income, spent $100,000, and his net worth went down the $100,000.

This method of analysis has great appeal to economists and FASB members. It has not been so readily accepted by investors and businessmen. Nevertheless, the FASB makes the accounting rules, not investors and businessmen, and those accounting rules are moving steadily toward a total balance sheet perspective. In fact, one of the projects of the FASB is called Revenue Recognition, which is sales revenue to the rest of the world. The project, in its current incarnation, asserts that companies should measure revenue, and hence income, by comparing beginning and end-of-year balance sheets. The FASB admits that a couple of conceptual issues are involved in measuring or valuing all items on a balance sheet, but that is the purpose of this book.

Every author has biases that he brings to the reader. At this point let me state clearly my bias on this topic. It is difficult to argue with the theory of the FASB's position on economic income. Admittedly, there are numerous problems in trying to match up revenue and expense, particularly for complex transactions involving many deliverables in the same sale (e.g., a major software sale and installation). The FASB feels that if one could measure the liabilities remaining at a point in time (e.g., installation and provision of future upgrades) for the company to complete its obligations to its customers, then one could measure income earned to date.

This approach requires faith that liabilities can be valued objectively and at minimal cost. Taking software as an example, a seller has promised to provide the customer with the next version upgrade of the software at no additional cost. What is the cost (value) to the seller of meeting this obligation? The answer is far from trivial, and may well derail the FASB project before it gets off the ground.

The FASB has continually stated that it is looking to a balance sheet perspective in making its determinations and that ultimately all assets should be shown at FV. As an appraiser, the author can state confidently that with only one exception (to be discussed in Chapter 4), he has never met an asset that could not be valued. Any asset *can* be valued.

UNREALIZED GAINS CAN BE MANIPULATED TO CREATE INCOME

A second thread running through the arguments of FV proponents is that some assets increase in value over time. The historical cost accounting model implicitly assumes that values either stay the same (e.g., land) or decline over time (e.g., machinery and equipment).

Taking land as an example, companies today cannot write up land values as and when they increase. The only way to realize any built-in gain on land holdings is to sell the land and receive cash. Although there is nothing wrong with a company selling assets, and it happens all the time, many critics argue that unrealized gains on assets such as land can, and are, realized in quarters when for some reason management needs additional income.

In other words, the unrealized gain was there all along, and accounting conventions dictate when the income shows up on the financial statements. This flexibility, some argue, gives freedom to management where the flexibility can be and, it is alleged, often is abused. One way of stopping the abuse would be to require companies to disclose the FV of its assets currently. That way the increase in land values would have shown up gradually over time. There would be no incentive for management, in a down quarter, to suddenly sell a valuable piece of property just to make the numbers look good, because under FV accounting there would be no realized gain in the month of sale.

Accounting critics in academia and financial journalists love to point out how unscrupulous managements constantly manipulate reported income, and it is assumed that this manipulation is at the expense of unsuspecting investors. That such manipulation can take place is beyond doubt, and the author worked for a company in such a situation. The following is factually true, although with time some of the details may have been forgotten.

In the 1890s a group of California businesspeople bought a lot of land in Kern County at approximately $1.00 per acre and utilized the land for agriculture. The company, Kern County Land Co., went public at some point, but it was not a particularly dynamic stock. Then oil was discovered and things got interesting.

The Kern County financial statements continued to show the principal asset was land, still at $1.00 an acre. Meanwhile, the oil revenues were pouring in, and management decided to invest in other companies. They bought stakes in Watkins-Johnson, Walker Manufacturing, and J.I. Case, among others. None of the investments had a rate of return equal to that of crude oil, but the company reported good net profits. In relation to invested capital, return on equity, management patted themselves on the back for producing outstanding results.

The return on equity at Kern County Land was boosted because the equity was the land at $1.00 an acre. Without oil, the land might have been valued at $1,000 or more an acre because with irrigation this was some of the most prosperous agriculture in the country. With the oil flowing, the income and returns seemed truly dynamic.

Then one day, totally out of the blue, Armand Hammer of Occidental Petroleum fame made a tender offer. He spouted the usual words about "unlocking shareholder value." What he really saw was land carried at $1.00 an acre that was worth 1,000 times as much. Effectively, the market had fairly priced the oil revenues but had totally disregarded the agricultural land.

Kern County management sputtered that Occidental was trying to steal a valuable asset, and the company was really worth a lot more. What they neglected to tell the shareholders was that if the land was truly worth $1,000 an acre, then management's return on that investment had been abysmally low. Management tried to have it both ways. Great return on investment (ROI) on original cost, but tremendous value currently. The obverse was terrible ROI and an undervalued stock that Mr. Hammer was willing to pay a slight premium over NYSE prices to acquire.

In a fit of desperation, Kern County management struck a deal with Tenneco and sold itself at a slight premium to the Occidental offer, but, of course, Kern County management was soon out of a job with their new masters!

The conclusion to be drawn is that if Kern County management had disclosed the current FV of the land, the stock would have been much higher. There would have been significant investor pressure for better returns on the current values, perhaps making management work harder. The moral is that in exchange for a very easy and comfortable life, at historical cost, Kern County management lost its job to true FV.

Proponents of FV financial reporting have numerous examples of this sort. Professor Baruch Lev of New York University has made a career arguing that intellectual capital (e.g., R&D, patents, trade names) drives shareholder value and that historical cost accounting and reporting disguises the real source of shareholder returns and corporate wealth. Lev argues that companies should develop values for their intangible assets and that such disclosure would put the stock market on much surer ground.

SHOULD WE HAVE FAIR VALUE?

The issue should be stated, rather, "*Should* all assets on a balance sheet be shown at Fair Value?" The fact that something *can* be done does not in and of itself justify doing it. We have one overriding objection to making companies develop the FV of all assets, showing the values on the balance sheet, and changes in value flowing through the income statement.

The standard definition of FV talks about a willing buyer and a willing seller. The fact is that for most operating assets of a company, the firm is *not* a willing seller. Wal-Mart owns most of its stores, and the fixtures in the stores have an original cost of more than $80 billion. How would it help an analyst to know that the current FV of Wal-Mart's PP&E is $75 billion or $85 billion? The fact is that if the company was to sell more than an insignificant number of stores, primarily to relocate to more desirable sites, it would go out of business. There is no way that Wal-Mart could be separate from its retail facilities.

There was no way that Kern County Land Company could sell its land at $1,000 an acre without going out of business. Of course, this is exactly what Occidental and Tenneco proposed and accomplished.

Nobody has ever put forth a convincing case that the FV of assets that cannot and will not be sold is relevant for decision makers. In a few instances, such as Kern County, the argument may be supportable. In most instances, it is not. Even the FASB's own concept statements propound the belief that the primary purpose of financial statements is to provide information to investors and creditors about future cash flows. So the real question is, "What cash flows are possible or realistic?"

What cash flow information is inherent in the FV of Wal-Mart's PP&E, when those assets cannot and will not be turned into cash? The cash-generating ability of Wal-Mart, and any retailer for that matter, is based on selling goods at a higher price than it bought them. The real estate and fixtures are necessary, but not sufficient, to generate income. They cannot be sold on their own without destroying Wal-Mart as we know it.

So while the FASB has a stated goal of going to FV, and this book discusses the development of such value information, no reader should believe that those in the appraisal profession are pushing this shift. Those of us closest to the development of FV information, we who make a living from valuation, are all too familiar with the problems of understanding the FV information that is developed. Frankly, there is great confusion in the business world between cost and value, as well as the difference between what we call value in-use and value in-exchange, both of which are discussed in Chapter 4.

Trying to develop FV information, and explaining its relevance to shareholders and creditors (not to mention to employees), is likely to be a monumental task for corporate financial executives. As will be discussed in Chapter 4, both the FASB and SEC, in the late 1970s and early 1980s, mandated disclosure of current value information, albeit in a supplemental form. Those experiments failed, and for good reason.

VOLATILITY

There is a fundamental difference in opinion between senior financial executives and the members of the FASB. Financial executives desire earnings to move smoothly, and they hate severe volatility of reported income. On the contrary, the FASB argues, with some justification, that business is not smooth, that gains and losses are normal, and that companies should simply tell it like it is.

Many of the financial scandals of recent years can be traced to desires to smooth out reported earnings. The catastrophe at the Federal National Mortgage Association (FNMA) traces back directly to management's unwillingness to live with Statement of Financial Accounting Standards (SFAS) 133 on financial instruments. Interest rate movements have corresponding effects on bond values, so a rise in interest rates will significantly affect bond values; when a company is highly leveraged, as is FNMA, a small interest rate change has a big effect on current values of securities. In efforts to prevent such swings being reported each quarter, FNMA management attempted to hedge its positions, but if the hedge is not effective, then the changes in values of the underlying bonds have to flow immediately through income, *and* there may be further changes in value of the derivatives that were bought in the hope of dampening the fluctuations. FNMA got caught in this trap and decided that in the interest of smoothing out income it would disregard the FASB rules that were part of Generally Accepted Accounting Principles (GAAP).

Now many executives have at times wished that GAAP caused a different result, and they have felt that the reported earnings and the true economics were at cross purposes. Few of these management teams, however, decided to simply disregard the rules. FNMA reportedly did choose to do so, and somehow persuaded its auditors to go along. When it was caught, top management of FNMA was fired and the auditors removed. In the final analysis, it was not that the GAAP rules were wrong, it was that the result of applying those rules resulted in unacceptable volatility.

An often overlooked consequence of going to FV financial reporting is that volatility of *reported earnings* will increase significantly. The
reason is simple: Values change fairly quickly, and small percentage
changes in asset values will necessarily be a much larger percentage change
of earnings. If a company has an 8% pretax margin on annual sales of
$100 million, it would be reporting $2 million each quarter. If it had a
similar $100 million of assets that went down 1% in the quarter, which
is not at all unlikely in many markets, then quarterly earnings would be
cut in half. Similarly, a 1% increase in asset value would increase quarterly earnings by 50%, which would make the next quarter hard to beat
from operations alone.

Much of the opposition to FV reporting by corporate executives
derives directly from their understanding of the impact of value changes
on reported earnings. Now the FASB, and other proponents of FV reporting, say that either the market will disregard such value changes or the
value changes are important and should be disclosed. Either or both of
these arguments fall on deaf ears of those financial executives who deal
daily with security analysts.

The overriding goal of sell-side security analysts is to try to predict
next quarter's earnings. The more accurate they are in their projections,
the more highly rated they are in the annual Institutional Investor analyst ratings. A higher Institutional Investor rating translates immediately
into greater prestige and higher pay for an analyst.

Thus anything that hinders an analyst from accurately predicting
future earnings is going to be treated as poison. Financial executives,
who take enough grief from analysts as it is, feel that earnings fluctuations from temporary value changes will simply distort longer-term
operating results. Executives want security analysts to focus on operating results over more than one quarter, but the analysts respond that
you have to make next quarter's numbers in order to get to the long run.
Both sides are correct, which is why financial managers dread having
a new complexity thrown at them in terms of changes in FV disrupting
actual or real operating results.

There is no evidence that the FASB, and other proponents of FV
reporting, are going to be dissuaded by these concerns of those who prepare financial statements. Unfortunately, the history of the last 35 years
is that virtually every proposal from the FASB for changes in financial

reporting—essentially increased disclosures—has been met with the cry that the new reporting requirements will have dire consequences, if not destroy the American Way of Life. Such alarms were raised with accounting for stock options, post-retirement benefits, pensions, financial instruments, and so forth. History suggests that very few of the predicted dire consequences ever turned out that way, so the FASB has become pretty cynical about complaints from companies.

Although the FASB can dismiss corporate complaints about added volatility that might arise from FV reporting, the problem would still exist. The real question, for which there is as yet no good answer, is whether *investors* would prefer the volatility in order to get an idea of FVs of the assets owned by the companies in which they have invested. We get back to the same question as before: what could investors do with the FV information? If it would allow better investment decisions, then the FASB will be forced to act and make companies provide the information. If, to the contrary, investors do not want, or need, FV information, then it will be difficult for the FASB to force it upon unwilling companies and shareholders.

The ultimate solution, which the FASB always disparages, is for companies to *disclose* the current FV of assets, but not necessarily run *changes in value* through the P&L statements. This has a double advantage of giving shareholders the information but not mixing up in the income statement the results of operations with external changes in asset values. We come back to the issue of disclosure throughout the remainder of the book.

CONCEPTS STATEMENT 7

The FASB's views on FV have been driven by their knowledge of, and familiarity with, financial instruments. Financial instruments, including stocks, bonds, and more complex options, futures and derivatives, derive their ultimate value from future cash flows of those instruments.

Determining the value of financial instruments, as a class, ranges from the simplistic to the complex. At one end of the spectrum, a corporate holding of 1,000 shares of GM or $100,000 of 90-day U.S. Treasury bills can be valued by going to today's edition of *The Wall Street Journal*. At the other end of the spectrum are complex derivatives developed for a specific client based on anticipated changes in interest rates or foreign exchange; these can essentially only be valued by the Wall Street firm that designed and sold them in the first place.

In discussing FV over the years, the members and staff of the FASB have been overly influenced by their understanding of the characteristics of financial instruments, and consequently have paid less attention to two other important aspects of valuation practice. The experience with financial instruments, in our opinion, is not necessarily transferable to other aspects of valuation.

As will be discussed in detail in Chapter 4, there are three (and only three) means of determining FV. These are often referred to as the market approach, the cost approach, and the income approach. Valuing financial instruments can be done in one of only two ways. One can determine the current market price from market sources, for example, *The Wall Street Journal*. That will tell you what others are paying today for a similar security. The second way is to use a Discounted Cash Flow (DCF) approach, which appraisers refer to as an income approach.

Essentially, the DCF analysis brings the anticipated future cash stream back to today's value by discounting at an appropriate discount rate. The choice of the appropriate discount rate is one of the two problems in using a DCF analytic approach. The other problem is getting a handle on the future cash flows.

Historically, appraisers have used professional judgment in selecting a discount rate for application in a DCF analysis. The choice of discount rate is based on current market rates plus a premium for the size of the company plus a premium for the perceived risk of the business or cash flows. So, if future cash flows are highly uncertain (risky), the appraiser chooses a *high* discount rate (which minimizes the value), while a highly certain stream of future cash can be discounted at a *low* rate (which increases the value).

Quite candidly, this system has worked well in practice, but it is always difficult to justify just why you as an appraiser chose a discount rate of 18%, when perhaps 16% would give a better answer. It is true that when using an income approach to valuation, utilizing DCF methodology, the answer is often sensitive to the choice of discount rate. Furthermore, some observers feel there is a false sense of precision in using a single discount rate, be it 16% or 18%.

Precision of values in an appraisal report is often questioned by readers. In the real world there is usually a range of values at which an item would sell. A perusal of the newspaper ads for automobiles would find a range of $1,000 to $1,500 between the top and bottom offer for a used 2006 Ford Escort. For an appraiser to come up with an exact number, perhaps to the next rounded hundred dollars, suggests that the appraiser has some unusual powers of analysis and foresight as to just who might offer the exact amount the car was valued at in his report. In reality, a range of values may be more useful to the reader of a report. Nonetheless, almost without exception, appraisers put an exact number in their appraisal reports and do not disclose ranges. Often, in the text of the report, appraisers will indicate that they have calculated a sensitivity analysis showing how much the final value might change with a different sales projection or a different discount rate.

When asked why appraisers insist on a single-point estimate of value, rather than a range, in their reports the answer is that usually the client needs a specific answer. So if you are doing an allocation of purchase price, the accounting department must make a specific entry debiting each asset at a specific dollar amount. If the appraisal report said that Patent #xxxxxx was worth between $250,000 and $300,000, then the only alternative for the accountant in practice is to take the midpoint, in this case $275,000. Consequently, over the years appraisers, knowing that clients often have to use a single number, have provided a point estimate rather than a range.

In reality appraisers are not so good that they can determine the FV of an asset to the third or fourth significant digit, much less to six or seven significant digits, but old habits die hard, and appraisal reports still are written with a single answer for each asset being appraised. This sense of precision, which is subject to question merely by questioning any one of the key variables, has led the FASB in CON 7 to develop a totally different approach, one that solves one set of problems with today's valuation methodology but creates a brand new set of problems.

Expected cash flow is not a term that many people are able to work into daily conversation. Yet if the FASB has its way, the specific concept embodied by this term will become very familiar. CON 7 defines expected cash flow as "the sum of probability-weighted amounts in a range of possible estimated amounts; the estimated mean or average."

As written, this is not exactly intuitively obvious, so an explanation is in order.

Assume that a company has had a lawsuit filed against it, alleging damages of $1 million. Although nobody can predict with certainty the outcome of a future jury trial, the firm's attorneys suggest the following:

Probability	Amount of Loss	Expected Cash Flow
.30	-0-	-0-
.25	$ 10,000	$ 2,500
.15	100,000	15,000
.20	400,000	80,000
.08	750,000	60,000
.02	$1,000,000	20,000
		$177,500

What this chart shows is that the expected settlement is within the range of zero to $1 million, and the weighted average of the expected outcomes, based on the probabilities, is $177,500. The single most likely outcome is zero, which is a win for the company; the worst-case scenario, of a total loss of $1 million, has only a 1 in 50 chance of occurring.

If the trial were being held tomorrow, according to CON 7 the company should book a liability of $177,500. If the trial were to be held, say, three years from now, the expected cash flow of $177,500 would be discounted at the three-year risk-free Treasury (3%) rate, so the present value today would be approximately $160,000. What CON 7 does is to apply a risk-free discount rate to a weighted average expected outcome. If the lawsuit were considered an asset by the plaintiff, and the plaintiff's attorney made the same estimate of probabilities of winning as the defendant had of losing, then the plaintiff would have an asset of either $177,500 or $160,000 depending on the date of the trial.

What CON 7 does is to substitute a certain discount rate (U.S. Treasury) for the appraiser's judgmental risk-adjusted discount rate, but there is a trade-off. Rather than using the most likely estimate of cash flow, CON 7 requires multiple projections of future cash flows. Even that multiplicity of possible outcomes is not too difficult to develop, albeit more work than a single most likely projection. The crunch comes in the assignment of probabilities to each of the three, four, five, six, or more outcomes that the analyst may prepare. The question that the FASB has avoided answering is, "Is the choice of probabilities any less judgmental than the choice of a single risk-adjusted discount rate?" Many of those who have looked at the issue believe that there is more work effort in applying the CON 7 approach, and it may not be more reliable.

Note: As early as 1957, in the first-year Control program at the Harvard Business School, the concept of Expected Cash Flow was presented and recommended as an analytical tool. Consequently, the FASB cannot even claim that CON 7 is original.

There is a further complaint made against the CON 7 approach, and this involves current accounting practice under SFAS 5, dealing with contingencies.

Contingencies, or uncertainties as to whether or not something will happen, are a perennial problem in accounting. Accountants are taught to be conservative, but is it conservative to set up a liability for something that is unlikely to happen? Most contingency issues deal with liabilities, but at least in concept there can be contingent assets, for example, the possibility of a plaintiff successfully winning a lawsuit. In terms of FV for financial reporting, we concentrate on contingent liabilities because that is where the controversy lies, and if we resolve the liability problem, presumably the same approach would apply to contingent assets.

With regard to contingent liabilities, the *current* SFAS 5 rule says that a company only recognizes a contingent amount on the balance sheet if two tests are met:

> It is probable *that an obligation has been incurred because of a transaction or event happening (1) on or before the date of the financial statements;* and (2) *the amount of the obligation can be reasonably estimated.*[2]

While the term "probable" is far from definitive, many accountants like to define it in terms of "more probable than not," which in turn leads to a working definition that if there is a less than 50% chance of something happening, it is not recorded on the balance sheet as a liability. Disclosure of the circumstance(s) in the footnote will undoubtedly have to be made even if the event is not likely to occur.

Taking the previous example for the lawsuit, there is less than a 50% chance of any significant liability occurring. Consequently, without the CON 7 approach, most accountants would not feel it necessary to set up any liability because any payment, if made at all, would likely be immaterial ($10,000), but the CON 7 approach requires setting up a $177,500 liability. Which of the two numbers, zero or $177,500, is correct? They cannot both be "correct" unless you accept the fact that GAAP is uncertain and totally flexible in the eyes of the preparer of the statements.

The FASB currently believes that the FV of the liability, based on the assumptions shown, is $177,500 if the lawsuit were to be settled in the short term. They have promulgated this idea in the draft SFAS 141R as a formal part of GAAP, so it is clear that the FASB is leaning this way. Many financial executives believe this CON 7 approach to the recognition and measurement of contingent liabilities is plain wrong. SFAS 5, which has been in existence for 30 years, is the correct approach, they believe, for financial reporting.

The argument against the FASB's position revolves around the paramount objective of financial reporting. As stated repeatedly by the FASB, the purpose of financial statements is to help investors and creditors understand future cash flows. Financial executives then ask, "How does it help a creditor or analyst to understand the future cash flows of the company by putting a $177,500 liability on the balance sheet?" The one thing that is virtually certain is that the firm will not pay out $177,500! It may pay zero, $10,000, $100,000, $400,000, $750,000, or even $1 million, but it is not going to pay $177,500.

By putting the $177,500 on the balance sheet, there once again would be a false sense of precision, that the liability is exactly the amount shown. Even more important, it would show the company is "on the hook" for that amount, when it is totally unlikely that amount will ever be disbursed. So, the argument goes, adopting and requiring an Expected Cash Value approach, in effect determining the FV of the liability, would be positively misleading in terms of helping readers of the statement to understand future cash flows.

Nonetheless, despite vigorous criticism from financial executives, and little support from users of financial statements, it appears as though the FASB is committed to an FV approach to contingencies. It is interesting to note that the International Accounting Standards Board (IASB) has gone even further in proposing that *all* contingent liabilities should be valued at the expected cash amount. In practice this means that a company would have to develop the expected value, and anticipated payment, for every lawsuit filed against it.

This logic follows from the belief that FV can best be derived from market transactions involving market participants. While the belief in, and the utility of, market participants is discussed throughout the book, at this point we are more focused on contingencies. As seen previously, the FASB's perspective on using the FV of contingencies represents a major change in financial reporting.

Their logic is that if Company A buys Company B, and finds out that B has a major lawsuit against it, A will make some estimate of the likelihood of the outcome and adjust its purchase price accordingly. Assume that B is worth $100 million without the lawsuit. Knowing B is being sued for $10 million, and estimating the expected cash value is $4 million, A would offer to buy B for $96 million. As will be discussed in Chapter 5, on allocation of purchase price, A would essentially have acquired (all other things being equal) $100 million of assets and a liability it estimated would settle for $4 million. In other words, in determining how much to pay, A took into consideration the range of probabilities that the lawsuit would be settled at an expected value of $4 million. Even though that exact figure is highly unlikely to be the specific settlement amount, nonetheless that is the amount that would be booked.

Where many analysts part company with the FASB is in the next step. Under the FASB's proposals for allocation of purchase price, any subsequent settlement of B's lawsuit will cause a gain or loss to run through the income statement. So, if the lawsuit actually settled for $1 million, A would show income that period of $3 million. So far, so good. But if the lawsuit settled for $15 million, A would have to take an $11 million charge. The FASB's accounting for expected value perhaps makes good theoretical sense. In practice, however, no company is going to willingly absorb an expense that could have been avoided by being more conservative in the original valuation of the lawsuit.

If B's law firm, or even A's law firm, said to management, "Gee, there is a 50% probability that you might lose all $100 million, and a 50% probability you will win totally, then the FV calculation of the expected cash value of the lawsuit would be $50 million, not the perhaps more realistic $4 million assumed above. Can an appraiser substitute his judgment for that of a law firm? Can an auditor substitute his judgment for that of the law firm and the appraiser? Can the SEC substitute its judgment for that of the law firm, the appraiser, and the auditor? And this does not even consider the Public Company Accounting Oversight Board (PCAOB), which may have the final word.

In a nutshell, by putting an expected cash value on contingencies that are not currently on financial statements and by making errors in the estimate a severe penalty against the acquirer, there is only one logical outcome. We will see new levels of conservatism in financial reporting, followed by several pleasant surprises when the worst possible outcome does not take place.

One further word on this subject: The greater the estimate of the FV of a contingent liability in a purchase price allocation, the more dollars that will appear on the asset side of the balance sheet, and, given current allocation procedures, the greater will be the amount recognized as goodwill. Keep in mind that goodwill is not amortized, although it must be tested for impairment, as discussed in Chapter 8. Consequently, by being ultraconservative in valuing contingent liabilities, the offset will be to nonamortizable goodwill. Then when the contingency is settled, and assuming it is settled for less than the previous expected cash flow, there will be a credit to income—and no charge for goodwill amortization.

If this sounds too good to be true, it probably is, but, as we already discussed, who, if anyone, will be able to second guess probabilities about future outcomes that are uncertain. Statistical validity can only be derived from many occurrences of the same or very similar circumstances. It is the essence of major lawsuits that the ultimate outcome will always be uncertain; hence assignment of probabilities will never be able to be validated. This is but one of the many reasons why FV financial reporting may solve some of today's accounting problems but will certainly create its own new set of problems.

FASB'S FAIR VALUE PROPOSALS[3]

In June 2004, the FASB issued an Exposure Draft (ED) titled "Fair Value Measurements." Contrary to conventional wisdom in the financial community, the ED did not, by itself, push the FASB or GAAP further in the direction of FV reporting. The ED attempted to standardize the way that companies determine and report FV information. The FASB felt that several previous Standards had called for FV information and had specified various definitions and measurement techniques. The ED would, hopefully, pull together into one source the recommended methodology for determining FV information, as and when it was called for by the FASB in past and future Standards.

That said, there is no question the FASB wants to move forward with FV reporting and that the ED represents a necessary, although not sufficient, first step. Undoubtedly, as it pushes for further FV disclosures, the FASB will refer to the final Standard derived from the ED as evidence that the information *can* be developed and that it has shown *how* to develop it.

In Chapter 2 we discuss how appraisers have traditionally developed what we refer to as Fair Market Value (FMV) and the FASB has started calling Fair Value. Some people claim to find differences in the two definitions, but we feel that for practical purposes what the FASB wants, and what appraisers develop, is essentially the same. Note that we are not supporting the methodology propounded by the FASB. Although the FASB and its staff are very competent accountants, they leave something to be desired in the area of understanding valuation.

Why does the FASB not understand valuation? Until recently, most of the FASB's determinations that FV should be used dealt solely with financial instruments. For the most part, the FASB recommends, and we as appraisers agree, that financial instruments should be valued on the basis of market transactions. In turn, market participants develop current transaction prices on the basis of estimates of future cash flows for those instruments. Appraisers are totally comfortable with this approach, and in fact use it every day. The problem is that the way financial instruments are valued is not necessarily the way that *other* assets are valued in practice. Yet the FASB's experience with financial instruments effectively blinded it to the reality that appraisers use other techniques and methodologies.

From an appraisal perspective, a cost approach, a market approach, and an income approach should all be used, and no one approach has primacy. In Chapters 4 and 5 we discuss these three approaches to value. For reasons that are not entirely clear, the FASB seems to have a prejudice against both the cost approach and the income approach, particularly when applied to company-specific assets.

For this reason the current version of the ED has developed a hierarchy of valuation methods, with the market approach being in Level 1 (the best) and the cost approach and income approach being in Level 3 (the worst). This flies totally in the face of more than 100 years of appraisal theory and practice, and can only be explained by reference to the FASB's primary experience with financial instruments.

Just one example here will suffice. In dealing with the subject of intangible assets and goodwill in SFAS 141, the FASB made an explicit determination that the value of the *assembled work force* in a company could not and should not be valued separately from goodwill. To quote from ¶B 169:

> The FASB observed that even if an assembled workforce met the criteria for recognition as an intangible asset apart from goodwill, the technique often used to measure the fair value of that asset is replacement cost [emphasis added]—the cost to hire and train a comparable assembled workforce. The FASB believes that replacement cost is not a representationally faithful measurement of the fair value." [emphasis added]

Since the author argued this point with the FASB, before issuance of SFAS 141, and lost the argument, all we can say is that we and the FASB have agreed to disagree. Replacement cost is the measurement attribute appraisers utilize in virtually all allocations of PP&E; in fact, the Fair Value ED grudgingly admits, some four years later, that replacement cost may be an acceptable approach, albeit it is still in Level 3, near the bottom of the FASB's FV hierarchy.

As a side note, in valuing In-Process Research and Development (IPR&D), which is discussed in Chapter 10, it is necessary to obtain a value for the assembled workforce, and GAAP permits—perhaps even requires—this determination. The problem is the FASB's blind spot to determining value in other than market transactions. This problem is not going to be solved until far more FV measurements are required in GAAP and preparers, auditors, the SEC, and the PCAOB all understand that limiting the determination of totally supportable values to the market approach is simply not possible.

Nonetheless, in conversations, speeches, and discussions, present FASB members make it clear that they have great reservations about any value determination that is not based on a clearly defined active market, hopefully one with many participants. The New York Stock Exchange and the U.S. Treasury securities markets both fill this bill, and the FASB and its staff are very comfortable opening up *The Wall Street Journal* and checking prices and values of financial instruments.

Unfortunately, if FV measurements are going to be permitted, or required, for other than financial instruments (e.g., stock, bonds, futures, and options), then the *The Wall Street Journal* simply does not publish prices of most tangible and intangible assets. For many, if not most, assets, active markets sufficient to determine value simply do not exist. That is why appraisers have developed and used these *other* approaches for more than 100 years.

CONCLUSION

Fair Value reporting is coming, whether we like it or not, as long as the members of the FASB continue their present thinking. That it will solve some of today's problems is certain. Equally certain, FV reporting will create a whole host of new problems.

Most readers of this book grew up on a traditional model of accounting and financial reporting. Income was determined based on matching revenues and expenses. Assets were stated at historical cost and depreciated over time down to salvage value. Gains were not recognized until they were realized. Losses were recognized immediately. Conservatism was at the heart of good financial reporting. Aberrations such as Enron and WorldCom could be traced back to optimistic reporting that bent the rules of conservatism.

It is apparent that the FASB favors FV disclosures, and corporate executives dislike it. The ultimate consumer of financial information, shareholders and creditors, have yet to be heard from. One solution is for companies to disclose information about the FV of assets that could be disposed of, and for which there is a market. That is, if assets could be converted to cash without adversely affecting the company's well-being, perhaps that information would give investors an idea as to how well management is utilizing the assets at its disposal.

Mandatory disclosure of FVs does appear to be on the horizon, and the primary purpose of this book is not to argue for or against. Rather, we want to explain to both preparers and users how the information can be developed and what it does and does not mean. Ultimately, the market will decide whether to accept FV.

ENDNOTES

1. FASB Exposure Draft on Fair Value Measurements ¶4.
2. Patrick R. Delaney, Barry J. Epstein, and Ralph Nach. *Wiley GAAP 2005: Interpretation and Application of Generally Accepted Accounting Principles,* Hoboken, NJ, John Wiley & Sons, p. 560.
3. The material in this section is based on the current Exposure Draft.

CHAPTER 4

How Appraisers Develop Fair Value

Management is responsible for its own financial statements. This statement will not surprise most readers of this book; many, if not most, nonprofessional readers of financial statements believe, however, that company financials are the work of the public accounting firm that has signed the audit certificate. The reason for bringing this point up is that when companies disclose Fair Value (FV) information in their financial statements, they are taking responsibility for the values disclosed.

Management may often be encouraged to utilize the services of an outside professional; at the end of the day, the outside appraiser is a hired gun. Although the appraiser has to take responsibility for his own work, hiring the appraiser does not absolve management of its ultimate responsibility. The obverse of this is also true. Management does not have to hire an appraiser to develop any FV disclosures made in the financial statements. Developing FV information is not recommended as a do-it-yourself undertaking; there is nothing in Generally Accepted Accounting Principles (GAAP) or Securities and Exchange Commission (SEC) regulations, however, that requires use of an outside appraiser.

It is important to note that this book is *not* a do-it-yourself guide for appraisals and valuation. We want financial executives to understand what appraisers do, understand why they do it, and understand what the resulting valuation answers mean. Thus appraisers, looking for guidance in implementing Financial Accounting Standards Board (FASB) FV pronouncements, can skip this chapter. We start with a brief review of the basic principles of valuation, followed by more detailed and substantive explanations of the tools and techniques that appraisers use.

BASIC VALUATION PRINCIPLES

Many books and articles describe the basic principles of valuation. Essentially, an appraiser uses one or more of the three approaches to value. Only three principles or approaches can be used to determine value, and every appraisal technique is simply a variation of one of these.

The *cost approach* asks what it would cost today to acquire the same or similar assets. If you are valuing a building, the upper limit on value is going to be the price you would have to pay a contractor today to build the same building. A rational buyer would not acquire an existing building at a price of $120 per square foot if a new building could be constructed at $100 per square foot. Similarly, in valuing machinery and equipment, we look to the prices of new assets from the manufacturer. Where necessary, adjustments are made for technology and productivity improvements. The cost approach is highly reliable in dealing with tangible personal property and real estate. It is not generally used by appraisers in valuing financial assets, such as the income stream to be derived from a security.

The *market comparable approach* looks to the market to see what the same or similar assets are actually selling for. If you have a 2005 Buick four-door sedan that you want to sell, how do you determine its value? You go to the classified ad pages and see how much other similar Buicks are selling for. Maybe no 2004 model is advertised, but 2003 and 2005 models are offered. You would then compare your car with those advertised and estimate what yours would bring. The market comparable method works very well when a well-established market exists. It is not ordinarily utilized by appraisers for intangible assets.

The *income approach* asks what investors are willing to pay for an asset with a given income stream in the future. Investors, and hence appraisers, adjust for perceived risk, so a U.S. Treasury bond with no default risk will sell at a lower yield (higher price) than a so-called junk bond. To value an asset using the income approach requires a good projection of future income or cash flows and choice of a discount rate. Whenever possible, appraisers prefer to utilize someone else's income projections, inasmuch as the specifics are better known by the principals. The appraiser, in turn, is usually responsible for the choice of the discount rate. The higher the discount rate that is chosen, the lower the value, and vice versa.

USE OF THE THREE APPROACHES

Generally speaking, appraisers are required by professional standards to use all three valuation approaches in every assignment. As a practical matter, this is not usually possible. So one of the first decisions that must be made is to determine how many of the approaches can be used. A brief anecdote highlights this issue:

For insurance purposes, appraisers are usually required to use a cost approach. This is because in case of loss, the insurance company is required to "make whole" the insured, essentially by replacing the lost or destroyed assets. So if you have a fire in your house that destroys the kitchen, to be back where you were before requires rebuilding the kitchen and providing replacement appliances. To make sure that the insurance companies receive sufficient premium, they require the insured (e.g., a homeowner) to buy coverage equal to the replacement cost of the house and contents. Then, in case of loss, the premiums paid in the past should be sufficient to restore the house to its condition before the loss. Consequently, for insurance purposes, the cost approach to value is used because that is the premise on which premiums will be collected and subsequent payments made for losses.

One time a prospective client came to a valuation firm and asked for an appraisal of his "Believe It or Not" Museum. We indicated to him that we could value the business based on revenue received from admissions, in other words, based on the income approach. The client indicated that was not satisfactory. What he wanted and needed was the insurable value of the museum for placement of insurance and proof of loss. Among other items within the museum were an Eiffel Tower built out of toothpicks and a shrunken human head from Peru. We indicated that maybe we could determine the cost to replicate the Eiffel Tower, but we simply were unable to support a determination of the cost to develop a new shrunken head! We lost the assignment and never did find out how he insured the shrunken head.

So at times we cannot use all three approaches to value. Now let us look at the other extreme, where we can use all three. Take as an example a commercial warehouse, one that is rented to several tenants based on the square feet utilized and the length of the lease. In this case we can value the warehouse by reference to current construction costs for structures of this sort, perhaps $70 per square foot for the sake of argument. If it is a 100,000-square-foot warehouse, the value of the building would be $7 million, plus the land. If the building site was ten acres, and land was selling for $20,000 in that neighborhood and with that zoning, we would add another $200,000 for the land, making a total Fair Market Value (FMV) utilizing the cost approach of $7.2 million.

We would also look at the rental income generated by the warehouse. Again, for purposes of example, assume gross rentals were $10.00 per square foot and net income after expenses was $8.50 per square foot, for a total cash return of $850,000. If investors in this area at that time were demanding an 11% return, then the building could be valued at $7.7 million. An investor buying the building for that amount might anticipate an 11% return, perhaps offset by some higher maintenance in the future and/or higher rental rates when existing leases expired. This would provide an indication of FMV utilizing the income approach of $7.7 million.

Finally, a competent appraiser would investigate actual transactions for warehouse facilities in the general area, going back perhaps three or four years. Obviously, there are not likely to be any 100,000-square-foot warehouses that have been purchased or sold locally, but there will have been a half-dozen sales in that period, of different sized warehouses, in different locations and perhaps different zoning. The appraiser has to take the historical transaction prices and adjust them for the differences between the so-called comparable transactions and the subject property. A premium or discount to the actual price of each comparable would be made for size, location, current interest rates, and several other variables. Making these adjustments requires the skill and experience of a competent appraiser and is the subject of review by a lending institution if the building will be collateral for a loan and the bank relies on the appraisal for valuation.

Utilizing the cost approach is pretty straightforward and can be performed by a competent businessperson. Utilizing the income approach can be, and often is, performed by a competent MBA. Utilizing the market approach for real estate, however, is never a do-it-yourself program for either a businessperson or an MBA. It does require a lot of experience, access to the right data, and an ability to make the proper adjustments. Assume for this example that the appraiser determines the current market for warehouses is such that the warehouse, given sufficient time on the market, could be sold for $7.4 million.

At this point we have three separate value indications for the same building, each different because of the separate approaches to valuation. There is nothing wrong with this discrepancy, perhaps contrary to conventional wisdom. While in theory perhaps all three approaches should provide the same answer, in practice they do not. In fact, the author has never seen a situation where all three answers are identical. Variations in the quality of information, if nothing else, will cause the answers to differ.

Nonetheless, an appraiser is hired to provide an answer to the question, "What is the Fair Market Value of the warehouse?" Most clients would not accept an answer, "Well, it depends." Neither would they accept as an answer to their question, "Well, I have three answers, which one do you want?" The appraiser is paid to make a determination in terms of a single answer, although as discussed in Chapter 2, inherent in any valuation is actually a range, plus or minus, to the reported value.

CORRELATING THE ANSWER

In the previous example, we ended up with three potential answers to the question about the FMV of the warehouse. One easy way of resolving the issue would be to take a simple arithmetic average of the three value indications. Unfortunately, this would be incorrect. In fact, the SEC has explicitly rejected arithmetic answers to values derived from various methodologies.

Appraisers are required, by professional standards, to evaluate the strengths and weaknesses of each value indication. Basically, we look at the information base utilized in each approach and weight more heavily the answer(s) that were derived from reliable sources. So, in the example, we might not weight the market comparable approach heavily if there were few comparable transactions, and the ones we had were for smaller buildings traded several years ago, and were no closer than 50 miles away. However, if there were ten sales within the last year, all of roughly the same size, we would weight the market approach more heavily. Similarly, the cost approach is often accurate for the building, but perhaps there is no land available in this business market, so the derived land value is relatively uncertain. The possible permutations and combinations are unlimited.

The bottom line is that the appraiser has to perform professional responsibilities by exercising judgment. Thus, in advance, it is probably unlikely that an appraiser will be able to say which of the three approaches is going to work out best in any specific situation. This gets to the heart of the issue discussed in the two previous chapters, between FASB and the appraisal profession. By setting up a hierarchy of valuation approaches, always putting the market approach on top, inevitably the FASB seems to downgrade the reliability of the income approach and the cost approach. From the author's perspective, the FASB is putting its thumb on the scale, in advance. It is telling valuation specialists, auditors, and financial statement users that using the income approach, much less the cost approach, is less reliable.

Yet Machinery and Equipment (M&E) appraisers have traditionally used the cost approach. In fact, using the market approach in an allocation of purchase price will positively give the *wrong* answer. At the time this book is being written, it appears the FASB may be rethinking its position on the reliability and relevance of the cost approach for M&E in the allocation situation.

VALUE IN-USE VERSUS VALUE IN-EXCHANGE

What may seem like an esoteric subject fit only for appraisers—how to determine FV—may turn out to have a greater impact on financial reporting than the adoption of SFAS 141 and SFAS 142. How should we determine the Fair Value of long-lived assets, usually Property, Plant, and Equipment (PP&E)? This is not an esoteric question because, as we will see, appraisers use two separate premises of value, and the choice will affect the amount allocated to PP&E. The fewer dollars allocated to PP&E, the lower will be annual depreciation charges, and the consequence would be that more would be allocated to goodwill, which is not amortized. Consequently, by choosing one premise of value over another, there will be a significant change in reported income. The issue, then, is what is the correct premise of value?

The difference between the two premises is as simple as whether you are buying or selling an asset. As shown in the previous chapter, if I am selling a 2002 Corvette to a dealer, I will receive some $29,000. However, if I go to the same dealer to *buy* a 2002 Corvette, the dealer will charge me some $39,000. The premise of value in this case is the answer to the question, "Are you buying or selling?" This concept is referred to by appraisers as determining a Value In-Exchange. It represents the current market price and requires specification of the appropriate market, in this case wholesale versus retail.

There is another premise of value, which appraisers refer to as Value In-Use. Over the last 35 years, appraisers have developed a standard methodology or approach to determine for purposes of purchase price allocation, the FV of PP&E on an accurate and cost-effective basis. We refer to this as a Value In-Use (VIU) premise of value, and it has worked well. The alternate approach, Value In-Exchange (VIE), seems now to be preferred by the FASB because of its emphasis on market participants and market transactions. VIE provides a *different* and usually *lower* value for PP&E. Although corporate financial officers might welcome this change in valuation concepts, because of its immediate favorable impact on reported income, as appraisers we raise the question, "Are we moving forward, or backward, if we adopt the FASB's VIE concept of FV, at least for purchase price allocation?"

The issue can be stated very simply:

> *Should M&E be valued for purchase price allocation assuming continued use by the new acquirer,* or *should M&E be valued based on prices in the open market, for example, used equipment dealers?*

WHAT IS VALUE IN-USE?

The following are the standard definitions used in appraisal reports to clients:

- **Value In-Use.** VIU is defined as an amount of money that would be exchanged between a willing buyer and a willing seller with equity to both, neither being under any compulsion to buy or sell and both being fully aware of the relevant facts, as of a certain date, *assuming that the assets will continue to function in their present capacity as part of an ongoing business enterprise at their present location.*

■ **Market Value (or Value In-Exchange).** Market value (or VIE) is defined as an amount of money that would be exchanged between a willing buyer and a willing seller with equity to both, neither being under any compulsion to buy or sell and both being fully aware of the relevant facts, as of a certain date. *(Market value excludes the cost of installation, transportation, foundations, piping, and power wiring applicable to each machine unit and does not consider its contributory value as a part of an ongoing business enterprise at its present location.)*

The italicized portions of the standard definitions highlight the two different concepts. VIU is premised on the assumption that, in a business combination, the buyer acquired a going concern. The buyer should identify what it would cost today to have the same or similar assets in place, up and running, and producing the output at the existing level.

Some of the equipment may be new state-of-the art, whereas others may be older technology, even fully depreciated, that is still capable of cost-effective production. The fact is that the day before the business combination, the assets were working and producing, and we assume (realistically) that no change occurs the next day simply because of new ownership. The purchase price for the business included as part of the going concern values the fact that the existing equipment has been installed, tested, and debugged and that the various components in, say, an assembly line are balanced. Although not handled in the SFAS 141 allocation, the fact that the seller has a skilled and assembled workforce also adds value.

In short, the VIU approach takes the perspective of the buyer. We look at the specific company and associated assets on an as-is, where-is basis. The purchase price for the overall business presumably was arrived at after due diligence by the buyer, which understands what it is getting and what it is not getting, in terms of productive capacity.

The valuation methodology for VIU is straightforward. In theory, we identify all of the assets, determine the *cost new* today, including freight in, installation, testing, and debugging. Then, based on physical inspection of the assets, the professional appraiser determines the age and actual condition of the subject assets and determines the depreciation from all causes.

The assumption is that while the assets *could* be replaced with new like-kind equipment, the fact is that they will not be replaced. Instead, the old assets will be retained, but by using the older assets that are both physically worn and may be less than current technology, there is a cost penalty for the existing assets in contrast to an all-new complement. It is the appraiser's duty to apply professional judgment as to the amount of depreciation from all causes that exists at the date of the business combination. Note that the appraiser's definition of depreciation is based on physical inspection and current technology, not on arbitrary accounting lives applied to original cost for purposes of financial reporting.

As a practical matter, appraisers usually do not determine the cost new of every asset, and separately determine the freight in, installation, testing, and debugging. There are not enough appraisers in the world to do this. As a shortcut, appraisers will often take the client's property record system. If the original cost of the assets is available, and the original date of acquisition, appraisers are able to apply either standard or proprietary indexes to that original cost. That provides the appraiser with a reasonable approximation of the cost today to acquire the same complement. Obviously, for major pieces of equipment, the appraiser has to test the indexing for accuracy by obtaining quotations from suppliers. The indexes are usually accurate, and appraisers find this approach provides a precise, yet cost-effective answer.

WHAT IS VALUE IN-EXCHANGE?

VIE takes a different perspective. It asks one of two questions: (1) what would it cost if we *bought* these assets in the open market, either from a dealer in used equipment or at auction? or (2) what could we *sell* the assets for, as-is and where-is to a dealer or at an auction? The answers to these two questions are obviously different as discussed previously with the example of the 2002 Corvette.

Before we can apply a VIE approach to meeting the needs of SFAS 141—if that is the desired methodology—someone has to tell us whether the exchange is *buying from* or *selling to* the market. In the used equipment business, because of relatively low asset turnover, the difference between the bid and ask price can go as high as 50%, while in our real-life example of the Corvette, the difference is just over 25%.

Historically, appraisers have *not* used a VIE approach very often in allocations of purchase price, but for financing, appraisers do use VIE. Why use VIU for allocation of purchase price and VIE for financing? The two different premises represent two different types of transaction. The allocation represents the interest of the buyer of the business, who will use the assets for the purpose for which they were acquired.

A bank, or other lending institution, does not want to run a business if the borrower is unable to meet the loan agreement. In the relatively rare cases when the lender takes over the physical assets in settlement of a loan, the first thing that is done is to try and sell the assets, usually piecemeal, to a dealer or through an auction.

Thus the lender wants an appraisal that tells it what is the maximum amount that could be realized if the assets were to be sold separately, and not as part of the going concern; at this point the concern is not going, which is why the bank now owns the assets. If the old management could not make a go of the business, the chances of the bank or other lender doing so are usually remote. In short, the bank wants a worst-case scenario, which means selling the assets on a more or less distress basis.

It is easy to see now that the two premises of value—in-exchange and in-use—each have their place. They are different in terms of the answer provided by an appraiser. They each are FV but to a different person for a different purpose. By and large, the VIE, even using the price *from* the dealer, is going to be *lower* than that developed from the VIU premise. The price of an asset new from a manufacturer always puts an upper limit on the used equipment price, but there is no lower limit. Particularly when the economy is far from robust, auction prices, and hence dealer prices, are often low. Auction prices are often determined in a bankruptcy or liquidation situation, where there is pressure on the seller. Dealers who buy at auction, and then resell to customers, have pressure to turn their inventory as quickly as possible.

A second difference occurs in how to deal with inbound freight, installation, and debugging. Present GAAP requires that these costs be capitalized as part of the "Cost" of an asset. This appears reasonable, because without the freight, installation, and debugging, no assembly line, or other production process, could conceivably work. GAAP, in effect, defines Cost as including everything necessary to make the asset fit for the function for which it was acquired.

These costs, and they can easily approach 10% or more of the vendor price, are going to be lost as and when the assets have to be sold to someone else. Obviously, a used equipment dealer will not pay for the original installation and freight because it now has to pay to deinstall the asset and pay freight to get it to the warehouse.

These commonsense issues require an appraiser always to ask the client, "What is the purpose of this valuation?" The appraiser's answer is going to depend on what he hears the client wants. So, contrary to cynical opinions, the fact that an appraiser provides answers useful to the client is not because he is selling answers, but because values do differ depending on the assumed transaction.

One word of caution to lenders: More than once, unscrupulous borrowers have given a lending institution an appraisal report that was requested for placement of insurance. Remember that insurance appraisal values are based on current replacement cost, not necessarily adjusted for physical and functional depreciation. Insurable values are usually at the highest end of the range of values for any asset, and values for collateral are at the lowest end of the range.

Put yourself in the place of an appraisal firm that gets a call from a very unhappy bank, stating that "Your appraisal report dated six months ago shows the asset values are X. We just took over the assets and tried to sell them and the maximum we can get is .3X. We want you, the appraiser, to make up the difference because of your professional negligence." This actually has happened, and the appraiser merely points to the wording in the appraisal report that clearly specified the premise of value, insurance placement, and said nothing about the value of the assets in the used equipment market that the bank really had needed.

In effect, the borrower understood the valuation business much more clearly than did the banker, and took advantage of this lack of knowledge. The appraisal firm did its job, and the misuse of the final valuation report could not be traced back to the appraiser.

FASB'S DILEMMA

Here is a direct quote from paragraphs 23 and 24 of SFAS 142:

> *Quoted market prices in an active market are the best evidence of fair value and shall [emphasis added] be used as the basis of measurement, if available. . . . If quoted market prices are not available, the estimate of fair value shall be based on the best information available, including prices for similar assets and liabilities and the results of using other valuation techniques.*

There is an active market for used assets in many, if not most, types of PP&E. This is what the FASB asks for and what many corporate financial officers are now starting to demand. However, auditors from several of the major national firms are totally used to the VIU approach, which has been utilized for the past 30 years. They are uncomfortable with a switch to a VIE, which they see is likely to place *fewer* dollars in PP&E and *more* dollars in nonamortizable goodwill.

Appraisers are in the middle. We can do either VIU or VIE or both. Tradition says that VIU is appropriate, and in our judgment fairly reflects the actual economics of the specific transaction. The FASB, however, is leery of company-specific valuations and much prefers looking to the market. Whichever approach is chosen, the one certainty is that future income statements will be affected. VIU has higher depreciation expense and lower reported earnings. VIE puts more into goodwill, which must be tested for impairment every year, but goodwill has zero impact on quarterly or even most annual operating results.

The real issue is that the FASB is leery of values developed from company-specific information. They much prefer the supposed objectivity of market prices. Auditors, too, are more comfortable with market prices that they can check and confirm. Even the Public Company Accounting Oversight Board (PCAOB) has weighed in on this topic. The Chief Auditor of the PCAOB, Douglas Carmichael, has given speeches in which he virtually says that in the absence of quoted market prices, most values are not auditable.

We discuss the subject of auditing of FV financial reporting in Chapter 13. The American Institute of Certified Public Accountants (AICPA) has issued guidelines on the topic. However, because those guidelines came out before the PCAOB weighed in on this topic, it is obvious that the last word has not been spoken on this issue.

CAN FAIR VALUE BE AUDITED?

If the PCAOB truly believes that certain FV information, essentially that derived from management's judgment or assertions about the future, cannot be audited, this puts the FASB in a tight spot. In situations where there is an active market, with several market participants, appraisers can develop the information and auditors can verify the data.

The problem is that for many types of valuation, particularly intangibles, there is no active market with market participants. Just a simple

example will suffice: Suppose that an appraiser is asked to value the Tide®
brand name, owned by P&G. As will be discussed in the next chapter,
the valuation of intangibles inherently requires projections about future
sales price and volume, as well as future expenses. In turn, this obviously requires some assumptions about future consumer demand, competitive conditions, and technology. Just imagine that some Japanese
technology company invents an ultrasound washing technique. What is
the impact on current models of washing machines and the demand for
detergents? What if Colgate comes out with a new detergent that really
is better than Tide? What happens if a new style of grunge clothing takes
hold and people wash their clothes less often? None of these scenarios
is particularly likely, but the chances of any one of them happening are
more than zero.

Getting back to the valuation of Tide, the appraiser would talk to
P&G management and obtain an understanding of their projections for
volume and price. The appraiser would discuss future demand, competitive conditions, and technology, and arrive at a judgment as to whether
P&G's own projections are reliable enough to utilize in valuing the brand
name.

The point is that appraisers make judgments every day, and in the
final analysis most valuations are based on the appraiser's judgment.
The PCAOB is correct: You cannot prove a judgment is correct. Similarly, you cannot prove a negative, but that does not stop people from
leaving their umbrellas at home because they do not think it will rain
today. You cannot prove it will not rain, but most people are willing to
go with the odds, knowing that once in a while they will be wrong,
and when it does rain they get wet. Meanwhile, they have not had the
bother of carrying an umbrella for at least 30 days when it truly was
not needed.

Put another way, anyone who makes a judgment call risks being
wrong, even though they are correct more often than not. Most judgment calls made by an appraiser—in this case the future sales revenue
and expenses of Tide—are correct. The values so derived are accurate
enough for most business decisions. That is why businesses in the United
States spend more than $1 billion on appraisals each year. It is cost
effective.

But to try and prove that any one valuation is correct is impossible.
A skeptical auditor can always pick holes in any appraisal report. There
never has been, and never will be, a totally bulletproof valuation—unless

someone wants the value of 100 shares of Cisco stock and you can go to *The Wall Street Journal* and get the closing price yesterday. Even that does not absolutely guarantee that you could call Merrill Lynch the next morning at 9:30 when the market opens and obtain that exact price to the penny.

When the PCAOB, or the FASB, states that they are uncomfortable with the judgments made in developing FV, they are correct. They should be uncomfortable—except for the alternative. More than one guru has stated that "It is better to be approximately right than precisely wrong." Valuing an asset at its original cost five years ago is precise and can be audited to the penny. Determining the true FV today is going to be an approximation, as noted earlier probably within a ±10% range.

Complaints about the difficulty of auditing management judgment, and appraisers' assumptions, have validity. However, one should not forget that today's financial reporting already has numerous assumptions, most of them based on management judgment. Somehow auditors are able to work around these imprecise values (e.g., future warranty expense or bad debt reserves) by looking at past experience and applying their *own* judgment!

The problem for an auditor today is that the PCAOB is coming in and auditing the auditors' work. Thus, anytime a financial scandal occurs, it is easy to review the audit work papers. After the fact, if something did go wrong, it is easy for the government auditor to question: "Why did you accept this value, this management assertion, this liability estimate?" Hindsight is easy, and auditors are trying to protect themselves more than ever; with the threat of a PCAOB review of each audit, there are going to be extraordinary efforts to verify values developed by appraisers. At the end of the day, this is impossible.

Ultimately, the choice is going to come down to auditors applying their judgment of the appraiser's judgment regarding management's assertions. Maybe it will be only one time out of a hundred, but all three will be wrong and the situation will have been set up for the financial press, Congress, the SEC, and the PCAOB to demand reform of the system. One of the prices we pay for useful and relevant financial information is the chance that once in a while it will turn out not to have been reliable.

Relevance and reliability are the touchstones of the FASB, according to its own Objectives of Financial Reporting. The fact is that tension sometimes exists between relevance and reliability. It is much easier for the business press to come up with numerous examples of the *unreliability* of certain information than it is to complain about the *relevance* of required GAAP disclosures, including FV.

Inasmuch as this topic has no permanent answer, we will not discuss it further. The reader, however, should keep in mind that at some point, the FASB is either going to have to change its attitude toward company-specific information or back off its commitment to FV financial reporting. We predict that more than 100 years of appraisal and valuation experience—showing that company information is usually valid—will grudgingly be accepted by FASB, and that their push for FV financial reporting will continue.

MARKET PARTICIPANTS

As noted earlier, the FASB holds strongly to the belief that the only valid value information is that derived from the market. They admit, indirectly, that there may be several different markets, with different prices (values). Appraisers, therefore, are supposed to select the appropriate market and derive transaction prices from that market.

This concept of the appropriate market, and market participants within that market, was illustrated previously with our example of a used car. An individual owner can sell his used vehicle privately through newspaper ads or to a dealer. These are two separate markets, with different prices and hence separate values to the owner. In one case, selling to the dealer, it is a quick transaction with little effort, but at a lower price. Selling a used car to a private party utilizing newspaper ads is going to take longer, involve numerous inquiries from buyers who may not be interested, and acceptance of risks involved in test drives and bad checks. On balance, however, one will receive a higher price. The reason is that the individual buyer will pay you less than he would have to pay for a similar car at a used car dealer. From the buyer's perspective, acquiring a car from a private party involves risk as to possible mechanical defects. Buying from a dealer, while not guaranteeing a perfect car, at least has the advantage that the dealer could fix something that subsequently turns out to be defective.

One more piece of the puzzle has to be addressed. From the perspective of a new-car dealer accepting a used car in a trade, there are two alternatives. The dealer can fix up the car, put it in inventory, and sell it at a price close to the Kelley Blue Book retail price. Alternatively, the dealer can decide to wholesale the car at a local auction, receiving less for the vehicle but not having to make repairs and cover the cost of keeping it in inventory until it is sold.

Essentially, what the FASB means by looking to market participants is first to identify the relevant market, and then do enough research to find out what such participants are actually paying for the subject asset(s). So far most readers would consider what we have said to be little more than common sense; although they might not have thought about these issues in these terms, it does not appear as though any difficult decisions have to be made.

Nonetheless, the question of just who is a market participant is often in dispute. As an example, consider an auto parts supplier, an Original Equipment Manufacturer (OEM) whose customer base is the ten major automobile manufacturers such as Toyota and Ford. The customer relationships the OEM has with the ten firms are clearly important. The ability to call on the appropriate buyers, the reputation for delivery and price, and the quality of the parts produced are all issues that, when performed satisfactorily, lead to more business in the future.

In deciding whether to acquire such a company, the prospective buyer would perform significant due diligence on the target's reputation in the industry, its product line, its workforce, and its proprietary patents and technology. Each of these attributes is an intangible asset identified by the FASB and discussed in greater detail in Chapter 6. For purposes of this discussion, market participants, we must focus just on the customer relationships.

What is the value of the target company's relationships with Toyota, Ford, and the other major auto makers? To another auto parts company, the relationships may not be worth much. Why? Because that prospective buyer already calls on the same ten buyers. In fact, there are only ten prospective customers in the world, and most of the major parts suppliers already sell to virtually all of them.

Thus, and this is the point, the customer relationships that the target company has are really worth very little, if anything, to another auto parts company. However, consider a financial buyer, a private equity firm, for example. These groups raise large amounts of money to invest in individual companies. They hope to turn around the target and sell it to someone else, or have an Initial Public Offering (IPO). To a financial buyer that is not already in the auto parts business, what is the value of the relationships the target has with its customers? Now the shoe is on the other foot. A financial buyer has no existing relationships with Ford and Toyota. If the acquisition of the target is going to work, the buyer *must* obtain the relationships; it must maintain the goodwill of the auto companies to this supplier or the buyout will be a failure.

Now comes the valuation dilemma. Are the customer relationships worth only a nominal amount to another supplier, or are they worth a lot to the financial buyer? As we have seen elsewhere from the perspective of an appraiser, the value of an asset is a function of who is going to use it for what purpose. So to an appraiser, either answer is correct depending on who the buyer is. However, having made this persuasive case—that the value is in the eye of the beholder—the FASB and the Emerging Issues Task Force (in EITF 02-17) have decided otherwise.

They have chosen to use the concept of market participants in the broadest sense. In practice, this means that the customer relationships have to be valued in relation to prospective buyers who are *not* already in the industry, even though for practical terms those may be the only realistic acquirers. Given the pressure the major auto companies are under, they are very reluctant to have a major supplier who is not already intimately familiar with the industry and its requirements. Thus, by far the most likely buyer for an auto parts company is another firm in the same industry, one to whom the target's customer relationships may have little value.

Lest this seem like an esoteric or theoretical point, keep in mind that the financial reporting consequences are far reaching. If one assigns a low or nominal value to the customer relationships in the purchase price allocation, then more of the total purchase price ends up in goodwill. Remember that goodwill does not have to be amortized, although it does have to be tested periodically for impairment (see Chapter 8). If a high value is assigned to customer relationships, then obviously less is assigned to goodwill. The downside, however, is that those customer relationships usually have a relatively short life, and the amount assigned must be amortized over that short life. Consequently, evaluating the value of customer relationships in terms of a broad concept of market participants will likely cause a significant decline in subsequent reported earnings. Accounting, unlike the physical sciences, is not based on uniform relationships like the laws of gravity.

Accounting is manmade, so it is not possible to say that one or another of the alternatives to valuing customer relationships in terms of market participants is correct and the alternative is wrong. Either is right and either can be considered wrong. The FASB and SEC have chosen the alternative that tends to lower reported earnings!

INCOME TAXES AND SUBCHAPTER-S CONSIDERATIONS IN VALUATION

Valuations for tax purposes are not all that different from valuations performed for financial reporting. The same concepts and definitions of FV are utilized. All three approaches to value—market, cost, and income—are properly utilized. There is, however, one major difference.

Most appraisals for financial reporting have an impact on reported earnings, and hence Earnings Per Share (EPS), as discussed in Chapter 1. In some cases the values may affect a company's actual cash flows, but in most cases—particularly for allocation of purchase price—the primary impact is on the *timing* of cash flows. Readers should keep in mind that under current tax law, *all* intangible assets are amortized over 15 years, irrespective of how they are handled on the books of the company. Thus, even a three-year noncompete contract has to be amortized over 15 years for taxes, although three years is proper for books. In short, how companies account for assets on their books does not really affect their tax liabilities.

The same situation does not hold true for valuations that are primarily utilized for taxes. There the taxpayer's interest is in direct conflict with that of the IRS. It is a zero-sum game. The lower the value allowed for estate-tax purposes, the lower will be the tax—and vice versa. This puts the IRS in an adversarial position in many, if not most, valuation situations. It has also led to an inordinate number of tax cases in the court system involving valuations, valuation theory, and application of those theories. Fortunately, all of those court decisions involving valuation for tax purposes can be disregarded by corporate managers and auditors. The SEC and the PCAOB, in reviewing filings, utilize the same valuation standards as do preparers and auditors. They may disagree about the assumptions, but they do not usually question the methodology.

In tax valuations, to the contrary, the IRS tends to challenge everything. The most common disputes revolve around gift and estate tax issues. For estate tax purposes, executors invariably want the lowest possible value assigned to the assets, usually shares in closely held companies. The IRS then argues that the valuations used in the estate tax calculations are too low. The disputes invariably center around two issues: (1) how much of a discount should be allowed for stock that is not freely traded and (2) how much of a discount should be allowed for lack of control.

The Discount for Lack of Marketability (DLOM) is well established. Obviously, if you had a choice of owning 100 shares of Dell or 100 shares of a privately held computer company for which there is no public market, you would choose Dell, even if everything else were equal. The ability to sell a stock with a phone call to your broker at Merrill Lynch is worth a lot. How do you sell 100 shares of the Smith Computer Company, founded and run by your brother-in-law? Who do you sell to? Why would they even want to buy?

That the liquidity of a publicly traded stock has value is beyond question, and the obverse, that an illiquid stock sells at a discount, is equally beyond question. The issue boils down to "How *much* of a discount can we support?" The answer to this question has been the subject of hundreds of studies, articles, and court cases. The final answer always ends up being, "It depends." This is not particularly helpful the next time the issue comes up. Consequently, the taxpayer's appraiser will pick the highest supportable discount, and the IRS will argue for a low DLOM. Both sides can cite studies, articles, and court cases, and some judge now has to make a determination; those decisions usually involve either splitting the difference or choosing the side that has made the most persuasive case. In short, the entire subject of DLOM is a mess and all because real cash is involved. One cannot blame either side for attempting to put its best foot forward. The only thing that suffers is the application of sound valuation principles.

The other dispute in tax valuations revolves around the appropriate discount applicable to minority interest, or lack of control. Particularly for privately held companies, the majority shareholder(s) hold all the cards. They control salaries, benefits, capital investment, and dividends. Minority shareholders occasionally go to court to claim they are being discriminated against and that the management is taking advantage of them. Go back to the early days of the Ford Motor Company and Henry Ford's treatment of his shareholders. Ultimately, they were bought out at an amount that many observers feel was significantly less than the true FMV of Ford at the time.

Consequently, again there is general agreement that minority shareholders are entitled to a discount on the value of their shares relative to their proportionate interest in the company. How much is it worth to have control over a company's direction and assets? This is the issue, and appraisers for taxpayers tend to assume a fairly large discount, whereas the IRS argues invariably for a smaller discount. Once again, the courts have to decide.

These issues about DLOM and control appear in some ways related for financial reporting, but because there is little at stake—other than the timing of income and deductions—these issues do not take up a lot of the time and effort of corporate executives and auditors.

Interestingly, but perhaps not surprisingly, when taxpayers are planning to make tax-deductible gifts to a charity, they often argue for higher values, and the IRS then argues for lower values. In this case the higher values equal a greater tax deduction and consequent tax savings for the donor. Once again, FV is far from precise; when money is at stake, perceptions of value often seem to change.

SELECTING AN APPRAISER

A strong argument can be made that as with other professional services, experience is the best teacher. In fact, experience is essentially the only teacher because very few formal college programs exist on appraisals and valuation. Virtually all appraisers today learned on-the-job. Just as you would want a surgeon who had performed many gall bladder operations if you suffered a severe attack, so too you should want an appraiser, or appraisal firm, that has had a lot of experience.

A humorous sidelight to this issue: Some 35 years ago, the author was just starting out in the business, and the senior professional in the firm, with about 20 years' experience told me, "You can't really understand valuation until you have had at least 15 years' experience." Five years later, in a conversation with another new hire, the same individual told the new hire in all seriousness, "You can't really understand valuation until you have had at least 20 years' experience." Upon mentioning this to another employee, he laughed and told me, "Yes, Sam always says you need experience that is five years less than he has worked!"

However, experience in the valuation business may not be the same as experience in valuing a specific type of asset. The single most common question asked of any appraiser by a prospective new client is, "What other companies in our industry have you appraised?" The implication always is that unless you have great familiarity with a specific industry, you probably are not qualified, and that assumption may be based on experience with other professions. You would not ask the gall bladder surgeon to do a heart transplant. You would not ask an injury lawyer to draft up a complex trust and estate plan. In short, in many professions there is specialization. Specialists often charge more but are assumed to have a higher degree of expertise.

Fortunately or unfortunately, this is not the case for business valuations. There are appraisers who specialize in real estate, or sports teams, or media, but any competent appraiser could readily perform an appraisal in any of those areas. The reason is straightforward: As we have seen, there are three, and only three, approaches to valuing any asset. Once you understand the principles and application of those principles (i.e., cost, market, and income), all valuations fall under one or more of these approaches. So, while the author has not performed many real estate valuations, he does understand the principles. Were he to undertake the valuation of a private residence, an apartment complex, or even a shopping center, he would apply all three approaches to valuation.

Where an appraiser who is experienced in a certain industry, or type of asset, has an advantage is in knowing the appropriate sources of data. What is the market for shopping centers? Who are the buyers and sellers? What shopping centers have changed hands recently and at what price? Any appraiser has to ask these questions. Someone in the real estate industry will be able to answer the questions quickly. An appraiser from outside the industry will have to do a little more digging. Both the experienced real estate appraiser, and say the author on the other side, are going to arrive ultimately at the *same* information and the same answers as to value.

The difference, from the client's perspective, is that the experienced real estate appraiser will not have to spend as much time on the engagement as would the author. If two appraisers were each to charge the same amount per hour, then the experienced real estate appraiser would be able to complete the engagement in less time, and for a lower fee.

There are two caveats: Ordinarily it will be two to three weeks from the time an appraiser accepts an assignment until he communicates preliminary indications of value to the client. Absent a specific rush assignment, which usually commands a premium fee anyhow, the two appraisers will actually deliver their reports at about the same time. Consequently, in normal circumstances the client will receive the same information in the same elapsed time, irrespective of which appraiser is chosen.

Regarding fee levels, the situation is a little more complex. Most appraisers, like most auditors or attorneys, have a standard billing rate. Appraisers estimate fees to clients based on an expectation about the amount of time it will take, in hours or man-days. Multiplying the time estimate by the rate provides an initial fee estimate. Some clients insist on a firm fixed fee in advance. Others are willing to pay based on actual time incurred.

In the situation described here, if the author were asked to value the shopping center, he would accept the fact that there will be some non-billable time involved in getting up to speed on current and recent transactions. Put a different way, to be competitive one would have to absorb some time as part of a learning curve. This is why clients always prefer to deal with an appraiser who is experienced in their industry, assuming that the fee will be less. That assumption may or may not be true. The one thing that is certain is that both appraisers can, and most likely will, arrive at similar—and correct—answers. What is the lesson to be learned?

If a prospective client is selecting an appraiser, make sure the individual or firm has significant overall valuation experience. In the author's judgment, ten years' experience is sufficient to have provided an appraiser with a sufficient range of issues and industries that he can take on virtually any valuation assignment. With regard to fees, although appraisers may not like it, there is nothing wrong with a client insisting on obtaining a firm fee estimate. In the unlikely circumstance that unforeseen things occur, the appraiser will come back for an additional fee.

Two examples will highlight what we believe are reasonable causes for a fee adjustment:

Example 1: In performing an allocation of purchase price, the appraiser relies on the target company's fixed asset record. Occasionally, a company has such poor records that they can not be used, and neither the client nor the appraiser knew this at the time of the engagement.

Example 2: Again, in an allocation assignment, more than once the buyer simply did not know the total extent of the target company's assets. In a not untypical case, we once found out that there were 22 plants to be appraised, not the 21 we were initially told about.

In both examples, and in similar circumstances, we have found that clients are perfectly agreeable to adjusting the original fee estimate. Nonetheless, the message for readers of this book should be: *Always obtain a firm fixed fee in advance, knowing that once in awhile it may have to be adjusted.* Anyone who has ever been surprised at a lawyer's bill, where every separate phone call is charged for, understands this advice. Most appraisers charge and bill on a per-day basis and simply do not keep track of time in ten-minute intervals. Obtain a day estimate and both sides will usually be satisfied.

CONCLUSION

Management is ultimately responsible for the FV information disclosed in financial statements. Although there is nothing in GAAP or SEC instructions that requires use of outside valuation specialists, most companies are choosing to delegate or outsource this task. Under current Sarbanes-Oxley Act requirements, a company's own auditors cannot perform any valuation that they will be auditing, so companies choose valuations specialists either from independent appraisers and appraisal firms or from one of the other accounting firms.

The one thing that should be clear at this point is that there is no such thing as "the" value of any asset. Is the asset going to be used for its present function or will it be sold? The value in each case is different. Will the asset be sold (or acquired) in the retail market or the wholesale market? The value in each case is different. Is the value being determined for insurance purposes or for loan collateral? The value in each case is different.

The FASB has asserted that so-called market valuations are more reliable and have a higher standing in their hierarchy than values derived from the cost or income approaches to valuation. We do not share this belief, and in the long run this unsubstantiated assertion is going to come back and haunt the FASB, but meanwhile they write the rules and we follow them.

Admittedly, it is difficult to audit professional judgment, and auditors are going to have to utilize their judgment in opining on FV information developed by others, either management or valuation specialists. We have asserted, and fully believe, that two appraisers given the same assignment will come within 10% of each other in their final value indications. This may or may not be close enough for auditors, the SEC, and the PCAOB. Nonetheless, given the judgment and assumptions inherent in any valuation, this appears reasonable, and furthermore, irrespective of one's desires, that is as close as it will get.

It is our further belief that any competent appraiser, with a minimum of perhaps ten years' experience, is capable of performing most valuations for financial reporting. Irrespective of the industry or type of asset, the final definition of FV assumes what a willing buyer and a willing seller might transact a purchase and sale. Appraisers use specific techniques and methodologies in developing these assumptions about market participants. These range from verifying actual transactions for similar assets to involving discounting future cash flows and income. In a significant number of valuations for financial reporting, those involving allocation of purchase price, appraisers determine FV through physical inspection and developing the current replacement cost of the asset(s).

Consequently, all three approaches to value (i.e., cost, income, and market) and the two major premises of value (i.e., Value In-Use and Value In-Exchange) are utilized by appraisers. As long as financial managers understand what these are and can provide proper direction to the appraiser, the resulting values will surely suffice for financial reporting.

Only when the results of a valuation are going to directly affect cash flows of the parties (e.g., divorce or gift tax) will appraisal reports from either party likely differ. This book is written for financial reporting, not dispute settlement, so we wanted to alert readers as to why two appraisers can at times provide widely different answers. In those situations, the differences can be narrowed, if not eliminated, if the same assumptions about the future are used by both parties. Perhaps that is wishful thinking when dealing with an ex-spouse or the IRS, but it does get to the heart of any questions about the answers or how the appraisers arrived at the answers.

CHAPTER 5

Allocation of Purchase Price (SFASs 141R and 142)

Both old Statement of Financial Accounting Standards (SFAS) 141 and new SFAS 141R require that the purchase of another company, for one lump sum, be broken down into its constituent parts. A basic Generally Accepted Accounting Principle (GAAP) is entering newly acquired assets (and liabilities) at their cost. In terms of a business combination, we usually assume that on day 1 cost and value are the same. Thus if target company is purchased for $100 million, including assumption of liabilities, then under SFAS 141 the acquiring company must determine how much of that $100 million purchase price properly pertains, on a separate basis, to working capital; Plant, Property, and Equipment (PP&E); and identifiable intangible assets. After going through this exercise, the difference between the sum of the Fair Values (FV) of each asset and the total purchase price shows up as goodwill. In this chapter we will go over the following points:

- Is the purchase price of target company equal to its FV?
- How do we handle synergies available to the acquirer that may have allowed it to pay more than other market participants?
- How does the new and revised GAAP, issued as SFAS 141R, differ from past practice?
- How do we identify each intangible asset and contingent liability?
- What happens if the acquirer has a true bargain purchase, buying target company for less than its true FV?

Then in the following chapter we discuss the specific methodologies that appraisers use in valuing working capital, PP&E, intangible assets,

Exhibit 5.1   Valuation of Contingent Lawsuit

Assumptions:

Plaintiff asking $50 million for patent infringement in a Jury Trial

Attorney thinks only a 30% chance company will lose; = 70% chance company will prevail and owe nothing

If plaintiff wins, attorney estimates $35 million damages would be awarded

CON 7 Analysis:

Scenarios	Probability*	Value
Company found not guilty, and no damages	70%	-0-
Company found guilty and damages awarded of:		
$1,000,000	2%	$ 20,000
$5,000,000	3%	$ 150,000
$20,000,000	5%	$1,000,000
$35,000,000	13%	$4,550,000
$50,000,000	4%	$2,000,000
$60,000,000	3%	$1,800,000
	100%	$9,520,000

*See narrative in text

and contingent liabilities as well as how to determine useful lives for calculating depreciation and amortization.

IS THE PURCHASE PRICE EQUAL TO FAIR VALUE?

If one refers back to the definition of FV (the price at which property would exchange between a willing buyer and willing seller, neither under compulsion and with full knowledge of both parties), then it would seem that the purchase price of a business is by definition FV. Virtually all business combinations are the subject of protracted negotiation, nobody is forcing the buyer to buy or the seller to sell, and the amount of due diligence assures both parties that there are few, if any, surprises.

Furthermore, what difference does it make in financial reporting if the final negotiated purchase price is *not* FV? In other words, why are we even discussing this topic as the first item in this chapter on allocation of purchase price? If the purchase price is greater than FV, there may have to be an immediate write-off. If the purchase price is less than FV, and we discuss this in a following section, there may be a pickup in income, but it will raise serious questions for auditors and the Securities and Exchange Commission (SEC).

How can the purchase price of a company differ from the true FV of the company? Several factors can make this happen:

- The prospective buyers engaged in a bidding war and the winner simply overpaid.
- In a stock transaction, the exchange ratio is fixed at one point, but when the deal closes, the buyer's stock has dropped precipitously.
- The buyer anticipated significant synergies that were not available to other buyers.
- The buyer had noneconomic motives to make the deal, for example, the CEO wants to run a larger company or wants to buy out a competitor, customer, or supplier.

Let us look at each factor in detail:

- *Overbidding* is a common occurrence. There are many situations where two or more buyers compete, each escalating their offer until the other party drops out. The term buyer's remorse often describes this situation. The fact is that more often than companies want to admit, they paid too much to prevent a competitor from winning; the fear is that if the competitor wins, the combination will be too powerful, so it is better to pay more today to preclude that from happening.
- *Stock prices collapse* sometimes when a deal is announced. Often the parties will have agreed to a collar; that is, the exchange ratio will be adjusted up or down by a certain percentage if specified events occur, but the range of stock prices may be outside the collar and the buyer still wants to move forward. Often there will be material adverse changes in the seller (lowering the value), but for one reason or another based on legal advice, the buyer cannot stop the deal.
- *Synergies* between the buyer and seller (e.g., the ability to eliminate duplicate expenses, sell more products, or reduce production costs)

are all motivations for business combinations. However, the basic principle of FV does not allow for unique synergies to be incorporated into the determination of FV. If only one company can achieve the synergies, then almost by definition there are no other willing buyers, and the final purchase price is not considered to be true FV.

- *Noneconomic motives* are almost impossible to quantify, much less get the buyer to admit to. Nonetheless, the history of some of the great conglomerates, like Tyco or ITT, suggests that acquisitions just for the sake of acquisitions are not all that infrequent. In such situations, in effect the seller has a temporary advantage and can obtain a selling price above true FV.

While the usual presumption then is that the purchase price equals FV on day 1, appraisers should test this assumption as part of their valuation. In Exhibit 5.2 we show such a test, albeit simplified for ease of explanation.

TESTING FAIR VALUE

Exhibit 5.2 shows a simplified test that should be undertaken both by the company and performed by an appraiser doing a valuation for allocation of purchase price.

Example A shows that the projected cash flows, when discounted at 12%, are equal to the purchase price of $100 million. So, if the Weighted Average Cost of Capital is approximately 12%, then one can be comfortable that the purchase price for the target was indeed consummated at FV.

Example B shows cash flows some 30% less than in the previous example. In order for the Present Value (PV) of the cash flows to equal the purchase price, it is necessary to discount them at 4%. Another way of looking at this is to say that the buyer will achieve only a 4% return on the investment in the target. Discounted at the same 12% rate, the PV is only $66.7 million. So if the business is worth $66.7 million and they are paying $100 million, there is obviously a disconnect. Virtually no companies are willing to invest in risky opportunities (e.g., mergers are considered risky) that have only a 4% potential return. Most companies have a minimum expected return of at least 10%, and many have hurdle rates of 14% to 15%.

Exhibit 5.2 Testing that Purchase Price Equals Fair Value

$ 000s omitted
Purchase Price = $100,000

Projected Income

		Year 1	2	3	4	5	6	7	8	Terminal Value 9
Example A:	Net Cash Flow:	$ 9,000	$ 9,450	$ 9,923	$10,419	$10,940	$11,487	$12,061	$12,664	$113,975
	Disc. Factor	0.94639	0.84764	0.75919	0.67998	0.60903	0.54548	0.48856	0.43758	0.39192
		$ 8,518	$ 8,010	$ 7,533	$ 7,084	$ 6,662	$ 6,266	$ 5,892	$ 5,541	$ 44,669
Net Present Value at:	12%	$100,177								
Example B: [−30%]	Net Cash Flow:	$ 6,300	$ 6,615	$ 6,946	$ 7,293	$ 7,658	$ 8,041	$ 8,443	$ 8,865	$ 70,918
	4% Disc. Factor	0.97917	0.93880	0.90010	0.86299	0.82741	0.79330	0.76059	0.72924	0.69917
		$ 6,169	$ 6,210	$ 6,252	$ 6,294	$ 6,336	$ 6,379	$ 6,421	$ 6,464	$ 49,584
Net Present Value at:	4%	$100,109								
	12%	$ 66,649								
Example C: [+40%]	Net Cash Flow:	$12,600	$13,230	$13,892	$14,586	$15,315	$16,081	$16,885	$17,729	$159,565
	19% Disc. Factor	0.91824	0.77424	0.65281	0.55043	0.46411	0.39132	0.32995	0.27820	0.23457
		$11,570	$10,243	$ 9,069	$ 8,029	$ 7,108	$ 6,293	$ 5,571	$ 4,932	$ 37,430
Net Present Value at:	19%	$100,245								
	12%	$140,248								

In Example B, therefore, one would reasonably consider that the $100 million purchase price was above the true FV of target company. The reasons why this could occur were discussed previously. If the purchase price were too high, it is very possible that an immediate impairment of the goodwill arising from this purchase would have to be made. We discuss testing goodwill, and other intangible assets, for impairment in Chapter 8. Suffice it to say that very few CEOs are comfortable with buying another company and immediately having to write off a significant portion of the purchase price, regardless of whether the purchase was made for cash or stock.

In Example C, with cash flows some 40% higher than in Example A, the target would provide a 19% rate of return. Discounted at the appropriate 12% discount rate, the PV is some $140 million. This suggests a bargain purchase. Buying a $140 million business for $100 million sounds too good to be true. As more than one observer has commented, if something appears to be too good to be true, it probably is not true. In the real world, absent compulsion on the part of the seller, there are few true bargains. If so, then how does one explain that certain acquisitions are in practice accounted for as bargain purchases? The FASB explicitly states, and we support the idea, that if it appears that assets are being sold for less than they are worth, other factors may be involved.

Typically, the seller may have certain contingent liabilities, such as environmental problems (think asbestos) or major lawsuits (think tobacco). Under present rules (SFAS 5), companies do not show such liabilities on their books unless there is considered to be a greater than 50% chance that payments will have to be made. Under the new SFAS 141R rules, the buyers will have to account for these contingencies. How to deal with these contingencies is covered in Chapter 7. The requirement that buyers fully consider all future contingencies may well, for practical purposes, eliminate bargain purchases.

Nonetheless, the type of analysis set forth in Exhibit 5.2 must be performed by the appraiser, and should be performed by the acquirer before closing, just to obviate any unpleasant surprises.

WEIGHTED AVERAGE COST OF CAPITAL

In the previous examples we discounted the projected cash flows at 12%, which we identified as the assumed Weighted Average Cost of

Capital (WACC). Financial theory, which we do not replicate here, suggests that the WACC is the appropriate rate at which to discount cash flows. The mathematical calculation of WACC is straightforward, although the necessary adjustments involve professional judgment.

The basic concept of WACC is that a particular company, or all companies in an industry, will finance its assets with a combination of debt and equity. Debt requires the payment of interest, which is usually deductible for taxes. Equity does not have mandatory payments, but usually requires a higher return. The equity holders bear the ultimate risk of failure of the enterprise. So the calculation of the weighted average of the two classes of funds requires an assumption about the appropriate percentages of debt and equity, the anticipated interest rate on the debt, and the required rate of return for the equity.

Exhibit 5.3 shows a simplified calculation for a company in the medical supply business. In one sense this example is not typical because the profit/earnings (P/E) ratios in this industry are so high that the cost of equity appears low. However, offsetting this is the fact that investors in this industry expect, even demand, high growth in revenues and continued high margins. Missing expectations even for one quarter will result in a severe drop in equity price, thus moving the company to a higher cost of equity. Nonetheless, for the companies selected for this example, one can see that the firms have relatively little debt, and a majority of the capitalization comes from equity. Consequently, the selected firms have a WACC of only 3.48%, which is significantly below the WACC for companies in most industries.

For the specific assignment for which this calculation was made, and the subject was a new and small company, we had to make two adjustments. First, large companies invariably have lower costs of capital than smaller ones. Studies show this point clearly, and appraisers often add a premium to the industry WACC if the subject company being valued is smaller than the typical industry comparable.

A second adjustment is often made to reflect the appraiser's judgment regarding the business risk inherent in the subject company. A start-up firm (the subject of the specific valuation) simply cannot command equity at the same return as can a well-established firm like J&J. In this case, with the subject's revenue at a small percentage of the publicly traded comparables, and with uncertain growth prospects, we felt it advisable to add a company-specific risk premium of 5%.

Exhibit 5.3 Calculation of WACC

Comparables:	Current Price	TTM Earnings	Price/Earnings Ratio	P/E Yield	[Millions] Equity Value	%	[Millions] Debt	%	Total Capitalization
Johnson & Johnson	$57.85	$2.86	20.2	4.9%	$171,000	98.0%	$3,453	2.0%	$174,453
Zimmer	$74.74	$2.08	35.9	2.8%	$ 18,000	95.4%	$ 869	4.6%	$ 18,869
Stryker	$46.09	$1.29	35.7	2.8%	$ 18,800	99.9%	$ 16	0.1%	$ 18,816

	Pre-Tax Cost of Debt	After-Tax [40%] Cost	Weighted Avg. Cost of Debt	Weighted Avg. Cost of Equity	Weighted Avg. Cost of Capital
Johnson & Johnson	5.23%	3.14%	0.062%	4.846%	4.908%
Zimmer	2.26%	1.36%	0.062%	2.655%	2.717%
Stryker	5.58%	3.35%	0.003%	2.797%	2.799%
				Average:	3.475%

WACC for above Companies:	3.47%	
Small Company Premium	6.00%	
Company Specific Risk	5.00%	
WACC:	14.47%	
say:	14.50%	

For this particular firm, it was our professional judgment that 14.5% was the appropriate WACC, and that was the rate used in our analysis. Company-specific values can range from 3.5% to 25% or more, but most companies we have dealt with seem to have a WACC between 10% and 14%. Having said that, it is imperative to develop a specific WACC for each valuation. Trying to use a WACC rate from one company or industry to evaluate a company in another industry is simply not supportable.

One point that should be dealt with here is that WACCs are usually built up from companies in the same industry as the subject of the valuation exercise. This is consistent with the Financial Accounting Standards Board (FASB) requirements that valuations should be developed from the perspective of market participants. In most industries there is a more or less standard debt/equity ratio, for example, but then what should be done if the subject company has a significantly different percentage of debt in its capitalization? Or, as a different example, it just emerged from bankruptcy and lenders are charging a much higher interest rate?

The pure theory says to use the industry WACC, almost irrespective of the company-specific situation. Practical considerations, however, usually dictate an adjustment to reflect the actual economics of the situation. So, for example, we were once evaluating an acquisition made by a Fortune 5 company that had an extremely low cost of capital. They insisted that their low WACC was derived from their exceptional operating success, that they used the company-specific WACC in their acquisition analysis, and that it would be misleading to use an industry-wide WACC for this particular acquisition. The client's logic appeared sound, and that was what we did, even though there were virtually no other firms with such a low WACC. The result was that the buyer could pay a premium for the target and justify it because of the lower cost of capital. As discussed previously, in theory perhaps the buyer overpaid relative to the real FV of the company from the perspective of other market participants. In practice, the buyer knew exactly what was being done, and it worked out very well for the shareholders.

Note: It is the application of this type of judgment that makes valuation an art, not a science. There is no substitute for the valuation specialist having knowledge of the specific facts and circumstances; he or she should not be totally bound by pure theory. Of course, any such adjustments must be justified and explained in the valuation report.

SYNERGIES

Both the FASB and valuation theory support the concept that FV is to be determined *without* regard for synergies that are unavailable to any market participant. Take a specific example, however, and this theory may not be as supportable as it seems. As an example, "Was the value assigned by P&G to Gillette increased because of unique (P&G) synergies?" In analyzing this transaction, the author has zero knowledge of the transaction or the parties, other than what is available in the business press.

At the time this book is being written, P&G made an offer for Gillette, offering to pay some 12% above the previous price at which Gillette had sold. The deal is being analyzed in the business press as allowing P&G to expand its line to include men's products, which will complement P&G's extensive line of women's cosmetics, detergents, and so forth. Thus there also might be the opportunity to expand internationally the sale of Gillette products in areas where P&G is strong. Finally, the parties anticipate reducing total employment by some 4%.

The reason for looking at this highly visible transaction is that it brings the issue into perspective. If P&G paid more than any other party, but an amount that is reasonable in relation to *its* synergies, then the excess should be carried as *goodwill*. If the so-called synergies, however, are available to any prospective purchaser, then there is a presumption that P&G has acquired, and paid for, some identifiable intangibles. Furthermore, there is a major difference in accounting treatment, and P&L effect, between goodwill and identifiable intangibles. Thus this discussion, which applies to all business combinations, has broad relevance.

P&G is one of the world's largest consumer goods companies, and the size of the Gillette transaction suggests that very few other companies, either in the United States or internationally, have the resources to undertake such a gigantic merger. In addition, few other companies could successfully integrate Gillette into their own marketing and distribution system, thus taking advantage of potential cost reductions. Look at it another way: Were Gillette to be acquired by a private equity organization, there are virtually no cost reductions (synergies) available, assuming as we do that Gillette's management is already running the company effectively and efficiently.

Without going into a detailed analysis of the international consumer goods industry (although a detailed appraisal would have to do so), it appears that the market participants who could seriously bid for Gillette number fewer than ten. Virtually every one of them has certain unique characteristics, such as management, recent changes in technology, or market share such that an acquisition of Gillette would be seriously considered, much less considered feasible.

In short, there are a limited number of market participants available to bid for Gillette, and hence little chance of a bidding war. The price offered by P&G appears to be as low as possible to encourage existing Gillette shareholders to tender their shares. Furthermore, the announced plans and cost reductions appear in line for transactions of this size. For comparison, think of the Bank of America acquisition of Fleet Boston, where B of A promised very substantial cost reductions and essentially was able to deliver on its projections. Certainly for bank acquisitions, there are many potential market participants, whereas for international consumer goods companies there are far fewer.

The conclusion we reach, with this superficial analysis, is that the prospective synergies or cost savings that P&G anticipates are fully in line with what market participants could expect, assuming that one of the maybe four or five other large international consumer goods firms actually was interested in Gillette. The consequence of this analysis, if it were correct, is to anticipate that a detailed analysis of the transaction after it closes, for purposes of developing the final allocation of purchase price, should be able to identify significant intangible assets that meet the definition of SFAS 141R. This type of analysis is required for every business combination, and the results will affect the subsequent reported operating results.

COMPARING SFAS 141R WITH ITS PREDECESSOR, SFAS 141

While we will discuss the valuation considerations of the following changes in Chapters 6 and 9, we highlight them here for readers who are more familiar with the provisions of the original SFAS 141 dealing with business combinations:

- Business combinations will be measured at the FV of the business acquired rather than the gross cost paid. Implications are:
  - Transaction costs must be expensed, not capitalized.
  - Contingent consideration must be recognized as a liability at FV, thus increasing the amount of goodwill.
  - FV of equity securities issued would be valued at the closing date rather than the date the deal was announced.
- Recognize assets and liabilities for contingencies
- Business combination accounting could no longer recognize future restructuring costs to be incurred.
- Partial acquisitions would require valuation of the total company at FV, and the minority interests would also be at FV.

TRANSACTION COSTS

At least until the current time, when assets are put on the balance sheet, one is supposed to capitalize all costs necessary to put the asset in working condition. Thus, for a major piece of production equipment, the cost includes inbound freight, installation, and debugging. Put a different way, what is the value to the buyer of a milling machine at the seller's loading dock? Very little. What is the useful value to the buyer of the same milling machine on its own loading dock? Some more, but still relatively little. What is the useful value of the milling machine bolted to the floor on the assembly line, but not set up and running? An increase in value but still not useful for actual production. Only when the machine is installed and running, producing the output for which it was acquired is the real FV of the equipment going to be realized. In short, it is well established that the FV must include all costs necessary to bring the unit to full production capacity and capability.

Now, in SFAS 141R, the FASB is turning this long-established concept upside down. The argument is that the transaction costs (i.e., investment banker fees, legal and accounting fees, valuation fees) are not part of the value of the enterprise to the buyer. The fact that any market participant is similarly going to have to incur investment banking fees, legal and accounting fees, and so forth is simply disregarded. It appears that the FASB's perspective is, again, market participants who might buy the newly acquired business from the buyer. Such a new buyer would not be interested in the now seller's transactions costs.

The short-term impact of the new FASB rule is going to be that in the accounting period of a major acquisition, the quarterly earnings are going to take a hit for all the accounting, legal, and investment banking fees. This will be explained to analysts, journalists, and shareholders, and in the long run may even help. Inasmuch as the costs will have to be expensed for financial statements, it might be reasonable to assume that the Internal Revenue Service (IRS) would allow the costs for the current period. Inasmuch as financial and tax accounting are related—but not identical—there is some chance that expensing for books may change the IRS view.

The longer-term consequence of this basic change to GAAP is going to be felt in PP&E. It will be difficult to have one standard for fixed assets and a different approach for business combinations. We shall simply have to see how this plays out over the next few years, but readers should be fully aware of the implication that this change in expensing deal costs has for PP&E.

CONTINGENT CONSIDERATION

Many potential transactions between buyer and seller founder because the parties cannot agree on what the target company is worth. The value of the business is dependent on future revenues and profits, and reasonable people will often disagree on their respective outlook. Invariably, the buyer is more conservative in its projections and the seller more optimistic, just as in the examples we cited in earlier chapters such as in divorce valuations.

There is nothing wrong with a disagreement, but without some mechanism for resolving the differences (think courts for divorce), few business combinations would be consummated. Sooner or later the same idea arrives to the parties in disagreement: "We'll buy your company at the valuation based on our projections, but if in fact you are correct and the business does as well as you think, then we will pay you, say, five times the increase in earnings over our base amount."

This solves the dispute, at least temporarily. We will omit the troubling issues that arrive three years later when the target has been integrated and the parties now try to figure out the real earnings of the company they bought three years earlier. There is substantial room for dispute, and this is ultimately a matter to be resolved between the cost accountants and the lawyers, but nonetheless some money is likely to change hands. Until recently the accounting solution was simple. Any contingent payments for the company, subsequent to the original transaction, were treated as goodwill. Subject to the usual impairment test (see Chapter 8), there was essentially no Profit and Loss impact of such contingent payouts.

Now the rules are different. Companies *must* estimate the payout most likely to be incurred and book this as a liability on day 1. Then, as and when a contingent payout is actually incurred, the amount is charged to the liability previously set up. That seems reasonable, at first glance. At second glance, however, this is a huge potential trap. The FASB further stipulates that if the ultimate payment is greater than the liability set up on day 1, the additional payment is charged to *current expense, not* charged to goodwill. Oops. An immediate P&L hit is incurred, perhaps not anticipated by security analysts and shareholders, or even creditors.

But wait, there is a solution. Just as any payment in excess of the amount accrued gets charged to expense, any amount paid *less* than anticipated now shows up as a *gain*, a credit to P&L. It does not take a genius to figure out that companies will want to be ultraconservative in estimating contingent payouts. The more they overestimate, the greater the favorable impact on subsequent P&L.

The members of the FASB have to be given credit for understanding the impact of their new rule. They know, and acknowledge, that companies will be tempted to overaccrue. The FASB believes, and they are probably correct, that the independent auditors, and certainly the SEC, are going to scrutinize closely the dollar amount set up on day 1. We discuss in Chapter 7 how to calculate this contingent payout. Suffice it to say here that if the parties cannot agree during the negotiations how things are going to turn out, how can they agree on the most likely anticipated payout? The short answer is that they cannot, and an independent valuation specialist will have to be called in to develop an independent assessment. As long as the appraiser has no bias, the independent auditors and the SEC will have no choice (other than to make their own assessment) but to accept this judgment, assuming it is well supported by analysis.

FAIR VALUE OF EQUITY SECURITIES ISSUED

This is a straightforward issue. As discussed earlier, if a deal is set with a fixed number of shares, and the shares change value significantly between deal time and closing, the impact of the change in value of the buyer's shares can be significant. There has been real controversy at times over this issue, and the new rule eliminates one area of dispute. It does suggest, however, that in consummating a deal that the parties absolutely anticipate the impact of a change in the value of the buyer's stock before closing. The usual way is to have a collar, saying in effect that the *number of shares* will be modified, up or down as the case may be, depending on the *price* of the stock during the waiting period.

Presumably, then, if the market is efficient, any change in the value of the deal will be reflected in the price of the buyer's stock. The number of shares will have been modified, and the deal will still close at something approximating Fair Value.

CONTINGENT ASSETS AND LIABILITIES

Perhaps the most significant change required by the FASB in accounting for business combinations deals with contingent assets and liabilities. Just as with the contingent consideration for a dispute between the buyer and seller as to the real value of the company, now buyers will also have to quantify the liabilities inherent in the seller. (See Exhibit 5.1 on page 98).

If the transaction is for the purchase of assets, the liabilities stay with the seller, so in theory buyers may now focus on asset purchases. As a practical matter, however, few sellers want to retain liabilities, no matter how remote, so most acquisitions are made in a way that the buyer assumes the liabilities. The FASB logic, in requiring buyers to quantify liabilities, is they assume, probably correctly, that buyers will have made at least a mental adjustment to account for the assumption of any liabilities.

The important point to keep in mind here is that SFAS 5, currently in effect as of the date this book is being written, states that contingencies must be accrued if two separate tests are both met:

1. It is *probable* that an asset has been impaired or a liability has been incurred; and
2. The amount of the loss can be reasonably estimated.

While a lot of thought has been given to the appropriate definition of "probable," in this circumstance most observers believe that the loss has to be more likely than not, or to be specific, over 50%. Also, what is a "reasonable estimation" of a loss?

Take a major lawsuit, such as the tobacco companies have faced. Will the tobacco company prevail? Its attorney writes a letter saying the company has a good defense and is not likely to lose. In fact, tobacco companies have lost relatively few such claims, so the attorney statement appears on the surface to be reasonable. Furthermore, even if the company lost, who knows today how much a jury might award and whether an appellate judge might not reduce damages awarded by the jury. These uncertainties, in line with the requirements of SFAS 5, have resulted in a large number of disclosures in financial reports, but relatively few accruals booked as a liability.

Most financial managers are comfortable with SFAS as written and typically interpreted. While judgment is required, both by the company and by its auditor, 30 years' experience provides excellent guidelines for practical application of these rules on contingencies. Having said that, the new business combination rules totally overthrow SFAS 5, albeit only for merger transactions. For all other purposes, SFAS 5 stays in effect at least for now, but for mergers, it is a totally new ballgame.

The FASB requires companies to quantify, and show on their books, amounts for *all* liabilities, irrespective of whether or not they meet the "probable" test or the "reasonably estimated" test mentioned earlier. SFAS 5 calls for the buyer to put a dollar amount on each potential liability (e.g., environmental liability such as asbestos, or lawsuits such as tobacco). Then when the contingency does come to pass and an actual liability can be quantified, the company will charge the payment to the previously set up accrual. As with contingent payments, if the expense is greater than anticipated, the net difference is charged to current expense. If the final resolution is for less than the accrual, the company must reverse the balance and credit income.

How to calculate the liability is shown in Exhibit 5.1 and also covered in Chapter 7, using the probability approach of Concepts Statement 7. So, in simple terms, if a company is being sued for $100 million, but the estimate is that there is only a 2% chance of the plaintiff succeeding, then the company sets up roughly a $2 million liability. If there were a large number of contingencies, and the probability estimates were reliable, this FASB approach is sound and defensible.

Critics argue, with some justification, that the one thing that is certain is the company will never pay out exactly $2 million. Either the suit will be dismissed with zero liability, or if the suit is lost the final settlement will be large, perhaps close to the $100 million claimed. The critics argue that putting $2 million on the balance sheet tells statement readers virtually nothing about the real economics or cash flows of the contingency. In fact, the current, and presumably continuing, SFAS 5 requirements do require a narrative disclosure. Such narrative in practice is going to be more useful than what essentially is an arbitrary number that everyone knows will never be paid.

Nonetheless, the FASB feels that by mandating quantification of contingencies in business combinations, a fairer picture of what was bought and what is owed will be made available. Whether the same logic will at some point be extended to *all* contingencies, not just those arising in a merger transaction, is as yet undecided. The FASB published an Invitation to Comment on this very topic, with comments to be received in early 2006.

Note: In fairness, it should be noted that virtually every proposal for change in GAAP accounting has been fought by constituents, most often financial executives of corporations and their bosses, the CEOs. The views with alarm fortunately have rarely turned out to be true, thus leading the FASB to take with a large pinch of salt comments that quantifying contingent liabilities will somehow destroy the American Way of Life—an assertion made by more than one respondent to the FASB views with regard to expensing stock options.

RESTRUCTURING COSTS

In the past, in an effort to predict synergies (cost savings) and then implement those savings, companies would set up as an initial liability the costs to be incurred in closing plants, laying off duplicate employees, and so forth. It almost appears superfluous to comment that in order to achieve cost savings one has to actually incur certain upfront expenditures. Rationalizing Production, Marketing, R&D, Human Resources, and Accounting is never easy and invariably incurs payments to the now redundant employees; yet the headcount reduction is at the heart of proposed savings to be achieved from a business combination.

Many managers believe that putting together a business combination involves several integrated operations. So if the purchase price is planned based on certain actions that will be taken, then such actions are actually part of the transaction. This has been the logic of setting up, as a liability, future expenses to be incurred for rationalizing operations. In other words, you cannot get the future savings, which have been incorporated into the transaction price, without incurring the upfront costs.

This logic has prevailed for many years, but with certain unfortunate consequences. The liabilities, incurred for future expenses, have on occasion been used to make subsequent quarters and years look better. The SEC, in particular, has been concerned about what it refers to as cookie-jar accounting. Companies have a cookie jar of accrued expenses, and they dip into the jar for just as much as they need to meet earnings targets; the amounts withdrawn from the liability and credited to earnings were not always directly related to true restructuring associated with the original business combination.

The FASB has stepped into the breach and in its revised SFAS 141 now precludes setting up restructuring charges as an initial liability. What happens to the expenses actually incurred, in effect the investment that has to be made in order to achieve the savings? The answer, while perhaps unpalatable, is simple. Expenses incurred after the deal is closed must be charged to expense at the time they are made. In short, you cannot anticipate future expenditures.

The immediate effect is to preclude cookie-jar accounting. So the FASB decision can be seen in terms of an anti-abuse approach. People did bad things with the old rules, so we will change the rules and now they cannot do that any more. This concept of making accounting rules to prevent abuse, and not based on sound concepts, has within it the seeds of its own destruction.

In requiring companies to set up a liability for contingent consideration and for contingent liabilities that may never be paid, the rule seems to be conservatism. So even if you do not think you will have to pay an amount on a lawsuit, you still have to set up the liability as though you will. But when it comes to actual expenditures that you *know* will have to be made, payments to employees who are going to be laid off as part of the rationalization of production, you can *not* set them up as a liability.

To many observers, the logic of these two positions appears to be in conflict. Certainly, the FASB members have explanations about the differences between the two liabilities; from the perspective of ordinary people, however, the two approaches to accounting practice are difficult to reconcile. Setting up a liability you know will *not* be paid, and not setting up a liability you know *will* be paid, gives critics of accounting theory and accounting practice a juicy target at which to take aim.

IDENTIFYING SPECIFIC INTANGIBLE ASSETS

In an Appendix to SFAS 141, the FASB has conveniently provided a list of some 29 different identifiable intangible asset categories. Many of these, such as trade names, patents, and noncompetition agreements, are intuitively obvious, and companies run into them all the time. Others, such as newspaper mastheads, song lyrics, ballets, and mask works, are almost by definition rare in the world of general business, and the author admits he has never valued any of the latter group.

In Chapter 6 we cover the specific valuation techniques appraisers utilize in valuing the most common identifiable intangibles. Here we only want to show how to identify the assets that have to be valued. The most common intangible assets, found in many acquisitions, are:

- Trademarks, trade names*
- Internet domain names
- Noncompetition agreements*
- Customer lists*
- Customer relationships*
- Licensing and royalty agreements
- Lease agreements
- Backlog
- Franchise agreements*
- Operating and broadcast rights*
- Employment contracts
- Patented technology*

*Specific valuation methodology is described in detail in Chapter 6.

- Software
- Unpatented technology

Some of these are obviously easy to identify and value, and others less so. Here we discuss briefly the issues involved in valuation.

Licensing and royalty agreements can be either an asset or a liability. As an asset, the acquiring company may have licensed its patents or trade names to others. The valuation is straightforward. The company should estimate future royalty income, for as many years out as the agreements extend, plus a reasonable estimate for likely renewals. The projected cash flow would then be discounted at a rate slightly above the WACC. The premium would reflect the business risk that the licensees would stop making or selling the licensed product(s).

As a liability, when the acquiring company has licensed someone else's patents or trade names, the same estimate of future cash flows should be made; that estimate should be for the difference between the license or royalty rate in the contract and what the rate would be if it were negotiated today. The discount rate most appropriately would be the company's own WACC. The lower the discount rate, the higher the liability amount that would be calculated. So it would be inappropriate to put in a business risk premium as the company has to make the payments.

Lease agreements, while very common, rarely present any valuation problems, because any agreement, say for office space, has little value unless the rental price is significantly above or below current market rates. So if the target company has a nine-year life left on a lease for 100,000 square feet, at $20.00 per square foot, this is not a $2 million per year liability for nine years. If current office rents in the area, for the same quality building (even better in the same building), are between $19.00 and $21.00, then one reasonably assumes that the $20.00 is a market rent. Because the future lease payments will correspond with future occupancy benefits, there is no present value to the lease. Theoretically, one can assert that moving expenses were paid to obtain occupancy and that this is an asset. However, the author has never seen this degree of precision applied. Market rents for leased assets, therefore, are virtually never booked as an asset or liability.

The situation can change in our example. If current rents are either $25.00 or $15.00, then the company either has an asset or a liability.

The *difference* between the current rate called for by the lease and the current market rent represents the amount of the benefit or cost. The valuation is straightforward again; the difference in rent per square foot, times the number of square feet, is the amount that is carried out for the remaining years of the lease and discounted at the WACC, with no premium or discount. This asset or liability is then amortized by the buyer over the remaining life of the lease. The effect of setting up an asset or liability in this situation is that future P&Ls will reflect current market rates. There will be no reduction in cost if current market rates are lower than the lease and no penalty if the current market rates are higher than the lease.

Our example has dealt with leases of office space, but the exact same approach applies to any and all of target company's lease agreements, including machinery and equipment, vehicles, and intangibles.

Employment contracts in our experience are treated exactly the same way as leases. If one has a five-year contract, say, with the Vice President of Marketing, this is neither an asset nor a liability if the total compensation is commensurate with the work performed. Again, theoretically, one could assign some value to the contract representing the cost of hiring the individual or a replacement, but because the FASB does not permit valuation of the assembled workforce, it would be highly unusual to assign a value to the fact that an individual was on the payroll. Experience suggests that most employment agreements or contracts are at market levels. It is difficult to conceive of a significant executive signing an employment agreement for *less* than he is worth.

In theory, again, a buyer may choose to pay part of the purchase price of an acquisition to one or more of the principals over time. This is usually structured as a noncompete agreement but does not have to be. We have seen situations where the seller has a five-year noncancelable employment agreement, where the future salary payments are in reality payment for selling the business. If such an agreement, effectively a no-work contract, is found, then it should be set up as a liability. However, it will be difficult to get the parties to agree that this is a no-work agreement that is really part of the purchase price. Both parties will assert that the agreement is real and that the seller will continue to work, consult, help, or be present as and when needed. For an appraiser to come in and assert that the agreement is a sham is going to take a strong stomach to argue with your own client. This is particularly true because both parties will assert the opposite, and the appraiser essentially is calling them both liars. Not good client relations!

UNPATENTED TECHNOLOGY

The calculation of savings accruing to the owner of unpatented technology, and the conversion of that annual savings to a FV, has few if any complications. The key point is identifying what in a company is proprietary or unpatented technology. Essentially, it is sometimes referred to as trade secrets. Several firms, as a matter of policy, do not wish to disclose what they are doing. The essence of the patent system is exactly opposite that—full disclosure in exchange for a limited time for protection against interference or copying.

We will discuss valuation of patents and patented technology in Chapter 6. Here we deal only with the identification of that asset. Now at one end of the spectrum, companies do the same common task (e.g., process accounts payable) in many different ways. Some use PCs on a local basis, some have central service units, and others try to handle everything via computer between themselves and their vendors. No one approach is correct, and each may have efficiencies in certain circumstances. In our judgment, none of these techniques would count as unpatented technology. The key element is that the process is secret, not known to others. Usually employees are required to sign a nondisclosure agreement. If the process really produces significant savings, perhaps only a few key executives have a full understanding of the entire operation.

So, unless a process has significant savings, and is kept secret, it probably does not qualify as unpatented technology. We had a manufacturing client we were appraising, and even though we had signed a nondisclosure agreement, the client felt that the benefits of the process were so great, and the risk of copying by others so severe, that it would not let us see the operation. At that point, we took their word for the fact that they had a secret, unpatented technology, took their word for the savings, and verified it by analysis of the P&L by product line and by customer. The savings were showing up as increased income, and we were able to value this intangible asset.

Exhibit 5.4 Determining the Value of an Assembled Workforce

[Assume a Professional Services Firm, without production employees
Annual Revenues assumed at $175 million]

Category of Employee	Number of Employees	Average Compensation*	Annual Payroll	Recruiting Cost**	Total Hiring Cost	Training Cost	Total Assembled Workforce
Senior Exec.	5	$250,000	$ 1,250,000	45%	$ 562,500	$ 625,000	$ 1,187,500
Senior Mgrs.	25	$150,000	$ 3,750,000	35%	$1,312,500	$ 937,500	$ 2,250,000
Supervisors	100	$100,000	$10,000,000	15%	$1,500,000	$1,667,000	$ 3,167,000
Administrative	1,000	$ 50,000	$50,000,000	$3,500	$3,500,000	$4,250,000	$ 7,750,000
	1,130		$65,000,000		$6,875,000	$7,479,500	$14,354,500

*Including Benefits
**See Text

BACKLOG

The FASB has required buyers to estimate the value of any backlog in place at the closing date. So if a target company has two months of sales already booked and in production, this represents an acquired asset and at least in theory must be valued. Buyers do not like this because the value assigned to that backlog must be written off over the same two-month period, thus suppressing normal margins. In other words, just by buying the company, the first two months of operation under the new owner will show substandard profitability.

Many buyers are unhappy when they realize the impact of valuing backlog. There is no good answer except to be highly creative in determining what are the normal expense and profit margins that any market participant would expect. If the appraiser uses a healthy imagination, it is sometimes possible to set the value of the backlog at little more than the selling expense that does not have to be incurred, because one is entitled, in valuing the backlog, to provide for a reasonable return on *all* investments in the company, including working capital, PP&E, intangibles (not including goodwill), and even the assembled workforce. Experience suggests that if this analysis is properly carried out, the value will turn out to be the foregone selling expense. It would be hard to argue with that approach, because the selling expense for the existing backlog was, in practice, incurred before the sale of the overall business.

ASSEMBLED WORKFORCE

For many years the IRS did not allow as a deduction in computing taxable income any charge for goodwill, which was considered by it to have an indefinite life and therefore no appropriate amortization period. However, it did allow deductions for amortization of intangible assets that could be demonstrated to have a definite life. An example was a subscriber base for a newspaper. A buyer of a newspaper could assign a portion of the purchase price to the subscriber list and then amortize that amount over the (supportable) life of the asset. In those cases, appraisers would determine how long individual subscribers continued to subscribe before they terminated. With some relatively simple statistical reasoning, the IRS and the courts agreed that a subscriber base could be quantified and aged, and hence was a wasting asset that could be deducted for taxes.

Because of the deductibility of identifiable assets with a finite life, and the nondeductibility of goodwill with an indefinite life, companies, their accountants, and their appraisers became highly creative in coming up with specific intangible assets. There were very favorable cash flow consequences for accomplishing this task for taxes.

As might also be imagined, the IRS took a rather jaded view of some of the assets, and their valuation, leading to innumerable discussions with the IRS and often ultimately to the courts. The time and effort spent on these analyses resulted in Congress passing Section 197 of the Internal Revenue Code. This put an end, once and for all, to all of the IRS and court challenges. Now, for taxes, all intangible assets are amortized over 15 years. Even if you can demonstrate that the life is shorter, such as a three-year noncompete contract, you still use a 15-year life for taxes. There is no distinction for taxes currently between goodwill and any of the intangible assets to be discussed in the next chapter.

As a practical matter, the then-applicable GAAP rules, particularly as interpreted by the SEC, did not distinguish among these various intangible assets, other than for In-Process R&D (see Chapter 10). Virtually all of the intangible assets (including goodwill) were amortized for book purposes, usually between 20 and 40 years. There was then, and still is now, almost a total discontinuity between accounting for books and accounting for taxes for assets acquired in a business combination, other than working capital and PP&E.

The reason for this discussion is to get to the topic of assembled workforce. This was one of the major intangible assets that virtually every acquirer claimed existed at the target. And, in fact, every company did have a workforce, that workforce had real value, and appraisers had no difficulty in putting a value and a life on the assemblage. In fact, if you ask most buyers why they are bidding for a company, they will state they are acquiring the people, the products, and the customers. No business can run without all three elements.

Now, as part of the FASB's original attempt at accounting for business combinations in 2001, the FASB arbitrarily decreed that an assembled workforce was not, in its definition, an identifiable intangible asset! This despite the fact that at least 50% of all company Annual Reports, in the Chairman's letter, have the following statement: "Our employees

are our most valuable asset." So[...] than the observance, nonetheless [...] employee base. This was proven i[...] virtually wiped out because so ma[...] Trade Center.

The FASB's logic was that there is [...] and therefore any valuation would [...] insistence that the only true measure o[...] market transactions. To give them cre[...] decree, people have not been bought [...] fact is that if you were going to start [...] spend a significant amount of resources i[...] training a staff. We discuss immediately [...] for an assembled workforce.

The nature of an assembled workfor[...] is really comparable to customer relationsh[...] erate income, and without them there wo[...] FASB chose to *exclude* assembled workfo[...] relationships in their master list of identifia[...]

How appraisers develop a supportable v[...] force is straightforward. In Exhibit 5.4 we s[...] the results of an assumed valuation. For simp[...] services firm with no production workers.

Recruiting cost is based on what a comp[...] to replace workers. For senior executives, th[...] would go to an executive recruiter; their fees a[...] compensation, plus, say, 10% for out-of-pocket [...] viewing, and moving. For senior managers, recru[...] 25% plus 10% for expenses. Supervisors, one ca[...] locally, perhaps from ads, word of mouth, and [...] event, the cost of hiring lower-level employees [...] for top management. Finally, for clerical and ac[...] nel, we assume the HR function would be set up[...] applicants.

Then to the total hiring cost we have to add an [...] breaking in the new staff to the requirements of t[...] assume for top management six months, for seni[...] months, supervisors two months, and for administrat[...]

month compensation for training. In our example, the FV of the assembled workforce would be more than $14 million. Although a rule of thumb can not be used, we often find that the value of an assembled workforce is between $8,000 and $12,000 per employee, depending on the mix of skills. If we are dealing with Ph.D. scientists, the cost might be higher, and if we were dealing with door-to-door salespeople, the cost could be significantly less.

The reason for showing the calculation of the value of an assembled workforce is that the amount can, and should, be used in valuing *other* intangibles. In a residual income valuation, a charge can be made for the value of the workforce, even though the value of the workforce is not allowed by the FASB to be shown as an asset on the balance sheet. Note: The chances of the present FASB reversing itself, and allowing the FV of assembled workforce to be shown on the balance sheet of the acquirer, is remote. Logic suggests that the change should be allowed, but logic and GAAP do not always go together.

BARGAIN PURCHASES

Can there really be a true bargain purchase? Can a company be acquired below its FV? Let us go back to the definition used by the FASB, which we quoted at the beginning of Chapter 2.

> *Fair Value is the price that would be received for an asset, or paid to transfer a liability, in a current transaction between marketplace participants in the reference market for the asset or liability.*

If both parties, buyer and seller, are "knowledgeable," if they are "unrelated," and if they are "willing," then why in the world would the seller accept less than FV? The answer is simple: they would not. Obviously, a transaction between related parties cannot qualify as FV, unless an independent appraiser, for example, determines the value, because if tax or financial consequences affect the joint owner, they are not acting at arm's length. They will arrive at a "price" that maximizes their financial position, but probably will not be true FV.

Similarly, if one of the parties is an unwilling seller, for example, to meet a short-term liability, the buyer may be able to extract a price concession. That is why the definition of FV uses the concept of a willing seller, to avoid just that situation.

Finally, the usual definition of FV uses the concept of "knowledgeable." Usually this is thought to cover the situation where the seller knows more about the business than the buyer, and the buyer overpays. Rarely will the buyer know more than the seller, but history is actually replete with such situations. Just for one example, a politician may know where a highway is going to be located, and buy right-of-way before the public announcement. If the seller had known what the buyer knew, he would have asked a higher and more reasonable price.

What happens is that an appraiser looks at the total purchase price of the target, then values all of the assets acquired, and finds that sum of all the values exceeds the price paid. The FASB has allowed for this contingency in SFAS 141R by first removing all goodwill and then allowing an immediate credit to income for the difference. The closer examination of the values derived for the individual assets in such a situation probably have to be thought through again. Furthermore, there has to be a much closer examination of real and contingent liabilities, including the competitive situation and outlook for the industry. It is reasonable to assume that if a seller sells for less than the business is worth, that maybe the business is not worth so much.

Frankly, it gets back to that old adage: "If something is too good to be true, it probably is!" The real chance of finding bargain purchases in the market, with the number of prospective acquirers that are out there, seems pretty remote. Rather than accept the fact that the buyer has put something over on the seller, perhaps what is really required is a closer scrutiny of the entire business model.

PARTIAL ACQUISITIONS AND NONCONTROLLING INTERESTS

In the past, when a company bought less than 100% of another company, yet controlled it because of more than 50% ownership, the accounting that resulted was often confusing. Exhibit 5.5 shows that the old accounting method picked up a proportionate share of the FV of acquired assets and consolidated the remaining minority interests at the target's original cost.

The effect was that, as shown in Column B, the PP&E amount shown on the target's books consisted of the cost value of the acquirer, plus the proportionate share of the FV of the acquired assets plus the minority

BACKLOG

The FASB has required buyers to estimate the value of any backlog in place at the closing date. So if a target company has two months of sales already booked and in production, this represents an acquired asset and at least in theory must be valued. Buyers do not like this because the value assigned to that backlog must be written off over the same two-month period, thus suppressing normal margins. In other words, just by buying the company, the first two months of operation under the new owner will show substandard profitability.

Many buyers are unhappy when they realize the impact of valuing backlog. There is no good answer except to be highly creative in determining what are the normal expense and profit margins that any market participant would expect. If the appraiser uses a healthy imagination, it is sometimes possible to set the value of the backlog at little more than the selling expense that does not have to be incurred, because one is entitled, in valuing the backlog, to provide for a reasonable return on *all* investments in the company, including working capital, PP&E, intangibles (not including goodwill), and even the assembled workforce. Experience suggests that if this analysis is properly carried out, the value will turn out to be the foregone selling expense. It would be hard to argue with that approach, because the selling expense for the existing backlog was, in practice, incurred before the sale of the overall business.

ASSEMBLED WORKFORCE

For many years the IRS did not allow as a deduction in computing taxable income any charge for goodwill, which was considered by it to have an indefinite life and therefore no appropriate amortization period. However, it did allow deductions for amortization of intangible assets that could be demonstrated to have a definite life. An example was a subscriber base for a newspaper. A buyer of a newspaper could assign a portion of the purchase price to the subscriber list and then amortize that amount over the (supportable) life of the asset. In those cases, appraisers would determine how long individual subscribers continued to subscribe before they terminated. With some relatively simple statistical reasoning, the IRS and the courts agreed that a subscriber base could be quantified and aged, and hence was a wasting asset that could be deducted for taxes.

Because of the deductibility of identifiable assets with a finite life, and the nondeductibility of goodwill with an indefinite life, companies, their accountants, and their appraisers became highly creative in coming up with specific intangible assets. There were very favorable cash flow consequences for accomplishing this task for taxes.

As might also be imagined, the IRS took a rather jaded view of some of the assets, and their valuation, leading to innumerable discussions with the IRS and often ultimately to the courts. The time and effort spent on these analyses resulted in Congress passing Section 197 of the Internal Revenue Code. This put an end, once and for all, to all of the IRS and court challenges. Now, for taxes, all intangible assets are amortized over 15 years. Even if you can demonstrate that the life is shorter, such as a three-year noncompete contract, you still use a 15-year life for taxes. There is no distinction for taxes currently between goodwill and any of the intangible assets to be discussed in the next chapter.

As a practical matter, the then-applicable GAAP rules, particularly as interpreted by the SEC, did not distinguish among these various intangible assets, other than for In-Process R&D (see Chapter 10). Virtually all of the intangible assets (including goodwill) were amortized for book purposes, usually between 20 and 40 years. There was then, and still is now, almost a total discontinuity between accounting for books and accounting for taxes for assets acquired in a business combination, other than working capital and PP&E.

The reason for this discussion is to get to the topic of assembled workforce. This was one of the major intangible assets that virtually every acquirer claimed existed at the target. And, in fact, every company did have a workforce, that workforce had real value, and appraisers had no difficulty in putting a value and a life on the assemblage. In fact, if you ask most buyers why they are bidding for a company, they will state they are acquiring the people, the products, and the customers. No business can run without all three elements.

Now, as part of the FASB's original attempt at accounting for business combinations in 2001, the FASB arbitrarily decreed that an assembled workforce was not, in its definition, an identifiable intangible asset! This despite the fact that at least 50% of all company Annual Reports, in the Chairman's letter, have the following statement: "Our employees are our most valuable asset." Sometimes honored in the breach more than the observance, nonetheless no company can survive without its employee base. This was proven in 9/11 when some companies were virtually wiped out because so many employees worked in the World Trade Center.

The FASB's logic was that there is no market in assembled workforces, and therefore any valuation would be suspect. This gets back to their insistence that the only true measure of FV has to be derived from actual market transactions. To give them credit, ever since Abraham Lincoln's decree, people have not been bought and sold in this country. But the fact is that if you were going to start a company, you would have to spend a significant amount of resources in recruiting, hiring, moving, and training a staff. We discuss immediately how we actually develop an FV for an assembled workforce.

The nature of an assembled workforce, as an asset of a company, is really comparable to customer relationships. Both are expected to generate income, and without them there would be no company. Why the FASB chose to *exclude* assembled workforce and to *include* customer relationships in their master list of identifiable assets remains a mystery.

How appraisers develop a supportable value for an assembled workforce is straightforward. In Exhibit 5.4 we show the methodology and the results of an assumed valuation. For simplicity, this is a professional services firm with no production workers.

Recruiting cost is based on what a company would have to spend to replace workers. For senior executives, the assumption is that one would go to an executive recruiter; their fees are 35% of the first year's compensation, plus, say, 10% for out-of-pocket expenses for travel, interviewing, and moving. For senior managers, recruiting firms often charge 25% plus 10% for expenses. Supervisors, one can assume, would come locally, perhaps from ads, word of mouth, and some agencies. In any event, the cost of hiring lower-level employees is obviously less than for top management. Finally, for clerical and administrative personnel, we assume the HR function would be set up and interview local applicants.

Then to the total hiring cost we have to add an amount for training, breaking in the new staff to the requirements of the specific job. We assume for top management six months, for senior managers three months, supervisors two months, and for administrative and clerical one

Exhibit 5.4 Determining the Value of an Assembled Workforce

[Assume a Professional Services Firm, without production employees
Annual Revenues assumed at $175 million]

Category of Employee	Number of Employees	Average Compensation*	Annual Payroll	Recruiting Cost**	Total Hiring Cost	Training Cost	Total Assembled Workforce
Senior Exec.	5	$250,000	$ 1,250,000	45%	$ 562,500	$ 625,000	$ 1,187,500
Senior Mgrs.	25	$150,000	$ 3,750,000	35%	$1,312,500	$ 937,500	$ 2,250,000
Supervisors	100	$100,000	$10,000,000	15%	$1,500,000	$1,667,000	$ 3,167,000
Administrative	1,000	$ 50,000	$50,000,000	$3,500	$3,500,000	$4,250,000	$ 7,750,000
	1,130		$65,000,000		$6,875,000	$7,479,500	$14,354,500

*Including Benefits
**See Text

month compensation for training. In our example, the FV of the assembled workforce would be more than $14 million. Although a rule of thumb can not be used, we often find that the value of an assembled workforce is between $8,000 and $12,000 per employee, depending on the mix of skills. If we are dealing with Ph.D. scientists, the cost might be higher, and if we were dealing with door-to-door salespeople, the cost could be significantly less.

The reason for showing the calculation of the value of an assembled workforce is that the amount can, and should, be used in valuing *other* intangibles. In a residual income valuation, a charge can be made for the value of the workforce, even though the value of the workforce is not allowed by the FASB to be shown as an asset on the balance sheet. Note: The chances of the present FASB reversing itself, and allowing the FV of assembled workforce to be shown on the balance sheet of the acquirer, is remote. Logic suggests that the change should be allowed, but logic and GAAP do not always go together.

BARGAIN PURCHASES

Can there really be a true bargain purchase? Can a company be acquired below its FV? Let us go back to the definition used by the FASB, which we quoted at the beginning of Chapter 2.

Fair Value is the price that would be received for an asset, or paid to transfer a liability, in a current transaction between marketplace participants in the reference market for the asset or liability.

If both parties, buyer and seller, are "knowledgeable," if they are "unrelated," and if they are "willing," then why in the world would the seller accept less than FV? The answer is simple: they would not. Obviously, a transaction between related parties cannot qualify as FV, unless an independent appraiser, for example, determines the value, because if tax or financial consequences affect the joint owner, they are not acting at arm's length. They will arrive at a "price" that maximizes their financial position, but probably will not be true FV.

Similarly, if one of the parties is an unwilling seller, for example, to meet a short-term liability, the buyer may be able to extract a price concession. That is why the definition of FV uses the concept of a willing seller, to avoid just that situation.

Finally, the usual definition of FV uses the concept of "knowledge-able." Usually this is thought to cover the situation where the seller knows more about the business than the buyer, and the buyer overpays. Rarely will the buyer know more than the seller, but history is actually replete with such situations. Just for one example, a politician may know where a highway is going to be located, and buy right-of-way before the public announcement. If the seller had known what the buyer knew, he would have asked a higher and more reasonable price.

What happens is that an appraiser looks at the total purchase price of the target, then values all of the assets acquired, and finds that sum of all the values exceeds the price paid. The FASB has allowed for this contingency in SFAS 141R by first removing all goodwill and then allowing an immediate credit to income for the difference. The closer examination of the values derived for the individual assets in such a situation probably have to be thought through again. Furthermore, there has to be a much closer examination of real and contingent liabilities, including the competitive situation and outlook for the industry. It is reasonable to assume that if a seller sells for less than the business is worth, that maybe the business is not worth so much.

Frankly, it gets back to that old adage: "If something is too good to be true, it probably is!" The real chance of finding bargain purchases in the market, with the number of prospective acquirers that are out there, seems pretty remote. Rather than accept the fact that the buyer has put something over on the seller, perhaps what is really required is a closer scrutiny of the entire business model.

PARTIAL ACQUISITIONS AND NONCONTROLLING INTERESTS

In the past, when a company bought less than 100% of another company, yet controlled it because of more than 50% ownership, the accounting that resulted was often confusing. Exhibit 5.5 shows that the old accounting method picked up a proportionate share of the FV of acquired assets and consolidated the remaining minority interests at the target's original cost.

The effect was that, as shown in Column B, the PP&E amount shown on the target's books consisted of the cost value of the acquirer, plus the proportionate share of the FV of the acquired assets plus the minority

Exhibit 5.5 Partial Acquisitions: Old versus New Treatment

[1] A (All-Stock transaction) Acquirer Buys 100% of Target for $60,000, Target's Book Value of All Assets is $35,000
[2] B Acquirer Buys 60% of Target with Stock for $36,000, Old Accounting with Partial Consolidation
[2] C Acquirer Buys 60% of Target with Stock for $36,000, New Accounting with Full Consolidation

	Target Co. Books (cost)	Target's Fair Value	Acquirer's Books	A Buy 100% of Target, Full Cons.	B Old Acctg Buy 60% of Target Partial Cons.	C New Acctg Buy 60% of Target Full Cons.
Other Assets	$25,000[a]	$25,000	$110,000	$135,000	$135,000	$135,000
PP&E	$10,000		$50,000			
Fair Value (Appraisal)		$15,000	N.A.			
New PP&E Book Value:				$65,000	$63,000[b]	$65,000
Goodwill		$20,000	-0-	$20,000	$12,000[c]	$20,000
TOTAL Assets	$35,000	$60,000	$160,000	$220,000	$210,000	$220,000
Minority Interest				-0-	$14,000[d]	$24,000[e]
Equity	$35,000		$160,000	$220,000	$196,000	$196,000
	$35,000		$160,000	$220,000	$210,000	$220,000

[a] Fair Value of All Other Assets = Book Value
[b] 60% of Fair Value of Target's PP&E (.6 × $15,000) + 40% of Target's PP&E (.4 × $10,000) Book Value + Acquirer's Book Value
[c] 60% of Goodwill
[d] 40% of Target's Original Book Value of $35,000
[e] 40% of Target's Fair Value

interest's ownership in the PP&E at the target's original cost. Another way of looking at it is to say that FV was calculated only on the proportionate share of the assets that were bought, and the original cost maintained on the remainder. This approach is good in theory, but it has two problems, one internal and the other external.

Internally, calculating depreciation becomes a nightmare because two sets of records are kept for each asset, at say the 60/40 ratio used in the example. Depreciation becomes even more complex if the company buys an additional 10% of the target at a later date. Now each asset will have three values associated with the separate pieces, and this goes on until 100% is acquired. Going the other way, disposing of assets causes complications in calculating gain or loss.

However, the partial consolidation at FV with the remainder at original cost has the advantage of showing the value of the minority interest at the straightforward amount of the assets that were not acquired. In Exhibit 5.5 in Column B, the minority interest is $14,000, representing 40% of the original $35,000 of assets on the target's books at the date of the sale.

The FASB has now changed this approach, which is shown in Column C. Under the new consolidation rules, the buyer will determine the FV of all the target's assets and show that FV on its own consolidated statements. That, in effect, writes up the amount(s) that were carried under the prior partial consolidation approach. Now the PP&E shows on the new consolidated balance sheet at the full $65,000, but the minority interest now goes up to $24,000. This minority interest increase of $10,000 over the other method of consolidation derives from the minority holders having 40% of the subsidiary shown now at the subsidiary's current FV of the total enterprise. In effect, then, the outside owners are given credit for a proportionate share of the total value of the target, even though they have not realized it by sale.

Another change, which is outside of the scope of this book, should be recognized. The FASB is mandating that the amount calculated as the minority interest be shown within the equity section and not as a separate element between debt and equity on the right-hand side of the balance sheet. Space does not permit a detailed examination of why the FASB made this change, or all of the arguments pro and con. This new approach will make the valuation much easier. In effect, any time the percentage of ownership of the company changes, the transactions will be booked at the then-current FV of the business. A question can be raised as to whether if 60% of a company is bought for $36,000 that the entire company is worth $60,000. There are usually control premiums and discounts for minority interests that affect value in the real world. In practice, one will probably find that 100% of the business enterprise value is assumed to be directly proportional to the amount paid for the percentage acquired. If there is strong evidence to the contrary, one should probably use the correct figure for the true FV of the target, if the acquisition price of the proportion bought is not closely proportionate to the overall enterprise value.

CONCLUSION

The FASB has made several changes that affect accounting requirements for business combinations. Many of these deal with FV, how it is calculated, and how the values are handled in subsequent P&L accounts.

The first step is to verify that the purchase price of the target is equal to the true FV of the company. This involves an analysis of what market participants would pay, or could pay, for the business. This, in turn, implies that an analysis has to be made of synergies inherent in the purchase. In effect, there are two types of synergies, or ways to cut costs. The first is available to any new owner of the target, and in effect is a rationalization of its business model. Inefficiencies are eliminated, costs brought under control, new product development speeded up, and so forth. Realistically, the advent of new management causes these changes to happen, with a consequent improvement in operating results. Put another way, this type of profit improvement was available all along, and could have been implemented by old management, but for some reason was not. Numerous business firms specialize in short-term or turnaround management. These managers are perceived as ruthless, but they are usually effective in rooting out inefficiencies. An acquirer that plans to make these changes can quantify what it plans to do, and in effect build this into the purchase price offered.

A second type of synergy is available only to a specific buyer, perhaps a direct competitor that is willing to pay a premium to eliminate competition, or a buyer that acquires a key supplier to reduce operating costs. These savings are not available to other market participants and allow the winning bidder (buyer) to pay more than anyone else. In theory, such a premium paid by the specific buyer, because it is not available to other market participants, makes the purchase price more than FV. In practice, if these unique savings can be quantified, they effectively end up in goodwill and will be reflected in the value of the business to the new owner. Given the methodology for calculating impairment of goodwill, such a payment will not trigger bad results.

Only if the price paid is truly excessive will there be a significant risk of a short-term or even immediate impairment write-off of goodwill. However, with increased scrutiny by auditors, the SEC, and the PCAOB, companies have to be very careful in documenting why they paid what they did and understand the impact of those decisions on the purchase price allocation.

The other major change imposed by the FASB deals with contingent payments and contingent liabilities. For the first time, companies are going to have to quantify, in terms of FV, liabilities assumed. SFAS 5 in the past has had in effect a more than 50% probability rule, so if a liability is less than 50% likely to be paid, no accounting entry is made. Now, in a business combination, a liability with even a 1% probability of occurring has to be accounted for. The challenges to the appraisal community in coming up with supportable values that will withstand challenges by auditors and the SEC is not going to be easy.

CHAPTER 6

Determining the Fair Value of Intangible Assets

In this chapter we provide detailed recommendations for the valuation of several specific identifiable intangible assets, specifically as listed in Statement of Financial Accounting Standards (SFAS) 141. It should be stated initially that there is probably not one single methodology, all others of which must be excluded. Different appraisers may utilize slightly different approaches. Each valuation assignment is specific, and the facts and circumstances will dictate the assumptions used. Having said that, the approaches used here probably can be used as templates in most valuation assignments.

TRADEMARKS, TRADE NAMES

We have successfully utilized two separate approaches to the valuation of trademarks and trade names. Attorneys tell us there is a technical difference between the two, but for financial reporting, most people use the terms interchangeably.

What does a trade name do? Essentially it increases sales volume, increases the selling price of the product, or both. Two examples will suffice: Although it is not generally known, in any geographic location most of the gasoline comes from the same pipeline. Well-known brands such as Conoco may have certain proprietary additives relative to unbranded gasoline, but essentially the product dispensed at the pumps of a Conoco station and an unbranded station are very similar. Yet there are often two gas stations on the same corner, one Conoco and one unbranded. Almost always the branded gasoline will sell for two cents or more per gallon premium. Why? Consumers have faith in the brand and the company behind it, and have no knowledge of the unbranded gasoline. The fact that the gasoline came from the same refinery and the same pipeline is not generally understood, and even if it were, consumers are willing to pay a small premium for the comfort of dealing with a familiar source.

One more example is soft drinks. Everyone uses the Coca-Cola® example in discussing brand valuation, and we will not be the exception. The point is that, faced with a choice on the store shelf of a two-liter bottle of Coke at $1.49 and a comparable bottle of a store brand or generic at $1.19, most consumers will pay the 30-cent premium for Coke. Why? In blindfold tests many, if not most, individuals have difficulty in distinguishing one cola from another. Yet the combination of familiarity and comfort with a known quantity leads people to make what for them is a rational decision to pay the seemingly slight premium.

Thus the advantage of an established brand is twofold: higher price *and* higher volume. Inasmuch as production costs are probably comparable for branded and unbranded products (e.g., raw materials, energy, labor), the gross margins are going to be significantly different. While the branded product will have a lot more marketing and advertising expense, branded goods often have higher overall profit than unbranded goods. An exception might be the house brand of a store like Wal-Mart, but in that case consumers are actually buying the Wal-Mart trade name, not Wal-Mart Cola.

If a trade name provides higher margins and higher volume, this leads directly into the valuation.

Method 1 is a direct cash flow analysis, and the worksheet is shown in Exhibit 6.1. It compares the cash flows of a branded item with the cash flows of a generic or nonbranded item. The *difference* in the cash flows is then discounted at a rate approximately equal to the Weighted Average Cost of Capital (WACC). The calculation of the WACC is covered in Chapter 5. The time period over which the projected cash flows are carried has to be relevant to the product and the industry. For a brand name like Ritz Crackers that has been in existence for decades, a 15- or 20-year time horizon makes sense. For a hot electronics product such as the Apple iPod, one might not want to go out more than perhaps five to seven years. This type of judgment is very specific to every valuation assignment, and it is virtually impossible to set up rules or "bright lines," as accountants use the term.

Exhibit 6.1   Direct Method of Valuing a Brand Name

Assume 5-year life for brand
  Decreasing 30% per year
Assume no tax effect
  Net Operating Losses apply

Per Unit	Branded Item	Generic Item
Sales Price	$1.000	$0.750
Cost of Sales	$0.250	$0.240
Gross Profit	$0.750	$0.510
Adv. & Mktg.	$0.150	$0.050
G & A	$0.100	$0.090
Operating Profit	$0.500	$0.370
Tax at 40%	$0.200	$0.148
After-Tax	$0.300	$0.222
Differential:	$0.078	
Sales Volume:	10,000,000 units	
Cash Flow	$780,000	

		Year				
		1	2	3	4	5
	Cash Flow	$ 780,000	$546,000	$382,200	$267,540	$187,278
Discount Rate — Assumed WACC 14%						
	Discount Factor	0.93659	0.82157	0.72067	0.63217	0.55453
	Present Value	$ 730,537	$448,575	$275,441	$169,130	$103,852
	Net Present Value	$1,727,536				
	Rounded:	$1,730,000				

Obtaining the information required by this Method 1 may or may not be easy. The company has often completed a make-or-buy analysis and obtained the costs and revenues of generic competition. In our example we assumed the production costs of the generic were slightly less than the branded item, allowing for higher-quality materials, for example. Also, we assumed slightly less general and administrative expense, related to the fewer customers that a generic manufacturer would typically deal with. We did, however, show higher advertising and marketing expenses for the branded product, reflecting couponing and all of the other tools of branded product sales and distribution.

The strength of this Method 1 is that if the information is available, or can be developed, the resulting Fair Value (FV) of the brand is fairly definitively derived. Put a different way, there are relatively few judgment areas that can be questioned by auditors and the Securities and Exchange Commission (SEC). Unfortunately, in valuing brands, it is sometimes necessary to utilize what we refer to as Method 2.

Method 2 is usually referred to by appraisers as the Relief from Royalty method. This methodology starts with the observation that many brand names are utilized by other firms on products different from the original product. So, for example, Harley-Davidson (H-D) motorcycles are truly an iconic brand with two-wheel aficionados. Some clothing manufacturers approached H-D and asked if they could license the Harley brand for a line of men's outerwear—jackets and boots.

The clothing company, once the licensing agreement was completed, sells the jackets and boots under the Harley name, even though the motorcycle company in no way manufactures clothing. The customer attributes the qualities of an H-D "hog" to the leather jacket carrying the H-D label. Presumably, the selling price of a Harley-Davidson leather jacket is sufficiently higher than the unbranded comparable jacket to allow for the licensing fee charged by H-D for the use of its name.

Appraisers are very interested in the royalty rates charged for different brands in different industries. These royalty rates are compiled by at least two organizations, and appraisers have access to those actual transactions. So, just pulling a single made-up example, suppose the H-D royalty rate for a leather jacket is 3% of the wholesale selling price of the leather jacket. Then suppose that Disney charges a sweatshirt manufacturer 7% for using Mickey Mouse printed on the sweatshirt. Admittedly, these are only two data points. But if we were evaluating the Bobby Jones trade name used on golf shirts, we might look at the Disney and H-D transactions and say that a reasonable businessperson would pay $4\frac{1}{2}$% royalty. The golf shirt sells for less than a leather jacket, and golfers like the Bobby Jones name, but kids like the Mickey Mouse name even better, and the sweatshirt is a lower-price product.

What is involved for the appraiser of the Bobby Jones trade name is to try and find the most comparable royalty rates that were derived from arm's-length transactions between two market participants, to use the Financial Accounting Standards Board's (FASB's) term. Once the appraiser determines what an appropriate royalty rate *would be*, the calculation of the brand value is straightforward. Assuming the $4\frac{1}{2}\%$ royalty rate is considered to be the basis of value, we would then apply that rate to the anticipated future sales of the product(s) using the Bobby Jones name. Notice that in this Method 2, relief from royalty, we do not get into cost of sales, selling expense, and so forth. All we need is an accurate estimate of future dollar sales.

The Discounted Cash Flow analysis would be the same as at the bottom of Exhibit 6.2. The anticipated royalty income to the owner of the Bobby Jones name would be discounted to today's Net Present Value. It might be appropriate to use a discount rate slightly higher than the WACC, allowing for the fact that the future sales volume could be uncertain.

This Method 2 is utilized when the company owns the trade name and only uses it itself. Certainly, if the company has arm's-length licensing agreements with third parties, the royalty rates actually charged to them provide a very good estimate, and therefore are highly supportable.

The term "Relief from Royalty" method applies when the owner of the brand, used only by it, has no definitive royalty agreements with others. So, in effect, the appraiser says, "If you did *not* own the brand name, here is how much you would have to pay someone else for the use of the name." The fact is that the company does own the name, but the relief from royalty method treats the name *as if* someone else owned it, and the *savings* from *not* having to pay a royalty to a third party is equal to the real value of the brand or trade name.

This explanation may be somewhat confusing at first glance, but the underlying concept makes very good sense. The only professional difficulty in applying it is the appraiser's choice of a royalty rate. Outside databases contain literally thousands of rates derived from actually licensing agreements, but in practice one rarely finds an identical product or licensing terms such as upfront payments or minimum royalties. Thus the appraiser does have to use judgment, and any outside auditor or the SEC can challenge the choice of royalty utilized. If the appraiser has examined a wide variety of royalty transactions, it soon becomes possible to estimate the range within which the actual rate will be chosen. Then the actual rate chosen will be a function of the appraiser's

Exhibit 6.2 Sample Company

Determination of Intangible Asset Values for Allocation
Customer Relationships

Valuation Date: January 3, 2006.

Pre-Tax Profit Rate: 22.0%

($000s omitted)

	2005	2006	2007	2008	2009	2010	2011	2012	2013	2014
Decrement Rate: 15%										
Sales of Existing Products to Existing Customers	10,000	8,500	7,225	6,141	5,220	4,437	3,771	3,206	2,725	2,316
Pre-Tax Operating Profit [22%]	2,200	1,870	1,590	1,351	1,148	976	830	705	599	510
Less Return on Working Capital [1.336% of Sales]	134	114	97	82	70	59	50	43	36	31
Less Return on Work Force [2.1% of Sales]	210	179	152	129	110	93	79	67	57	49
Less Return on Trade Name [3.75%]	375	319	271	230	196	166	141	120	102	87
Available:	1,481	1,259	1,070	910	773	657	559	475	404	343
Less Taxes at 40%	593	504	428	364	309	263	223	190	161	137
After-Tax Cash Flow	889	756	642	546	464	394	335	285	242	206
Discount Rate: 14%										
Discount Factor	0.87719	0.76947	0.67497	0.59208	0.51937	0.45559	0.39964	0.35056	0.30751	0.26974
Present Value:	780	581	433	323	241	180	134	100	74	56

Value Indication: $3,471

Tax Benefit: = $2,902 $\times$ FV $ 568

FAIR VALUE $3,471

Value Indication/(1−((tax rate × annuity factor)/tax life))

Annuity Factor: PV(Discount rate, tax life, −1) $6.14

(continues)

134

Exhibit 6.2 Sample Company (*Continued*)

Employee Workforce			Weight	Working Capital Charge
Method A:	Annual Payroll	$5,000,000		Accounts Receivable + Inventory = 2 months or .1667 of Sales
	$\frac{1}{3}$ year [4 months] for hiring and training:	$1,650,000	0.6667	8% Return Required on Working Capital
				Percent = .16 × .08 0.01336
Method B:	Cost to hire employee:			
	$12,000 per employee	$1,200,000	0.3333	
	100 employees			
	Fair Value of Workforce	$1,500,015	10-year Life	
	Absorption Rate =	2.10%		
	1st Year's Sales × Annuity factor			

assessment of the strength of the brand name, the competition, the future of the product, and perhaps technological changes anticipated in the product line.

INTERNET DOMAIN NAMES

Valuing Internet domain names is often a challenge. Who would ever think that the name "Amazon" has anything to do with books, "Google" with search engines, or "eBay" with online auctions?

The days on which each of these Internet businesses were started, the respective domain names not only were worth no more than the registration cost, say $1,000, but many individuals thought the founders were crazy for choosing names that had no relationship to the product or service. Yet five to ten years later, these three domain names are truly invaluable. How much of the value of Amazon.com, Inc. is due to the business model and how much to the name? How much of Google's value is due to the business model and how much to the name?

At this point, Internet users automatically think of Amazon if they are going to order books (and other products) or Google if they are performing an Internet search. Originally, the business model attracted customers who used whatever name the principals had given the site. Later, the name itself drove customers to the site and hence the business.

As we have seen elsewhere, there is often one cash flow stream related to the entire business. Many factors make up the success of such a business, and it may be arbitrary to try and split up one stream of cash flow into several separate elements. Taking Amazon as an example, the company has software that quickly locates a book, additional software that helps perform a quick checkout function, and other software that handles the shipping function. In addition, Amazon has possibly the largest inventory of books in the country. Each of those elements drives business to the Web site. The name Amazon has truly become generic for ordering books on the Internet, just as Kleenex has become generic for facial tissues. How much of Kleenex's market share today is related to its name? Probably a large portion. Similarly, how much of Amazon's volume is derived automatically because people punch in that word to order books?

The SEC has issued a statement that says one *cannot* value an intangible asset by capitalizing the total net income stream of a business, subtracting a required rate of return on all other identifiable assets (e.g., working capital, property, plant, and equipment [PP&E], and intangibles). Thus we cannot value the Amazon domain name by taking the income stream for the company, providing for a return on the inventory and the value of the software systems, and say that is the domain name's value.

If we are truly required to value the domain name on a separate basis, then our choices are limited. Recall that there are three, and only three, approaches to value: (1) market, (2) income, and (3) cost. While there is a limited market in domain names, each transaction is unique, and if Stamps.com were sold for $200,000 (totally made up), that would tell us nothing about what Amazon.com would sell for. Different businesses, different customers. There is no market for the Amazon name, and it is highly unlikely there ever will be.

We could look at the cost of recreating as well known a name that would have the same public recognition. Recall that the Japanese car maker Datsun at one time changed its name to Nissan. It took years and cost many millions of dollars before consumers were comfortable with the new name. That was just the advertising and marketing cost. What was the impact of the name change on lost sales? It probably will never be known, but one could look at sales volumes before and after the name change and make some judgment.

So if we were forced to put a value on the Amazon domain name, we might attempt to develop a cost for an alternative name, taking into consideration advertising the new name plus an amount for lost sales during the changeover process.

Finally, we might try to value the Amazon domain name from our Relief from Royalty method, which is a variation of the income approach. Amazon sells products on its Web site for other vendors and charges them a fee or royalty. Part of the charge may be for use of the software, but certainly a major reason other vendors pay Amazon to use their domain name and Web site is the popularity of the name. From Amazon's records, if one had access to them, it appears that you could develop a royalty rate and then apply that to Amazon's own book sales. Remember that valuing an intangible used by its developer always involves a savings in not having to pay someone else—hence the *relief* used in the relief from royalty concept. So if we determined that independent third parties, on an arm's-length basis, paid Amazon.com Inc. 3% of sales for

Exhibit 6.3   Valuation of a Noncompetition Agreement

Assumptions:

$000s omitted

5-year life of the agreement

With the agreement, sales grow 7% per year
    Net Income = 5% of sales

Without the agreement, sales grow 4% per year
    Net Income = 4% of sales

Weighted Average Cost of Capital = 10%
    Discount Rate = 12%

		Year				
		1	2	3	4	5
With	Sales	150	165	182	200	220
Agreement:	Net Income	8	8	9	10	11
Without	Sales	150	156	162	169	175
Agreement:	Net Income	6	6	6	7	7
Difference:		2	2	3	3	4
P.V. Factor at 12%		0.94491	0.84367	0.75328	0.67257	0.60051
Present Value		1.42	1.70	1.95	2.17	2.38
Value of Noncompetition Agreement:		9.61				

use of its name, then we would apply that rate to its own book sales. At that point, as with our other examples, we would project out future sales, take 3% of the sales, apply a tax rate, and discount the after-tax cash flow. The discount rate would be the WACC. The methodology would be identical with that shown in Exhibit 6.3.

Again, for this example, we would have one value indication derived from a cost approach and a second from a relief from royalty approach. At that point, undoubtedly the two indications would differ, and the appraiser would have to use professional judgment to correlate the two numbers. We cannot provide guidance here for the exercise of that judgment because it is totally specific to the fact and circumstances.

NONCOMPETITION AGREEMENTS

Almost every merger transaction involves a commitment by the seller's principals, officers, and key employees that within a stated period of time, they will not go into business and compete with the new owner. This makes sense, if you look at the example of a hospital. It pays $1 million to buy a pediatric practice of four doctors. Then six months later, one of the doctors does not like the new arrangement, quits, and opens an office next door. His patients knew nothing about the sale of the practice to the hospital. Neither do they know about the doctor again starting to practice on his own. The doctor would keep all of his old patients; the hospital would have nothing and would be out $250,000 for each of the physicians. Naturally, the hospital in acquiring the practice would have required each doctor to sign a legally binding agreement not to compete.

It is outside the scope of this book to discuss the legalities and enforceability of noncompete agreements. Suffice it to say that the courts will enforce them as long as they are not unreasonable. A reasonable restriction on the doctor might be that he cannot open an office within 25 miles of the hospital. An agreement that the doctor could not practice anywhere within the United States would not be enforceable because the hospital cannot prevent the doctor from making a living practicing his profession.

As a consequence, most noncompetition agreements are carefully drawn and scrutinized by the attorneys for each side. Having said that, not all such agreements have real economic value. In one case, the founder of a business was 85 years old and retired by selling his business to a publicly traded company. The company, rightfully, had the seller sign a noncompetition agreement. Upon close examination, however, the real chance of that individual going back into business to compete with the new owner of his old business was extremely remote. The seller was wealthy and had no interest in, or intention of, going back to the day-to-day world of buying and selling. The true FV of the agreement could not be valued at more than a nominal few thousand dollars.

There are actually two types of agreement. First, those where the seller retires from the business and has the time (and money) to go back into business in the absence of the noncompetition agreement. The second type occurs when the seller accepts employment with the buyer, and the noncompetition agreement becomes effective upon termination of employment. In the first instance, there is often a real possibility of the seller going back into business. In the second instance, the longer the seller remains with the business after the transaction closes, the less likely he is to suddenly quit and start over.

In valuing noncompetition agreements, the first step is to evaluate just what the buyer acquired, in terms of potential future competition from the sellers. Unlike the aforementioned 85-year-old, we have seen what we can call serial entrepreneurs, individuals who have a knack for starting new businesses, building them up, and selling out. Such an individual, if he were 45 years old and had already started and sold three other businesses, might have to sign an extremely restrictive agreement in order for the buyer to close the deal. In short, each agreement stands on its own, and the facts and circumstances have to govern the determination of FV.

Assume now that we have a valid agreement, where there is a real possibility of the seller being able to compete with the buyer in the absence of the noncompetition agreement. The typical life of such an agreement is three to five years after the individual leaves his original business, and before he would be allowed to go into the same line of business.

In Exhibit 6.2 we lay out the recommended methodology. This approach is sometimes referred to as the "with and without" method. First, we project the business as planned in the due diligence planning phase, which undoubtedly contained the assumption of an effective agreement. This is the base case. Then as Step 2 we make an alternate projection assuming the noncompetition agreement is *not* present and the seller(s) immediately goes into the same line of business. We are only interested in the financial outlook for the buyer and do not analyze the prospects for the seller(s)' new business venture.

It is usually clear, if the seller were allowed to start up a competing business, that the buyer's outlook would be adversely affected. What we do is prepare an alternate scenario showing the sales, expense, profit, and cash flow outlook if two separate companies are now competing in the same market. Invariably, the new acquisition, from the buyer's perspective, is going to perform less well than if there was no competition. A certain number of customers, and perhaps employees, will want to affiliate with the old principal and his management team.

For the valuation, we then compare the two financial projections, one with and one without competition. The *difference* in cash flows is discounted over the period of the noncompetition agreement, so if there is a three-year term, we take three years' results, and if the agreement is for five years, we take the projection over the longer period. While perhaps subject to debate, we recommend that the discount rate be slightly above the WACC, because if the competition did take place, the business acquired would end up being higher risk than originally anticipated.

One last point should be considered: If the noncompetition agreement applies to the old management, who become employees of the acquirer, then the starting period for the analysis would be pushed out into the future; this requires some estimate as to when the employee(s) might leave and go into competition. The farther out the estimated date, the less the value of the noncompetition agreement, solely because of the time value of money.

For financial reporting, the FV of the noncompetition agreement would be amortized over the life of the agreement, whereas for tax purposes a straight 15-year amortization is required. Under the Internal Revenue Code, all intangibles are amortized over the same 15-year period. It may make little sense to have a three-year noncompetition agreement amortized over 15 years, but the offset is that goodwill, which is not amortized at all for financial reporting (it is tested for impairment as discussed in Chapter 8), is written off and deducted for taxes also over 15 years. Taxpayers lose on one point and win on the other. As an historical footnote, until the Internal Revenue Code was changed some 10 years ago, there were interminable fights between taxpayers and the IRS over the value of intangibles and whether they could be amortized at all. Those days are past; the 15-year time horizon seems to work well. As a matter of interest, when the FASB was contemplating what are now SFAS 141 and SFAS 142, many commentators suggested using the same 15-year life for amortizing the FV of all intangibles for financial reporting. The FASB did not adopt that suggestion, but it did make sense to many people.

CUSTOMER LISTS AND CUSTOMER RELATIONSHIPS

The FASB has identified two separate intangible assets that it called "Customer Lists" and "Customer Relationships." There is confusion in the minds of many people as to the difference or distinction. The way we explain it is as follows:

Customer List refers to a computerized list that can be sold, or more likely rented, to a third party for use in its advertising and marketing efforts. An example would be an airline list of frequent fliers; airlines often let credit card companies use this list to solicit for new accounts. Presumably, the credit card company pays a fee to the airline to use the list, or reimburses it based on successful sales. The point is that the list is developed by one company and used by another.

Customer Relationships are far more amorphous and are often difficult to define crisply. Basically, the FASB uses a two-test basis for determining if a customer relationship exists: (1) either the customer has a *contractual* relationship with the company and future business can be expected, or (2) the relationship is *severable* and can be acquired by someone else. We will discuss this in detail in the next section.

The basic distinction in our mind is that the Customer List can generate direct cash flows from rental or sale of the list, whereas Customer Relationships have value based on future sales to those customers, with no third-party involvement.

The valuation of a customer list is very simple. If it is a list that can be rented out, you project the actual or potential rental income (say names are rented at $50 per thousand). Because the valuation is as of the purchase date, we believe that a relatively short life should be assigned to the list, inasmuch as perhaps a minimum of 10% to 15% of the names turn over each year, so the half-life of a typical list might not be more than three years.

An argument can be made that one should carry out the income projection much further into the future, and then subtract the cost of keeping the list up to date. Using that assumption, the customer list for *Time* magazine might have a realistic life of 20 years. But the cost of obtaining new subscriptions, which adds new names to the list to offset the natural losses, may well show that on a straight rental list basis, the subscriber list for the magazine is not making money. But if you disregard the marketing costs of obtaining new replacement names, you are not looking at the true cost.

There are companies who, for a fee, will *compile* a list (e.g., Corporate Treasurers of the Fortune 1000 companies). This list is not a by-product of anything else, but would have been developed specifically to meet a customer demand, say from a large commercial bank. Such lists have a very short life, and if the company compiling it were acquired, it is questionable whether the lists in their files on day 1 had much if any value. The real value of a company that compiles lists for others would be the customer relationships with their clients, and their know-how in being able to develop lists of almost any sort.

While mail-order, magazine, credit card, and e-mail lists do have value, close examination usually reveals that there is relatively little value as of the acquisition date. But whereas customer *lists* rarely have significant value, customer *relationships* have a lot of value, as discussed in the following section.

CUSTOMER RELATIONSHIPS

This intangible, identified by the FASB in SFAS 141, is perhaps the single most difficult to value. The problem is not the valuation methodology, which we shall see is based on future income, but rather it is that reasonable people differ markedly on just what is meant by a "relationship."

In its original incarnation, the FASB specified that customer relationships should be valued if they are based on "contractual relationships." Alternately, the relationships should be "separable," that is, capable of being transferred to a third party. The FASB used as an example bank deposits, which occasionally are sold during an acquisition to another bank, primarily to avoid antitrust problems. It is true that there is a modest market for bank deposits because of the unusual legal aspects of banking.

But to draw conclusions that therefore most customer relationships meet the FASB's original test—separable or contractual—flies in the face of reason. Take an original equipment manufacturer (OEM) auto parts supplier to Ford. Ford may be buying taillights from this company, but there is no long-term contract requiring Ford to purchase part or all of its taillight requirements from the company. Neither is the relationship "separable" in the sense that the company could go to Ford's purchasing department and tell it, "from now on you are buying your taillights from Company Y, to whom we just sold our relationship." It takes little imagination to see just what the response would be.

At least to this appraiser, when the FASB talks about "contractual" relationships, we think of the ordinary use of the term "contract," something that both sides have willingly signed, and if drawn properly is enforceable in a court of law. The fact is that very few business relationships are contractual, enforceable in law. Certainly long-term leases are enforceable. Employment agreements are enforceable. "Take or pay" contracts are enforceable.

But we have never seen a normal business relationship between buyer and seller where if one party or the other is dissatisfied that the other party can go to court and secure judicial enforcement of the agreement. Certainly, many buyers switch suppliers, and many suppliers choose to drop customers. These changes in relationships are usually a result of quality, service, and price. And if either party is dissatisfied with any of those criteria, there is almost always a mutual agreement to dissolve the relationship; no contractual relationship remains other than the buyer having to pay for the goods and services already delivered.

This analysis led to the conclusion that very few customer relationships met the FASB's test of contractual and separable. Thus, for about a year and a half after issuance of SFAS 141, most allocations had very few dollars assigned to this particular intangible. Yet common sense suggests one of the main reasons that encourages Company A to acquire Company B is to obtain the relationships, even if they are not contractual and probably not separable without full concurrence of the buyers.

Furthermore, the SEC became concerned because if few dollars are assigned to the customer relationship intangible, then more dollars are left in goodwill. Keep in mind that goodwill does not get amortized, while customer relationships may have a high value and a relatively short life—perhaps five to eight years. Dollars assigned in an allocation to customer relationships are going to have to be written off quickly, reducing ongoing reported income.

The FASB was not in a position to amend SFAS 141 shortly after it had been issued, but the SEC was not satisfied with the outcome. So, to solve the problem caused by the way SFAS was written, the Emerging Issues Task Force (EITF) was charged with coming up with a solution. In EITF 02-17 the group effectively concluded that if a seller had received even a cancelable purchase order, that this met the SFAS 141 test of "contractual" and therefore one would have to value not only the value of the current Purchase Order, but also the value of all expected future business between the parties. Carrying this one step further, even if a recent purchase order (P.O.) had been fulfilled, and none were open on the acquisition date, the expectation that a *future* P.O. *might* be issued was enough to bring in a required valuation of customer relationship.

Before describing the methodology that should be used, we must face up to one more difficult definitional issue. This occurs frequently when a company buys a competitor that is selling to the same customer base. P&G in buying Gillette fits this scenario. Gillette's customer base of grocery stores, discount stores, drug stores, and warehouse stores is identical to that of P&G. It is hard to conceive of a distributor of Gillette products that does not deal with P&G.

From the perspective of P&G, the buyer, does Gillette's relationships with, say, Wal-Mart have any real value? P&G sells more to Wal-Mart than Gillette and already has a very close relationship with Wal-Mart. It is hard to believe that in practice Gillette is bringing *anything* to P&G in the way of customer relationships; in practice it may be the other way, P&G may be able to expand Gillette's sales through it sales operations.

The same issue arises with the OEM auto parts supplier mentioned previously. There are only ten or so automobile manufacturers in the world, and many suppliers already deal with all ten, in one way or another. So if one OEM buys another OEM, and this happens frequently, the buyer argues, correctly in our opinion, that it already deals with all ten manufacturers and the target's relationships *per se* have little or no value.

Unfortunately, this commonsense analysis also is not accepted currently. The argument is not that Gillette's relationships with Wal-Mart have zero value to P&G—because it has no value. Rather, the current interpretation says, do not look to the specific buyer, in this case P&G, but analyze the customer relationship value from the perspective of the infamous market participant. So if a private equity firm, not an operating company with existing Wal-Mart relationships, were to acquire Gillette, then Gillette's relationships with Target, Wal-Mart, Walgreen, and 10,000 other stores would have value.

Right or wrong, we must value customer relationships from the perspective of a theoretical buyer, not the actual buyer. By the way, the same logic has been applied to trade names. Often, Company A will buy Company B and immediately cease using B's trade name, substituting its own larger and better-known name. In such situations, for many years the buyer allocated nothing to the acquired trade name because it was not going to be used.

Recent interpretations, however, are forcing buyers to recognize a value for the trade name it will not use, on the basis of what another company *might* have done with that name if it had acquired the target company. Even worse, after assigning a value to the unused trade name, the buyer may have to recognize an almost immediate impairment loss because the trade name is not generating any income! Truly, this is a triumph of accounting theory over economic reality, but as long as the SEC, and by extension auditors, require this approach, all that appraisers can do is point out the folly, and then get on with the valuation assignment.

The value of a customer relationship involves estimating future sales from existing clients or customers. As we saw, even customers who are not doing business on the acquisition date must be included in the analysis. The sales projection starts with the sales of the company's present product line to those existing customers. Then an allowance must be made for anticipated losses in customers.

Basically, customer losses come from two directions. Competitors steal away existing customers, either through better price, service, and quality or through introduction of new products. A second source of customer losses comes from mergers and changes in business strategy of customers. If Circuit City stops selling white goods, because it is too competitive and unprofitable, the major manufacturers have lost a customer. True, if the same number of washing machines is sold in the country, then some other retailer's sales will increase, but sales increases on the one hand and distributor losses on the other are not necessarily directly correlated. Any analysis of a company's sales of five years ago compared to today's sales will show a significant turnover in customers.

In short, companies inevitably lose customers every year; just to hold their own they have to add new accounts, and to grow they need to add even more. To handle this attrition, appraisers put in a decrement factor to current-year sales in projecting the future. Ideally, the decrement factor would be derived from actual historical experience. Given the large number of customers that many firms have, it may be impractical to perform a statistical analysis, so we often discuss this with the firm's sales management team and arrive at a decrement rate that appears reasonable.

The real issue then becomes, what sales projections can we make of *new* products or services to those same old customers? At one extreme would be a television manufacturer who comes out with a "new" line every six months, but a Best Buy or Circuit City is very likely to put the "new" models on sale in place of the older models. At the other extreme is a chemical manufacturer whose customers change the basic make-up of their product and require a different chemical molecule. Can the chemical manufacturer count on obtaining the new business just because they have sold some other product to that same company? Probably not.

Purchases of a new product (not yet for sale on the date of the transaction) are more than likely to be competitive; the customer is going to contact two or three potential suppliers before deciding who will be the preferred supplier. For this reason, we typically are very careful about projecting sales of new products to existing customers. Almost every industry is competitive, and at the first sign that a buyer is considering a new product, several suppliers will approach them.

Past performance obviously is a critical element considered by the typical purchasing agent in selecting a supplier of a product that was not purchased previously. In reality, however, if DaimlerChrysler changes specifications, *all* the bidders will have had prior relationships with DaimlerChrysler, and probably all of them would be considered qualified. Consequently, if we are evaluating future sales of our target company to DaimlerChrysler, we typically only project out sales of existing products or models.

We do *not* anticipate sales of possible or potential future products that are going to be competitive at the time they are first purchased. Thus if a target sells fashion clothing to retailers, the future sales should include forthcoming designs. If Chanel were the target being allocated, it is unlikely that Neiman Marcus is going to drop the Chanel line in the near future. However, in industries where price and delivery are important, the future sales are far more uncertain, and we often choose to be quite conservative in our projections.

The reason for this lengthy discussion of what might at first glance seem to be a minor item is that, in practice, this is far from a trivial exercise. The SEC, and hence auditors, insist that companies minimize the amount of residual that goes to goodwill; the area they often scrutinize most closely is the value assigned to customer relationships. As noted earlier, a large amount assigned to this particular intangible, with a relatively short life, is going to substantially affect future profit and loss (P&L).

The final area in the valuation of customer relationships that deserves attention is the dull and boring subject of cost accounting. Developing a sales projection may be difficult, but at the end of the day, most observers will agree that the final determination is as good as you will get. But just having a sales projection of existing products or services to existing customers is not enough. One has to develop the anticipated income and cash flows associated with those future sales.

First, a brief story:

> One of the very first allocations we performed after introduction of SFAS 141 was for a major petroleum company that had acquired a large refiner and marketer of gasoline. We determined that the relationships the company had with its service stations fit the FASB definition of customer relationships because they were contractual. The service stations had each signed contracts that allowed them to use the name of the oil company in exchange for acquiring its gasoline from the company at a specified price. Gasoline being gasoline, there was no question of new products coming in, although occasionally a service station would go out of business, thus leading to a decrement percentage. The issue was this: What was the basis of calculating the appropriate profit margin on the anticipated gasoline sales over the next ten years?
>
> Assume that at the refinery level, there was a $.10 per gallon gross margin. The first assumption was that we could determine the FV of the customer relationships by applying the $.10 margin to the total future sales of gasoline over the next ten years. After all, that was how much the oil company was going to "earn" on the sales.
>
> The company's retail sales manager turned pale immediately when he heard this computation. He said, "But if you do that, I won't show any profit for ten years." [Since the $.10 amortization would offset the total reported gross profit.] "Worse, I won't get any bonus!"

This answer, that there would be no profits for ten years if we followed the FASB's new rules, was simply unacceptable—and wrong! However, the correct answer was not intuitively obvious, so we called the FASB staff with responsibility for interpreting its own work.

"You have to allow the company to obtain a normal Return on Investment (ROI). You cannot assign all future profits from the customer to the customer relationship intangible," was the answer. We were pleased to get this guidance, but it still did not solve the underlying issue, which is: what is the *appropriate* measure of cost or profit?

What has developed over time is to project out the sales of existing products to existing customers. Then we apply a full charge for Cost of Goods Sold and a full allocation of General and Administrative expense. We would not apply a full charge for selling and marketing expense because we are dealing with existing customers who presumably know the company and its product line. There would be a charge for appropriate marketing costs associated with normal customer service.

Then, after arriving at a preliminary operating profit, we have to put in charges for a normal return on assets employed. These are separate charges, related to sales volume, that provide for a required rate of return on:

- Working capital
- Property, Plant, & Equipment
- Other Intangible Assets, such as:
  - In-process R&D
  - Assembled workforce
  - Software
  - Patented and unpatented technology
  - Trade names and trademarks

In Exhibit 6.3 we show the worksheet for calculation of the value of customer relationships. It starts with $10 million sales of existing products to existing customers and shows a 15% decrement each year as existing customers, or products, cease to purchase. We assumed a 22% pretax profit rate for all Selling, General & Administrative (SG&A) expenses other than direct sales costs that need not be incurred for existing customers. We then show a required rate of return for working capital, assembled workforce, and trade names. No charge was made for a required return on PP&E, assuming this was a service business without a material investment in such assets.

The choice of the required rate of return on, say, working capital is related to the risk of that asset category. So, for example, we allowed for an 8% return on working capital because most observers feel that this is a low-risk asset category. Cash, receivables, and inventory can usually be converted to cash quite readily. While we do not show PP&E, we probably would have used a required rate of return of the WACC, here 14%, as representative of the risk. For the return on the workforce, we used the WACC. For the return on the trade name, we took a straight 3.75% of sales, representing a relief from an assumed royalty rate of 3.75%.

In coming up with the final FV of the customer relationship, we also have to adjust for the tax benefit of setting up the intangible as an asset and amortizing it for taxes over the 15-year life the IRS allows.

FRANCHISE AGREEMENTS

Do you wish that your grandfather had obtained a half-dozen McDonald's franchises from Ray Kroc 40 years ago? In all likelihood such an investment would have turned out to be profitable. Maybe, instead, your relative could have become the local Cadillac dealer in New York City. Probably that investment would have helped provide for your family. What would have been wrong with a Coca-Cola bottling franchise acquired back in the 1920s?

What do a Cadillac dealership and McDonald's have in common? They are both franchises, provided by the franchisor to an investor. In exchange for obtaining the right to use the franchisor's name, and distribute its product, the franchisee commits to upholding certain business standards (product service for Cadillac, cleanliness for McDonald's). Finally, in a typical franchise, a royalty or franchise fee must often be paid based on sales volume.

Another type of franchise agreement is held by a cable-TV firm to provide service to a locality. Comcast, for example, has a renewable franchise in many Virginia localities. They had to commit to string cable to all the homes in the community and then in exchange have a monopoly in service. Virtually no communities have competing cable-TV or competing electrical service, simply because the capital costs of providing the physical infrastructure is so high that two firms could not each earn a decent ROI in the same community.

Finally, we can categorize TV stations as franchisees, although the federal government provides the license. Without a Federal Communications Commission (FCC) license, no radio or TV station can broadcast.

With the license they are in business and can immediately start selling advertising. We discuss broadcast and operating rights in the next section. In this section we are discussing the valuation of commercial franchise agreements that range from lawn services to auto lubrication, and from restaurants to auto dealerships.

The principal value of a franchise is the exclusivity it provides. As an aside, Subway sandwich franchises are very easy to obtain, and the company has a reputation of setting up new locations very close to existing locations, thus diminishing the real value of a Subway franchise. At the opposite extreme probably would be a National Football League (NFL) franchise, where individual teams sell for hundreds of millions of dollars, compared to maybe $50,000 for a Subway. So exclusivity is the key element.

Just as it takes two blades of a scissors to cut, it takes two aspects to make a franchise valuable. On top of the value to the franchisee of the exclusivity provided by the franchise is the requirement that customers want or demand the product or service offered by the franchisor. How valuable today is a franchise to sell Plymouth or Hudson automobiles?

The valuation of the intangible aspect of the franchise agreement is fairly straightforward. Taking a restaurant franchise as an example, one would value the land, building, and hard assets (e.g., kitchen equipment, signs, furniture, dishes) on the basis of the cost approach, what you would have to pay today to acquire those assets.

For the franchise, the ability to use the name McDonald's, one would look at two aspects. First, what does McDonald's charge new franchisees for a restaurant in that type of location with that sales potential? So, perhaps, McDonald's would require an upfront fee of $250,000 to sign the agreement.

The real FV of the business to the franchisee, however, is probably significantly more than $250,000. The fact is that there is not going to be another McDonald's restaurant at that particular interstate highway interchange. The volume of business that a McDonald's will generate will exceed the volume of a no-name hamburger restaurant because of the name and the sign and the perception of uniform quality that travelers have of McDonald's.

This increased sales volume, less the required current franchise payments based on sales, perhaps 5% of revenues, represents the gross benefit of the franchise. As in all these intangible valuations, it is necessary to subtract the relevant cost of sales and normal operating expenses that any well-run restaurant requires. Then one would provide for the required rate of return on the other assets employed in the business, as we have done previously. At that point the remaining cash flow would be discounted at the WACC appropriate for the restaurant industry, and the present value of the cash flow would properly be considered the FV of the franchise agreement.

That is the easy part of any valuation of franchise agreements: coming up with an FV number. The real difficulty is in determining whether the franchise agreement has an indefinite life or a finite life. As we have seen, the difference in accounting treatment is substantial and definitely affects the reported earnings of any acquirer. Whether earnings are going to be accretive is one of the major criteria in many merger and acquisition (M&A) decisions, so how the FV of franchise agreements will be handled for accounting purposes becomes critical.

The FASB's guidance on what characterizes an "indefinite life asset" is in paragraphs 11 and 16 of SFAS 142, and a brief explanation of "indefinite" is given within paragraphs B 49 through B 66. Most franchise agreements are written for a definite term, say ten years, with provision for renewal if both parties agree. Therefore, one argument is that the franchise value should be determined over, and amortized over, ten years. This does not make sense, however, if history suggests that most franchise agreements are renewed pretty much automatically in practice.

Effectively, SFAS 142 says that if agreements are historically renewed, without significant additional cost, the life can be considered indefinite, and the FV so determined will not be amortized. A lot of language suggests that periodic testing of the indefinite assumption, and of the FV itself, is required; if a finite life is later determined, then amortization should begin, and if the value is impaired, a writedown must be made.

Having said all this, should a McDonald's franchise be considered to have an indefinite life? Certainly the company occasionally, and often the franchisee, decides to cease doing business, particularly in a geographic location undergoing socioeconomic changes. So renewal is not automatic or without some cost based on past experience. However, a successful profitable location will certainly be renewed because it is generating a good return.

Some companies will voluntarily choose to assign a finite, albeit a long, life to a franchise agreement to avoid the risk of having a sudden impairment. The feeling is that if a 40-year life is assigned, then only 2.5% of the FV will be charged off each year, and that is more conservative accounting. Other companies, with the same fact situation, assert that the life of the franchise agreement is truly indefinite, that few if any costs will be associated with renewal, and that they will *not* amortize the FV.

In the final analysis, this is an accounting determination to be made by the company, and an appraiser is not considered an expert in accounting. So, while appraisers may have an opinion, it is ultimately between the company, its independent auditor, and the SEC whether a franchise agreement can be treated as having an indefinite life.

OPERATING AND BROADCAST RIGHTS

The same essential issues as with franchises apply to cell phone, cable, radio, and TV licenses granted by governmental units. In exchange for promising to supply a service to the community, the operator is granted a local monopoly.

The valuation of these entities is a little easier in one sense, because there is an active market in buying and selling radio and TV stations, cellular networks, and to a lesser degree cable systems. Rules of thumb have been developed as to an appropriate selling price based on certain demographic factors. The more active the market, the easier is the valuation.

In the absence of a local market, appraisers value the operating and broadcast rights on the basis of anticipated cash flows, after allowances for returns on all other assets. Once again, the issue comes down to the expected life. The life affects the dollar amounts assigned to FV, because if a franchise expires in four years and one carries out the financial projection only for four years, the dollar value will be low. But since renewal is highly likely, and directly affects the value, the FASB has required appraisers to consider two factors: (1) the likelihood of renewal and (2) the costs anticipated with any renewal.

Take the example of a cable franchise that is about to expire. The local city or county government may well require the operator to upgrade the system for digital or two-way communication. Such an upgrade may involve substantial capital expenditures, probably offset by future revenue increases. In this situation, what is the life for purposes of first calculating the FV, and second, determining the amortization period? Assuming the franchise will be renewed, the cash flow projection, the basis of determining current FV, would incorporate the future cash outflows for the anticipated capital expenditures. That still leaves open the life, and while some would argue for an indefinite life, given the growth in satellites and competition from telephone companies, it might be hard to support an indefinite life.

The SEC has taken exception for television stations as to the life of the network affiliations (e.g., NBC, CBS, and ABC). In the past they have been renewed almost automatically inasmuch as very few stations change affiliation. However, during the renegotiation process, certain changes are sometimes made relative to the amount of advertising to be shown from the network, versus the amount of local advertising the station can broadcast. The SEC has interpreted such changes as preventing the use of an indefinite life for the network affiliation value. By the way, the value of a network affiliation for a television station can be determined by comparing the economics of several nonaffiliated stations with more or less similar network affiliated stations. While an independent television station can be valuable, the network affiliation increases the station's value substantially, and that increase is appropriately allocated to the network affiliation, not the station.

PATENTED AND UNPATENTED TECHNOLOGY

Although most people would recognize that some patents have value, that *un*patented technology also has value may come as a surprise. Patents have two types of value. They provide a unique, even monopolistic, technology to the owner of the patent, or to a licensee, thus reducing cost or increasing sales. Second, the patent can generate direct revenue through licensing agreements with others. Consequently, an inventor, whose patent is granted by the Patent and Trademark Office, can use the patent and let others use it for a fee.

However, not all patents generate meaningful savings or revenue. Many companies file for and obtain patents solely as a defensive move, either to prevent others from doing the same thing or to use as bargaining chips if a competitor tries to claim infringement. Furthermore, the commercial outlook for many product patents never develops as the inventor had hoped, while many process patents end up on the shelf.

All of this is to say that just because a target company has a long list of patents it owns does not mean the patents have a lot of value. In practice, with the possible exception of the pharmaceutical industry, relatively few patents have truly significant value. Put a different way, a few critical patents have great value, and most patents have little value. For patents that are truly unique and provide a significant advantage, say a major drug patent, the value is going to be determined based on the overall profitability of the product, less an allowance for the required return on all ancillary assets.

Alternatively, some appraisers value patents on a relief from royalty basis, similar to the technique used for trade names. We ask: if you did not own the patent, what royalty rate would be charged by a third-party owner? We then utilize the databases of royalty agreements for patents to develop a supportable royalty rate. This royalty is then applied to the projected sales of the product utilizing the patent, carried out to the future either when the patent expires, or the product's sales diminish because of competition. The FV calculation would be made using the WACC.

Unpatented technology is valued in exactly the same way. The problem is that trade secrets, how a product is made, are often difficult to keep secret. Some companies are so concerned about the disclosures required in a patent application that they prefer not to patent an invention or a manufacturing method and hope that news does not get out to competitors. Valuing unpatented technology in straight financial terms is identical to the patents described previously, although we would recommend a higher discount rate to reflect the fact that there is always a risk that the secret will somehow be revealed and the company's current advantage would be lost.

SOFTWARE

Valuing software is fairly straightforward. There are three types of software that commonly have to be valued in a business combination. The first is purchased software, such as an Enterprise Resource Planning (ERP) system like those sold by SAP. The second is internally developed software used for the firm's own internal operations, and an example would be a quality control system, recording successes and failures. The third would be software developed for sale to third parties. Each of these requires a different type of analysis.

Purchased software is becoming far more common than it was even ten years ago. The complexity of business, combined with the increased power of PCs, has led many applications to be performed on PCs rather than on mainframes. But as business becomes more complex (e.g., payroll), it is far less expensive for a company to buy software from a specialist rather than write its own. So for a large company, many of the major systems will have been purchased and often customized for the firm's specific unique requirements.

Furthermore, for major applications, such as ERP, the cost of the software is only a fraction of the total cost, which has to include implementation. Thus in valuing a major software system, one that costs several million dollars, it is imperative to determine how much cost was involved in the original implementation. Many consulting firms have charged as much as five times the software cost to help install a major system for a large client.

In determining today's value of a simple payroll system, for example, or a general ledger application, it is probably sufficient to determine from the vendor the cost today to purchase the latest version of the system. If the company has maintained its original acquisition through subsequent upgrades or versions, the current cost from the vendor closely approximates the FV. However, if the company has chosen, for whatever reason, not to upgrade to today's latest version, a discount from the new cost is warranted. This amount can be determined by asking the vendor how much it would charge to bring the client into compliance with the latest version, and subtracting that amount from the new system's cost.

This approach assumes that the company's own staff handled the original implementation and would do so again. While theoretically an amount could be imputed for reinstalling the existing general ledger or payroll system, in practice this refinement may not be necessary. The reason is that unless incremental people would have to be added to the staff, one assumes that any normal installation would be accomplished by people who are already on the payroll with no incremental out-of-pocket cost.

The issue in valuing major purchased systems, such as an ERP system, is how much to attribute today to the value of the consultant's original efforts. Assume, for example, that three years ago the software cost $2 million and the consultant charged $10 million for help in installation, and further assume that the costs today for the software and consulting would be similar. The question is whether the value of the total installation should assume a full $10 million for the consulting.

Keep in mind we are trying to determine the FV of the intangible asset to the new owner, the buyer of the company. Would the existing staff of the target company be able to perform more of the installation effort itself the second time around? The answer is probably yes. For the sake of discussion, assume that the day after the purchase of the company, a freak accident occurred and the entire ERP system was lost and had to be reinstalled.

You might have to pay for the software from the vendor, and might well require outside consulting help for the reinstallation, but would you need as much help this time as the first? A strong argument can be made that only a fraction of the capitalized installation effort should be attributed to the system's value today. How much of a "haircut" to attribute to the learning curve is a matter of professional judgment. The fact is that the FASB precluded putting a value on the assembled workforce; nonetheless the workforce is in place and has a lot of knowledge and skills, including knowing how to make an ERP system work.

One last point on purchased software: Most appraisers do not separately value PC operating systems and standard office systems such as Excel or Word. The assumption is that new PCs come with this complement of software, and the embedded software is typically included in the replacement cost of the PCs.

Internally developed software typically is valued on the basis of the current cost per man hour, or cost per line of code to replicate the existing software. Interestingly, most appraisers do not discount the learning curve at all in valuing internally developed software. Presumably, if the programmers who wrote the program are still there, they could re-create it a second time with fewer hours. They would, if nothing else, be able to avoid pursuing approaches that did not work and could proceed straightforwardly and efficiently, but there is usually relatively high turnover of programming staff, so the assumption of requiring the same hours today as it did originally is probably supportable.

One has to be careful in determining which internally developed software has value. Since the test is what market participants would do, presumably then very common simple programs, say an internal phone directory, would have little value because *every* prospective buyer would already have such a program.

In our experience, the only internally generated software that is separately valued relates to the specific business practices of the target company. So-called generic software that performs common tasks, and that most buyers already have on their own, is not given status as an identifiable intangible, but an actuarial program developed by an insurance company would definitely be considered. As with many other valuation issues, professional judgment has to be applied.

With both purchased software and internally generated software, the question of the appropriate life must be looked at. Perhaps ten years ago, when PCs were not as well developed, much software had a relatively short life. As new versions came out, the older version that had been valued now had little if any value. Thus short lives were the rule rather than the exception.

Whether it is progress or not, newer versions of most software systems, both purchased and internally developed, are being released much less frequently. Instead, minor changes are made on a more or less continuous basis. Thus determining the true life of a software program acquired on day 1 of an acquisition is more a matter of definition than anything else. If an insurance company has a complex actuarial program, or if a manufacturing company has an SAP ERP program, it is almost certain that modifications will be made at least once a month. When do these updates and minor changes become so numerous that the program is no longer comparable to that acquired originally? Certainly, fixing a small bug does not count as showing the end of the life of the original program, but maybe 300 such changes later, the program now has significantly greater throughput and functionality—and most observers would agree that it is now a new program.

One final factor in setting a life for software is the fact that many business processes today are in fact developed to meet the needs of the software, not the other way around. One of the complaints many years ago was that too much software simply carried forward old and inefficient processes. Now we are 180 degrees the other way. Processes are driven by the software.

The consequence is that changing a software system, going from Oracle to SAP, or vice versa, is impossible for practical purposes. Many companies that have grown through acquisitions report having a half-dozen different general ledger programs still operating many years later. The cost of change is perceived as higher than the benefits of focusing on one best-in-class program.

The true cost of changing software is such that, in the author's judgment, long lives for software can be justified and should be used. We have seen cases where a ten-year life is assigned and no questions are raised. All other things being equal, buyers prefer the longer life because this reduces the yearly amortization charge.

SOFTWARE DEVELOPED FOR SALE TO OTHERS

Valuing software that is used commercially by others is based almost entirely on the projected income stream. In effect, the cash flow received from customers for a software license is little different from royalty income for use of a trade name by licensees. Software is hardly ever sold outright; payment by a customer is actually for a license, thus preventing the buyer from reselling to others.

There are numerous problems related to revenue recognition by software vendors, relating primarily to what services have yet to be delivered or performed. For example, a customer of Oracle may pay one amount up front and a second fee for consulting services related to installation and access to new updates and revisions when issued. Just when income is earned, and what are the exact milestones for revenue recognition by the seller, have caused a lot of problems. These issues, however, do not significantly affect the valuation of the software, because the FV is based on the Net Present Value of future cash flows, both revenue and expenses. So theoretically it may make a difference as to exactly in what month a new version is issued, but for practical purposes a software firm is continually updating existing products.

Thus the valuation issue really revolves around future cash inflows, not the exact timing of ongoing expenditures. Given the relatively high margins in software, and a more or less even level of expenses for R&D, sales, and marketing, the key question to be answered is how long the existing program can be expected to be viable. Because the FASB allows for expected renewals, and the expenses associated with those renewals, one can probably assign a fairly long life in this time period. A long life, of course, increases the value of the software, but by the same token, the total amortization is spread over more years. In practical terms, there may be little difference in terms of annual expense between an eight-year life and a ten-year life.

The discount rate appropriate for a particular software program is going to be a function of the competitive situation. As an example, take software for personal income tax calculation. It is virtually 100% certain that Americans will be paying taxes on income for many years into the future. Equally certain is that the complexity of tax calculations will cause many taxpayers to look to software for help in filing. Effectively, there are only two or three consumer tax preparation packages, and they have ended up being quite similar. The cost for someone else to enter the market is high. Put these factors together, and one could justify a fairly low discount rate (effectively a higher FV) if one were valuing an existing personal income tax package.

At the other extreme might be software used on the Web to help customers get information on new and used-car prices and identify local dealers who might sell such cars. Numerous such programs are available, and one can easily assume that every developer of such software is constantly trying to get a competitive advantage through improvements and updates. This is a highly competitive market that has not settled down into a two- or three-way race. Thus a valuation today of such software would use a much higher discount rate, reflecting the uncertainties affecting any one market participant.

CONCLUSION

The FASB has identified several intangible assets that must be valued in every business combination. Although the FASB provides general guidance in developing FV information, each specific situation must be looked at in terms of its unique characteristics. In short, there is no known software into which one can plug a couple of variables and out will come the true FV. The reason is that one may have to look at all three approaches to value—cost, income, and market—and determine which of them is relevant. Then the valuation specialist, working with the client, has to develop an understanding of the intangible asset and determine just what it contributes to the overall value of the business.

Care must be taken not to double count the same stream of income in valuing two seemingly independent intangible assets. For a consumer goods company, shelf space on the grocers' shelves is valuable, as is the product formula; both share the same cash flows with the manufactured product (not an intangible) and the trade name by which the public buys the product.

Absent the detailed analysis, one might try to value the trade name, the product formula, and the shelf space. All three are necessary, and no one of the three is sufficient to cause customers to buy the product. Thus developing the present value of the intangible(s) for this product requires clear delineation and professional judgment as to how to allocate the single stream of cash provided by customer purchases. The same thought process has to be used in evaluating customer relationships for machinery and equipment suppliers, relative to patents and unpatented technology.

The overall goal of the FASB, and by extension auditors and the SEC, is to assign as much value as possible to identifiable intangibles. This has the effect of minimizing goodwill, which is not amortized. Thus the second important point in valuing identifiable intangibles is to determine the life over which they will be amortized. While in some cases the life affects the total FV, by and large the value is determined first, and the amortization period determined afterward.

Under the current rules, intangible assets with an indefinite life are not amortized, although they must be tested for impairment periodically to make sure that the current FV is equal to or above the carrying amount. As mentioned, the FASB and the SEC have worked hard to reduce the assets that qualify for indefinite life treatment, and now essentially only trade names seem to pass muster. All other intangibles must be given a life and amortized. Companies want the longest supportable life; many appraisers feel it is part of their professional responsibility to aid management in the selection of the appropriate life. Other valuation specialists feel that the choice of life is an accounting issue and should be left solely to management and its accounting advisors. The author is in the camp that says valuation specialists are most familiar with the issues and understand how the calculations and assumptions were developed. Therefore, the appraiser's recommendation for the useful life should carry a lot of weight.

One final point about the life and amortization period: SFAS 142 specifies in paragraph 12, "The method of amortization shall reflect the pattern in which the economic benefits of the intangible asset are consumed or otherwise used up." What this means is that straight-line amortization may not be the most appropriate means of writing down the asset each period. It is beyond the scope of this chapter to get into the specifics of any one situation. Companies should be aware, however, that at any time the SEC and Public Company Accounting Oversight Board can look at amortization methods, and the company will bear the burden of proof of supporting a straight-line, rather than an accelerated method.

CHAPTER 7

Valuation of Liabilities and Contingent Payments

In 1970 the then Accounting Principles Board (APB), the predecessor to today's Financial Accounting Standards Board (FASB), issued APB 16, which dealt with "Business Combinations." In 20 pages, accountants were told how to handle the accounting for mergers and acquisitions (M&As). The FASB came out in 2001 with SFAS 141 and in 125 pages told accountants how to handle business combinations. In 2006, the FASB is coming out with SFAS 141R [Revised], containing some 236 pages.

In 35 years has the world grown that much more complex? Probably not. What has happened is that accountants, management, and the financial community as a whole have become far more sensitized about the importance of reported earnings and earnings per share (EPS). Every nuance in Financial Standards is explored and tested, to see if some advantage can be gained in terms of reported earnings.

The FASB, responding to this pressure, has attempted to improve the practice of financial reporting; it tightens up standards, either when they are initially issued or after they have been issued. Many details of recent Standards issued by the FASB seem to be based on an antiabuse philosophy. One only has to look at the history of financial reporting for leases or financial instruments to see how far this has been carried. The number of pages of regulations and rules on these two topics alone is mind-numbing, but the FASB and Wall Street are not the only ones to blame for this complexity.

Public accountants are forever searching for more guidance so they can tell their clients "here is the way you must report this transaction." Rather than exercise professional judgment, it appears easier, at least in the short run, to refer to rules. That way, if the client does not like the answer or the accounting treatment, the auditing firm can blame the FASB and the Securities and Exchange Commission (SEC), rather than taking responsibility for allowing or disallowing the particular accounting treatment. Unfortunately, the consequences of this approach, carried out over 35 years, is an ever-greater complexity in accounting rules, too much disclosure, and an almost total disconnect from what many observers feel is the real world.

The final straw, in terms of financial reporting complexity, which may be the one to break the proverbial camel's back, is the ever-increasing trend toward Fair Value (FV) reporting, the subject of this book. So far we have concerned ourselves primarily with the FV of assets. Now it is time to turn to liabilities and contingent claims.

In the past 35 years that the author has been in the appraisal and valuation business, virtually 100% of client assignments have dealt with assets. Very few clients have asked us to determine the FV of liabilities. The basic assumption was that liabilities—debt, if you will—are denominated in a specific dollar amount, and there were few valuation issues. If a company owes a bank $5 million, or has $50 million long-term debt outstanding, the values of those liabilities are generally assumed to be, respectively, $5 million and $50 million. Some academic theorists would argue that if the long-term debt had been issued with a coupon of 6%, and current rates were 7%, that the true FV of the debt was, say, $46 million. If rates had gone down to 5%, the FV would go in the opposite direction and be worth $53 million. But this type of theoretical consideration was usually disregarded, and in financial reporting a $50 million bond issue would be reported as a $50 million liability, irrespective of current rates.

Similarly, if a company faced a lawsuit and the plaintiffs claimed $100 million damages, the company would report the lawsuit in the financial statement footnotes, with a comment stating: "We believe the lawsuit is without merit and are vigorously defending against the claim." Under current Generally Accepted Accounting Principles (GAAP), as promulgated in SFAS 5, companies have to quantify the contingency *only* if *both* of two conditions are met, as shown in paragraph 8 of SFAS 5:

1. *"It is probable that an asset had been impaired or a liability had been incurred; and*
2. *The amount of loss can be reasonably estimated"*

Furthermore, the Statement goes on, "It is implicit in this condition that it must be probable that one or more future events will occur confirming the fact of the loss." The Statement defines "probable" as: "The future event or events are likely to occur." In practice, accountants have basically agreed that in this situation, "likely" means a "more than 50% probability"; thus lawsuits where the attorney opines that the plaintiff is unlikely to prevail do not have to be quantified and set up as liabilities on the balance sheet. This system of determining when liabilities should be recognized on a balance sheet, and an amount determined, has seemingly worked well for the past 30 years.

In practice, for things like environmental liabilities that may not be paid for many years in the future, accountants had argued that "the amount of loss could not be reasonably estimated." It is fairly certain that if a building has asbestos, it will have to be remediated some time in the future, but with no plans to abandon the building, nothing has to be spent until a change in usage occurs, and who knows how much it would cost 30 or 40 years from now? So under SFAS 5, such a liability was not put on the balance sheet. Now, under SFAS 143, the FV of the future obligation must be determined and shown on the books.

In short, most accountants have been comfortable disclosing contingent liabilities in footnotes, but without having to attempt to quantify what is essentially an uncertain amount. Put a different way, many people feel that putting a definitive amount on a balance sheet for an uncertain liability provides the reader(s) with a false sense of precision. Most contingencies can *not* be estimated precisely, and financial statements do not use ranges. The basic consensus has been that good disclosure alerts readers and permits them to make their own determination, using their own judgment. What has worked well for more than 30 years is about to change totally.

FASB'S NEW APPROACH TO LIABILITIES: "EXPECTED VALUE"

At this point the FASB's new concept can best be understood by a simplification. If a plaintiff is suing a company for $100 million, and there is only a 5% chance that the plaintiff will prevail, the new accounting would put a $5 million liability on the balance sheet, even though there are 19 chances out of 20 that there will be no payment and 1 chance out of 20 that the full $100 million would have to be paid out. As many observers have pointed out, the one number we know that will *not* be incurred or paid out is $5 million, the only amount shown on the balance sheet! Looked at a different way, the balance sheet will show a number we know is wrong, and will not be experienced, while the overwhelming probability that nothing will be paid is in effect overlooked or disregarded.

How did we get to this point, and what does it mean for financial reporting? The concept of expected value comes from statistics, where there are a large number of chances and a large number of occurrences. So, as an example, if a roulette wheel has 36 numbers (1 to 35 + 0) but only pays off at 35:1, the expected value of a $1.00 bet is $.972. The $.028 difference between the amount bet and the payoff is the profit earned by the house. Put a different way, as long as the payoff at roulette is 35:1, and the odds are 36:1, bettors as a whole will lose and the house will inevitably win. We all know this, either from school or intellectually or from experience.

But what the expected value at a roulette wheel does *not* tell us is what will happen on the *next* spin of the wheel. When we place a bet on number 23, and the croupier spins the ball, only one of two things will happen. The ball will hit 23 and we win 35 times our bet, or it falls in another number and we lose our money. On any one roll it is all or nothing, not an expected value of .972. Some have referred to this as a "binary outcome."

If we play enough times, we know that the house odds will prevail, but that does not stop some lucky bettors from coming out ahead at any particular point in time. Yes, the house almost always wins in the long run, but bettors are in Las Vegas having fun in the short run. Consequently, most bettors do not pay attention to the long-term probabilities and focus solely on their own immediate play. But carried out over thousands of bettors, the house inevitably comes out ahead, despite a certain number of players who go home as winners.

Looked at this way, the concept of expected value makes very good sense, and obviously is applied by businesspeople, particularly those in the gaming industry. Having said that, it is not immediately intuitive that what works in casinos will work equally well in financial reporting. Nonetheless, this is what the FASB is requiring.

For those readers who were never fortunate enough to have studied statistics in school, or more likely to have forgotten what they learned, expected value can be shown in a very simple example. Assume a range of outcomes for an investment in a new gold mine. After reviewing the geological reports regarding ore content, economists' forecasts about the future price of gold, and mining engineers' forecasts about the expenses of mining and refining the ore, the following estimates are made:

Initial Investment: $15,000,000
Potential Outcome: [1st Estimate]

Net Profit/Loss	Probability	Expected Value
($25,000,000)	5%	($1,250,000)
($5,000,000)	10%	($500,000)
Break-even	15%	-0-
$1,000,000	20%	$200,000
$5,000,000	23%	$1,150,000
$25,000,000	20%	$5,000,000
$99,000,000	7%	$6,930,000
	100%	$11,530,000

Potential Outcome: [2nd Estimate]

Net Profit/Loss	Probability	Expected Value
($25,000,000)	5%	($1,250,000)
($5,000,000)	10%	($500,000)
Break-Even	15%	-0-
$1,000,000	5%	$50,000
$5,000,000	20%	$1,000,000
$25,000,000	20%	$5,000,000
$99,000,000	25%	$24,750,000
	100%	$29,050,000

Disregarding the time value of money, for a $15 million investment the first estimate shows a loss would most likely be expected, while the second estimate shows a probability of a positive, in fact very good, return on investment (ROI). Which of these is correct? Should the investment be made or passed?

The answer to the investment decision depends on which set of potential outcomes you have most confidence in. In the real world, we are not dealing with a whole series of gold mine investments. Rather, we are dealing with a single investment, which is either going to succeed or fail, and in advance nobody knows the outcome. So the real question is, "Where do we get these seemingly precise probabilities?" Unlike roulette wheels, where there are literally millions of tosses so the laws of probability can work themselves out, for most investments each stands on its own.

Yet the FASB's Concept Statement 7 (CON 7), the basis for valuing assets and liabilities based on future cash flows, is totally dependent on the ability of the valuation specialist or analyst to project the range of possible outcomes and assign probabilities to those outcomes. In our gold mine example, the range of outcomes is from a total loss to a six times return. Those numbers probably are a reasonable range with which most investors would feel comfortable. But where do we obtain the probabilities? Moderate changes in the probabilities can have a total change in the expected value, going from a loss to a reasonable ROI. Are the probabilities in Estimate 1 better than Estimate 2? Certainly they are more conservative, but that does not make them better, inasmuch as belief in Estimate 1 would result in no investment. If it turned out to be a profitable investment, not investing because of conservatism would have been diametrically wrong.

Certainly optimism, per se, is not undesirable in and of itself. As a broad generalization, accountants and appraisers, afraid of being proven wrong, are usually more conservative than entrepreneurs and marketers. So the question is, in performing this valuation analysis, whose projections and assumptions do you use?

The reason for this seeming digression is that in terms of valuation and financial reporting, the application of expected value, as set forth in CON 7, is going to have a significant impact on reported results. It will not take long, after companies and their managers understand the ramifications of the expected value concept, for abuse to occur.

It should be noted that the FASB's approach is that in a business combination, once the amount of the initial liabilities has been determined, then any adjustments upon final determination are going to be charged, or credited, to current period income. So if a company estimates its liability for a lawsuit that the target company had outstanding at acquisition at say $10 million, and it is settled for $1 million, then there will be a $9 million pickup. Conversely, if the loss estimate is $1 million and the lawsuit settles for $10 million, there will be a $9 million charge to expense. Even a fifth-grade student can figure this one out. It will *always* be preferable for a company to overestimate any possible loss than underestimate it. While the accounting entries arithmetically are reciprocal (overestimate equals income and underestimate equals loss), the behavioral impact will be vastly different.

How will this unbelievable bias built into the system be controlled? The FASB's answer is that management has to do a good job, and that auditors will have to exercise professional judgment. Both assumptions are reasonable, and in theory can work. In practice we believe that appraisers are going to be under strong pressure to adopt conservative assumptions about future contingencies. Corporate management will definitely want such conservative assumptions. How will either appraisers, or auditors, substitute their judgment for that of the client?

Keep in mind that estimating a loss from a lawsuit, or an environmental clean-up, involves a judgment about future outcomes. It is a fundamental premise that *nobody* can foretell the future, much less prove it. It is extremely likely that the sun will rise in the East tomorrow morning, but in our present state of knowledge, this can not be proven beyond a reasonable doubt. There is some chance, remote as it is, that the sun will become a super-nova tonight and we will all be toast before the morning. So there is a difference between having confidence that something will happen and acting on that confidence, on the one hand, and being able to prove that same thing will happen with 100.00% certainty on the other hand.

So, for example, if a company's attorney says, "There is a 40% chance you will lose the lawsuit" (plaintiff asking for $100 million) versus "there is a 20% chance you will lose," how does any nonlawyer judge which of the two assumptions is better? Yet the difference, if the company prevails, is a credit to income of $20 million. How will attorneys be able to respond to client management when asked for a conservative estimate?

In the insurance business, many companies require that their actuaries determine reserves for future losses *independently* of management. The actuaries are then judged, and paid, on the subsequent accuracy of their estimates. Thus there is no pressure on the actuaries to over- or underestimate future losses, with a consequent impact on current quarter's earnings.

This model, however, will not work for business combinations. Met Life insures millions of lives whose behavior follows well-known actuarial tables. Allstate's car drivers similarly have relatively predictable patterns of outcome. But how do you forecast the outcome of a single large tobacco or asbestos tort lawsuit? The law of large numbers simply does not apply to a single instance, and that is what individual environmental liabilities or tort lawsuits are: individual events.

Having just said it is difficult, if not impossible, to predict the future, the author will stick his neck out and make a prediction. After two to three years of experience with the FASB's expected value approach to valuing liabilities, and having subsequent resolutions impact then current income, he predicts that the FASB will change. The FASB is unlikely to go away from the expected value approach, but it will be forced to have the impact of subsequent final resolutions charged or credited to goodwill. Impacting one quarter's income because of an inability to foresee the future several years in the past simply will not be acceptable to companies, management, analysts, and shareholders. The old system, of the charge or credit for subsequent resolution going to goodwill, was not considered theoretically elegant by the FASB theoreticians, but it did not encourage game playing. The FASB has compromised in many areas in the past, and we predict they will be forced to compromise here.

ESTIMATING AND VALUING LEGAL LIABILITIES

Having said that, there are and will be built-in bias to any estimate of contingent liabilities such as a lawsuit; nonetheless, companies will have to follow the FASB's requirements. Furthermore, because of the scrutiny that all such estimates of liabilities undoubtedly will incur, companies and their valuation specialists will have to be prepared to defend every one of the key or critical assumptions that go into the valuation.

In the case of lawsuits, it will be incumbent upon the company's attorneys, those handling the litigation, to develop an informed opinion about their client's chances of winning or losing, and if they lose, an approximate estimate of the probabilities. Based on evidence to date, attorneys are going to resist making these estimates, but someone will eventually have to, and management ultimately will pressure the lawyers to come up with a figure.

There is a possible solution to the problem of the inability, or unwillingness, of a company's own attorneys to estimate the potential loss from a major lawsuit. There are many retired judges who often act as arbitrators in what is called "alternative dispute resolution" (i.e., arbitration). Such former judges, with no relationship to the company, could be hired to provide a professional opinion as to the chances of the plaintiff or defendant prevailing. While possibly somewhat expensive, this would be a solution to the argument raised by opponents of the FASB's position.

One of the key concerns of the attorneys, and management, is that an estimate of the amount of possible loss may provide a roadmap to the opposition team. Companies do not want to show their tax accrual work papers to the IRS, for fear of showing where the company feels it has a weak position. Similarly, no rational executive is going to tell the other side, "We expect to have a 40% chance of losing, and therefore expect to settle for $15 million." You might as well write a check to the other side immediately if that appears in the financials.

Undoubtedly, the footnote disclosure, and the placement of the liability on the balance sheet, is going to be the subject of intense discussion. It is unreasonable for a company to voluntarily expose its strategy and expectations, so the information on the acquired lawsuits somehow will be lumped in with all other disclosures on the consolidated balance sheet. Having received the attorney's best estimate of the outcome—and this has to be for each and every significant lawsuit on an individual basis—the appraiser will then have to put the data into a CON 7 format.

Suppose a plaintiff is asking for $50 million for a patent infringement. The attorney, reluctantly and after much prodding, finally concedes that there is only a 30% chance of the company losing, and that if it does lose, the most likely damages would amount to no more than $35 million.

On the surface, the concept of expected value might at first suggest taking 30% of $35 million as the most likely expected outcome. However, that is *not* the approach used in CON 7. Exhibit 7.1 shows, using assumed outcomes and probabilities, a valuation of this lawsuit, starting with the attorney's assumptions. We start by using the 70% chance of not having to pay anything. A question at this point would be related to legal defense costs. Even if we do not lose the case, there undoubtedly will be substantial legal costs just to go to court. If the best estimate today is that approximately $1 million will be charged by the law firm, the question arises as to whether this amount can be, or even should be, accrued.

Looked at in one sense, the lawsuit is a liability under the FASB's definition, and it is impossible to defend against the lawsuit without incurring the $1 million in defense costs. Put a different way, if you do not spend the million dollars, you surely will lose the $50 million requested by the plaintiff. It would appear, however, that by analogy to other future expenses at closing that the company cannot and should not accrue the $1 million in anticipated legal defense costs. We are not justifying this position, and believe it is wrong, but we would be surprised if auditors and the SEC would permit such an entry.

Exhibit 7.1 Valuation of Contingent Lawsuit

Assumptions:

Plaintiff asking $50 million for patent infringement in a Jury Trial

Attorney thinks only a 30% chance company will lose; = 70% chance company will prevail and owe nothing

If plaintiff wins, attorney estimates $35 million damages would be awarded

CON 7 Analysis:

Scenarios	Probability*	Value
Company found not guilty, and no damages	70%	-0-
Company found guilty and damages awarded of:		
$1,000,000	2%	$ 20,000
$5,000,000	3%	$ 150,000
$20,000,000	5%	$1,000,000
$35,000,000	13%	$4,550,000
$50,000,000	4%	$2,000,000
$60,000,000	3%	$1,800,000
	100%	$9,520,000

*See narrative in text

Back to Exhibit 7.1: If there is a 70% chance that no damages will be assessed, then the expected value of that outcome (absent legal fees) is zero. It is then necessary to look at the entire range of outcomes if the plaintiff prevails. In other words, the attorney's estimate of only a 30% probability of the plaintiff succeeding in no way is determinative of the actual award by the jury. So, for example, the company may lose but the plaintiff only be awarded a nominal $5 million in damages. Likewise, without showing every possible number between zero and the upper limit, we pick several possible outcomes, in this case $5, $10, $20, $30, and so forth up to $60 million. Note that while the plaintiff is asking for $50 million, it is *possible* that the jury can award *more* than is requested. This may not be likely, and we assigned only a 1% probability, but the history of awards does show that awards above the amount asked for do occur.

The critical question is how we arrived at the probabilities for the 30% range where an amount would be owed. For the example, we had to make them up because this is not based on a real case. In practice, the valuation specialist doing the analysis would either have to use his own judgment, try to elicit something from the attorney, or do a tremendous amount of research on jury awards.

It is possible that after the FASB pronouncement on valuing contingent liabilities is being used that someone will develop a database that can be utilized for this purpose. In valuing license agreements, at least two competing databases capture the essential elements of thousands of such agreements. It is highly likely that if there is a demand for information about damage awards, that some entrepreneur will offer this service. At present, however, we are not familiar with any usable source for appraisers.

The basic problem is that anyone can file a lawsuit, and the defendant must defend itself, irrespective of the merits of the case. In the United States, we do not have a "loser pays all expenses" concept as is common in other countries. Consequently, many lawsuits are filed where the odds are that the plaintiff will not prevail, but from the defendant's perspective there is always some chance greater than zero that the plaintiff will in practice prevail. Thus, in trying to estimate probabilities of loss, when there will never be a directly comparable lawsuit with which to compare, the answer ultimately involves judgment. Whose judgment should be used? Ideally, it would first be the attorney, then company management, and finally, third out of three, is the appraiser. However, experience suggests that in the actual day-to-day effort to allocate a purchase price, the appraiser actually develops the probabilities.

As noted earlier, there is no market with which to test the probabilities, so unless the amounts used are *prima facie* unreasonable, we presume that a reasonable range developed by the appraiser will be used and probably not revised. Auditors, the SEC, and even the Public Company Accounting Oversight Board (PCAOB) can question the assumptions, but the one thing that is certain is that none of them have any *better* database or support for their assumptions. As so often happens, the first person to prepare an estimate in good faith is likely to see those numbers used by all parties.

Using the example, an auditor could say to the management and the appraiser, "I don't think there is a 1% probability that the award will be in excess of the original amount asked for. I think you should only use .005%. Where did you get your 1%?" There are really only two responses. First, "This is our best professional judgment. Where did you get your .005%?" The second response is, "OK, Mr. Auditor, we will use your .005% estimate, but how are you going to audit your own number?" We would expect a moment of dead silence from the auditor, who in all likelihood will then say, "Well, if you feel that way about it, go ahead and use your 1%."

In Exhibit 7.2 our expected value is $13.65 million. This amount, according to the FASB, is what should be set up on the opening balance sheet. Let us just follow things through for a moment. Assume that 12 to 18 months later, the case settles, and to avoid further legal fees the defendant agrees to a $1 million payment. The attorney still feels that following a jury trial the plaintiff will lose, but the defendant does not want to take a chance, spending in the process perhaps $1 million in further legal fees for the risk of a much higher penalty. So the $1 million settlement is arranged.

At the date of final settlement, the company will charge $1 million to the $13.65 million reserve already established. The remaining $12.65 million will be reported as income in the period. Remember that the amount of the settlement is very different from the amount on the balance sheet that represented the expected value. A reasonable question can be asked whether defendants, having set up a relatively large reserve, will now feel pressure to settle lawsuits for a small amount in order to pick up a large credit to income.

Exhibit 7.2 Application of CON 7

Assumptions:

Plaintiff is suing for $50 million
Attorney believes only a 30% chance of losing

Potential Loss	Probability	Expected Value
$60,000,000	1%	$ 600,000
$50,000,000	1%	$ 500,000
$40,000,000	8%	$ 3,200,000
$30,000,000	20%	$ 6,000,000
$20,000,000	12%	$ 2,400,000
$10,000,000	8%	$ 800,000
$ 5,000,000	3%	$ 150,000
-0-	47%	-0-
	100%	$13,650,000

The true answer to this question lies outside the scope of this book. In fact, the FASB deliberately eschews, in determining accounting policy, whether there will be social or economic consequences. They feel that accounting can be neutral. GAAP accounting, in their view, should not affect management judgment to undertake a particular course of action, just to obtain a particular accounting result. That is the theory. In practice, the world does not work that way. Our prediction is that having large reserves on the balance sheet for contingent lawsuits will encourage more and perhaps higher settlements.

At this point someone will raise the question, "Well, if you settled for $1 million, why did you put 13 times that amount on the balance sheet as a liability, what amounts to a more than $12 million cushion?" The answer is that first the FASB does not let us accrue legal fees today to pay for future litigating expense. Second, the concept of expected value in CON 7 explicitly requires consideration of all possible outcomes. In retrospect one could argue that a more than 2% probability should have been assigned to a $1 million potential outcome, but that is the beauty of 20-20 hindsight; you always know today what you (or they) should have done yesterday.

We predict that in the case of large lawsuits, with major amounts set up as liabilities, there will be substantial post-settlement sniping at companies by analysts, and possibly the SEC, when after the fact the initial estimate from CON 7 turns out to be wrong. Certainly, many of the estimates will turn out to be wrong, mostly on the side of overestimating the liability, not underestimating the amount.

VALUING ENVIRONMENTAL LIABILITIES

Just as lawyers are the primary source for preliminary estimates of how lawsuits may settle, so environmental engineers have to be the source for valuing environmental liabilities. Whether it is to exit a landfill or coal mine, remediate a Superfund site, or remove asbestos contamination, there are two common threads: (1) the timing of the remediation is in the future, and (2) the amount of the final settlement is unknown. Unlike a liability for a bond issue, where the timing, interest, and principal are clearly delineated in advance, the liability for environmental issues will not be determined until the final expenditure(s) are made.

Adding to the uncertainty is the fact that the legal requirements, usually promulgated by the Environmental Protection Agency (EPA) or comparable state agencies, shift over time. And such shifts rarely reduce the requirements. Consequently, the timing for the expenditure may slip, but at the same time the dollar amount to accomplish the requisite clean-up also increases.

In SFAS 143, which deals with Asset Retirement Obligations (including future remediation costs), the FASB states:

> *The fair value of a liability for an asset retirement obligation is the amount at which that liability could be settled in a current transaction between willing parties, that is, other than in a forced or liquidation transaction. Quoted market prices in active markets are the best evidence of fair value and shall be used as the basis for the measurement, if available. If quoted market prices are not available, the estimate of fair value shall be based on the best information available in the circumstances, including prices for similar liabilities and the results of present value (or other valuation) techniques.*

FAS143, Par. 8

> *A present value technique is often the best available technique with which to estimate the fair value of a liability. If a present value technique is used to estimate fair value, estimates of future cash flows used in that technique shall be consistent with the objective of measuring fair value.*

Concepts Statement 7 discusses two present value techniques: a traditional approach, in which a single set of estimated cash flows and a single interest rate (a rate commensurate with the risk) are used to estimate fair value, and an expected cash flow approach, in which multiple cash flow scenarios that reflect the range of possible outcomes and a credit-adjusted risk-free rate are used to estimate fair value. Although either present value technique could theoretically be used for a fair value measurement, the expected cash flow approach will usually be the only appropriate technique for an asset retirement obligation. As discussed in paragraph 44 of Concepts Statement 7, proper application of a traditional approach entails analysis of at least two liabilities—one that exists in the marketplace and has an observable interest rate and the liability being measured. The appropriate rate of interest for the cash flows being measured must be inferred from the observable rate of interest of some other liability, and to draw that inference the characteristics of the cash flows must be similar to those of the liability being measured. It would be rare, if ever, that there would be an observable rate of interest for a liability that has cash flows similar to an asset retirement obligation being measured. In addition, an asset retirement obligation will usually have uncertainties in both timing and amount. In that circumstance, employing a traditional present value technique, where uncertainty is incorporated into the rate, will be difficult, if not impossible.

FAS143, Par. 9

The cash flows used in estimates of fair value shall incorporate assumptions that marketplace participants would use in their estimates of fair value whenever that information is available without undue cost and effort. Otherwise, an entity may use its own assumptions.

Those estimates shall be based on reasonable and supportable assumptions and shall consider all available evidence. The weight given to the evidence shall be commensurate with the extent to which the evidence can be verified objectively. If a range is estimated for the timing or the amount of possible cash flows, the likelihood of possible outcomes shall be considered. An entity, when using the expected cash flow technique, shall discount the estimated cash flows using a credit-adjusted risk-free rate. Thus, the effect of the entity's credit standing is reflected in the discount rate rather than in the estimated cash flows.

FAS143, Par. 10

A liability for an asset retirement obligation may be incurred over more than one reporting period if the events that create the obligation occur over more than one reporting period. Any incremental liability incurred in a subsequent reporting period shall be considered to be an additional layer of the original liability. Each layer shall be initially measured at fair value. For example, the liability for decommissioning a nuclear power plant is incurred as contamination occurs. Each period, as contamination increases, a separate layer shall be measured and recognized.

"The fair value of a liability for an asset retirement obligation is the amount at which that liability could be settled in a current transaction between willing parties" is the basic FASB assumption on valuing liabilities. But the fact is that except for insurance markets, there is no market, and hence no transactions, for most liabilities, whether current liabilities or contingent future liabilities. Thus the FASB wants companies (in practice, valuation specialists) to construct a what-if scenario, based on market participant assumptions. Unlike the valuation of assets, where there is a market for virtually any asset or asset type, there is no ultimate market where one can test the validity of liability valuations. Whether we are dealing with lawsuits or asbestos remediation, there simply are not a lot of potential buyers or potential sellers, the necessary requirements for any market to function.

This gets to the primary criticism of the FASB's approach to FV of liabilities by corporate financial officers. They feel, with substantial justification, that going to an FV balance sheet, with the concomitant changes in value affecting the income statement, is intrinsically unreliable. This argument about reliability of information versus the usefulness or relevance of such information has been going on for a long time. Certainly a cash-based accounting system is going to be a lot more reliable than an accrual system with its multitude of judgments. Most statement users, and management itself for that matter, prefer accrual data that more closely tracks economic substance rather than cash.

This usefulness of accrual data is used by the FASB to justify the *relevance* of FV data, which most observers agree is one step removed from normal accrual information. The FASB argues in this case that relevance of FV trumps the potential unreliability of FV information. This argument will never be resolved because of the inherent imprecision of FV information, particularly for the valuation of liabilities. Having said this, companies will still have to comply with the FASB's mandates, and the valuation of liabilities, both actual and contingent, at FV is going to be required.

VALUATION OF CONTINGENT PURCHASE PRICE

In many business purchases, the buyer and seller simply cannot agree on what the business is worth. The seller has an optimistic outlook of new products, customers, sales, and profit potential. The buyer, because it is his money that is being paid now for that rosy future, normally is quite skeptical about optimistic projections.

Obviously the buyer must have some favorable outlook, or the transaction would not have been entered into in the first place, but there is usually a difference of opinion about just how good things are going to be in the future. Rather than have the deal fail because the parties cannot agree, the usual result is that a base price for the acquired business is agreed to, with *additional* compensation to be paid as and when certain agreed-upon milestones are met.

This is often a very reasonable compromise, although it must be said that defining the milestones, and measuring them unambiguously, is never as easy in practice as it seems sitting around the negotiating table. Discussing the cost accounting and profit measurement techniques that should be used in setting up the formula, and subsequently applying it so as to avoid controversy, is outside the scope of this book. What is necessary here is to look at the change in accounting practice the FASB is requiring. This change is being made in the name of FV. Before the recent pronouncement, accounting for any subsequent payments was very simple. The subsequent consideration paid out, cash or stock, was offset by an identical charge to goodwill. Because goodwill was not amortized, although tested for impairment, in theory the impairment risk was increased by subsequent payments.

But such payments were only made when the target exceeded the original projections made by the buyer; in effect the additional payments were made because things were going *better* than expected, which effectively obviated any downside risk of an impairment charge. In effect, most buyers were happy to make the additional payments because, without a bad payout formula, it meant that the acquisition was working out better than expected, and the additional payment did not affect earnings in any way.

Now the FASB has decreed that the FV, at date of acquisition, of any contingent payout has to be shown as a liability on the balance sheet. Many observers have pointed out that if the parties to an arm's-length transaction cannot agree on the price—and that is the reason for the contingent payout in the first place—how can a definite amount be determined for inclusion in the financial statements?

The answer has to be that the two parties probably cannot determine this amount themselves, certainly not on an objective and verifiable basis, but that does not preclude an independent appraiser, one who has no financial interest in the outcome, from developing a reasonable estimate. At the time this book is being written, we have not undertaken such an assignment, but here is how we believe it should be performed. In every case the buyer will have made some projections as to the future sales and profits expected from the acquisition. It will have assigned some sort of multiple to those earnings, representing what it is willing to pay. The expectation has to be that the new combined company will be able to meet the projections. Once the deal is consummated, the sellers are no longer at risk if performance expectations are not met. Consequently, there usually will be little upside contingent payments unless performance exceeds some sort of normal range.

The sellers, during the negotiation, will have made their own projections. The upper limit of their projections, which the buyer probably was not willing to accept on an outright basis, formed the baseline for the potential maximum payout. At this point there will be two projections: the buyer's normalized expectations and the seller's optimistic assumptions. Each will have sales, gross margin, Selling, General, & Administrative (SG&A) expenses, R&D commitments, and estimates of new markets to be opened, new products developed, and so forth.

The appraiser will take both sets of projections and independently evaluate them for reasonableness and likelihood of outcome. To an appraiser, the fact that the parties could not agree on the most likely outcome is neither a surprise nor an impediment to performing the valuation. In effect, the appraiser will be performing what is referred to in the valuation profession as a Business Enterprise Valuation (BEV). This involves looking at the company's history, its projections and outlook, its financial position, competition, and new product/service development. Weighing all those factors, both the discounted cash flow and comparisons with other publicly traded firms provides preliminary indications, which then form the basis for the appraiser's final valuation judgment. By performing an overall BEV, the appraiser in effect can then identify the target company's performance requirement and see whether, in the appraiser's judgment, it will be fully met. Assume that the appraiser values the combined companies such that the target company's contribution is somewhat less than the amount for the maximum payout, but above the minimum threshold. It should be possible therefore to provide a supportable yet independent objective assessment of the most likely outcome and how much additional contingent payment would be due at that level.

With no pressure from the client, there is no reason why the independent auditor, the SEC, or the PCAOB for that matter, could not rely on the appraiser's professional judgment. With no claim at stake, the appraiser will provide as good an estimate of the expected final payout as can be found. In other words, there *should* be no bias either up or down in the appraiser's estimate of the final liability. But, let us look at least hypothetically at what will be the real-world situation. If the client (the acquirer) books the appraiser's estimate of the future contingent payment as a liability, there should be an equal probability that the appraiser is either too high, or too low, when the final outcome is known. While appraisers usually do not provide ranges of value, the final single-point answer that is provided actually is the midpoint of a symmetrical range of possible outcomes, but with no way of knowing in advance where within that range the true number lies.

Unfortunately, the accounting treatment required of the acquiring company by the FASB does not provide equal results, albeit they are symmetrical. The new accounting is that if the amount of the liability booked is ultimately found incorrect, the difference (either a debit or a credit) is booked at that time. So absent any bias on the appraiser's part, half the time there should be a debit (charge to expense) and half the time a credit (credit to income).

The accounting theory is unassailable, but ask any CFO: "Are you indifferent if you have an equal likelihood of a charge to expense or a credit to income?" Every reader of this book can answer this question without thinking about it. The bias, and it is a bias, is to avoid charges to income at all costs and take a credit to income if it occurs, without specifically arranging in advance for a credit to happen.

The penalty imposed by the stock market and security analysts when companies miss estimates by even $.01 a share is severe. A responsible CFO will do everything in his power to prevent an unexpected charge to expense, just because the appraiser was too conservative two or three years earlier. What does this mean to the appraiser at the time he is asked to estimate the contingent payout liability? Professionally, he will give his best and most objective answer, one that is supportable upon review by the independent auditor, the SEC, and the PCAOB. Nonetheless, as we have seen elsewhere, valuation is not an exact science.

In projecting the future results of the combined companies, dealing in other words with future events that are unknowable, most appraisers are likely to support optimistic rather than pessimistic assumptions about future sales, profits, and cash flows; such optimism will increase the apparent likelihood of a larger payout, which leads to a larger liability having to be booked.

What will happen is that the company and the appraiser will be in the position of being challenged, and having to support projections that nobody, repeat nobody, knows today whether or not they are going to occur. A review appraiser for the auditing firm can, and will, argue persuasively that the company is being overly optimistic simply to preclude a future charge (and pick up a credit to income). The company and its appraiser will vehemently defend their assumptions, and the argument can go on for a long time. The truth is that no power on earth can provide the correct answer because of the human limitation about foreseeing the future.

Now if a company has made ten acquisitions and on all ten they ended up with a credit to income because the contingent liabilities were overestimated, an auditor could persuasively argue that there likely is bias on the part of the company and its appraiser. But on any one acquisition, and one valuation estimate of a future payout, neither the auditor nor the company will have a track record to use as support for its respective position.

The reason we are focusing on this subject so hard is that this will be an unintended consequence of the FASB's switch in accounting theory. Under the old theory, subsequent payments went to goodwill and there was no liability estimate. Now there has to be an estimate of that liability, with serious consequences to the company if an error is made on the low side. An appraiser can do a better and more objective evaluation of the contingent liability than can either party to the transaction, but it will be a rare appraiser (one who is retiring from practice the next week?) who will not be aware of the consequences to his client if he has erred on the low side.

The FASB, having made the basic change in accounting, will not be a party to these discussions. Companies, their appraisers, and their auditors will. All we can do here is point out the built-in conflict and hope for goodwill (no pun intended) by all parties.

CONCLUSION

Appraisers and valuation specialists have had many years of experience in valuing all types of assets for all sorts of purposes. In its new GAAP accounting for business combinations, for the first time companies and their valuation specialists will have to value liabilities and contingent payments. For many liabilities, such as accounts payable and current bank debt, the face amount and the FV will be the same. This is usually true of many working capital valuations that book value equals FV.

For other liabilities, particularly contingent liabilities such as for asbestos mitigation or plaintiff lawsuits, the old standard in SFAS 5, that the amount must be both probable and capable of estimation, no longer applies. For the first time, something with a small probability of a large loss will have to be quantified and put on the balance sheet.

Further complicating the issue is that the new GAAP accounting will penalize companies if the estimated amount of the liability acquired in a business combination turns out to be higher than first thought. The company will have to take a charge to expense upon final resolution if the actual amount is higher than that previously estimated. However, to achieve symmetry, the FASB also allows companies to take a credit to income if the estimated liability turns out to be higher than the amount actually paid out.

This impact will put substantial pressure on companies, and appraisers, to be conservative in estimating all such liabilities. If you estimate too high, there is no downside, but if you estimate too low, your stock will take a hit. This one-way street, however, is going to be a target for auditors, the SEC, and the PCAOB to ensure that companies do not overestimate liabilities just to build in future gains.

The problem is that valuing liabilities involves estimating the future, and so far in recorded history, no mortals have been able to accomplish this feat regularly and reliably. Perhaps Greek oracles once did a pretty fair job, but they are not currently available for day-to-day consultation. Consequently, there will be continual controversy among appraisers, auditors, the SEC, and companies as to whether the accruals for future liabilities are reasonable or realistic. The trouble is that it will always be one person's opinion against another's, with no reliable basis for settling the controversy.

Time will pass and there will be ultimate resolution of each separate liability, but even that historical perspective will not tell whether a new estimate made today, of a totally different liability, is equally accurate. For probability estimates to be mathematically reliable there have to be many similar situations with comparable outcomes, something that does not exist in the world of lawsuits, environmental liabilities, and contingent purchase price adjustments.

Companies are ultimately responsible for their own financial statements, and we predict that most financial managers will choose, quite rationally, to be conservative in estimating liabilities. This will put pressure on appraisers, who will then have to defend the necessary assumptions against challenges from auditors and the SEC.

CHAPTER 8

Testing for Impairment

There are three different approaches to testing assets for impairment. For fixed assets (i.e., Property, Plant, and Equipment [PP&E]), SFAS 144 requires the use of undiscounted future cash flow. For identifiable intangible assets, one determines Fair Value (FV) based on current methodologies. Finally, for goodwill, impairment involves a two-step process.

TESTING GOODWILL FOR IMPAIRMENT

Recall that as part of the grand compromise that did away with pooling of interest accounting for business combinations, the Financial Accounting Standards Board (FASB) permitted companies to treat goodwill as having an *indefinite* life. In practice, this means that rather than amortizing goodwill over a maximum of 40 years, as in prior Generally Accepted Accounting Principles (GAAP), goodwill no longer has to be amortized. In fact, it cannot be amortized.

Common sense suggests that no asset can stay on a balance sheet forever, and goodwill is not an exception to that rule. Since, by definition, goodwill is an intangible asset, how do we determine that it still has the same value that it had on day 1? Unlike PP&E, which we can physically inspect, goodwill is perhaps the most amorphous of assets. There literally is nothing to look at, no documents that can be referenced, and no market transactions to be tested. While it is often easy to criticize the FASB and how they have developed GAAP over the years, every once in a while they show a great deal of imagination and do get it right. Testing goodwill for impairment is one of these cases.

Remember that goodwill is not an asset that can be valued separately. It is simply an arithmetic product, or residual, between the total purchase price of a company, and the sum of the values of all the identifiable assets, including working capital, PP&E and identifiable intangibles. Looked at a different way, if the true FV of all three categories of assets is $1.7 million, then the dollar amount assigned to goodwill is the difference between $1.7 million and the total purchase price. So if the acquirer paid $2 million, the books would subsequently reflect $300,000 of goodwill. If the purchase price was $2.3 million, then goodwill would have been $600,000 or double the amount. And if the buyer had paid only $1.7 million, there would be no goodwill.

Consequently, goodwill is totally a function of the price the buyer paid for the company at the date of acquisition and the FV of the underlying assets. Keep in mind that the FV of the underlying assets is totally independent of the price paid for the entire company, so in our example here the $1.7 million FV of the underlying assets should be the same for every total buyer, irrespective of who bought the company and what was paid for it.

This means that in valuing goodwill at a subsequent date, one cannot go back and re-create the purchase transaction and pretend a new purchase price for the company and new FV for all the assets and liabilities. Some other mechanism must be developed, particularly because after most acquisitions the buyer integrates the new unit into its existing businesses.

In fact, this integration is what allows subsequent cost savings and synergies to be realized, but you cannot integrate operations and then one year or two years later say, "what would the old stand-alone target company be worth today?" The acquired company will have lost its identity and can never be re-created again. Yet the goodwill based on the original purchase price remains and must be tested to see if it has retained its value or lost value. Keep in mind, however, that U.S. GAAP does not permit write-ups of most intangible assets; absent another business combination, if the current FV of goodwill has actually *increased,* then no accounting entry is required or even permitted. All that can happen to goodwill on the balance sheet is for it to remain constant or be written down.

The FASB solved the problem of present identification of previously acquired goodwill by creating a new concept, called a reporting unit, which is similar in many respects to the segments that companies have to use to report basic financial data about operating units of the business. Reporting units and how they differ from segments are discussed in the next section.

VALUING REPORTING UNITS

Most readers are undoubtedly familiar with the idea of business segments. All publicly owned companies must file with the Securities and Exchange Commission (SEC). One of the GAAP requirements that the SEC monitors closely is segment disclosure. In addition to a consolidated profit and loss (P&L) and balance sheet for the total firm, companies must de-compose their operations into business segments and report financial information separately regarding those units. While only abbreviated information is required, essentially sales revenue, operating profit, total assets, and capital expenditures, this data is usually sufficient for analysts to compare a business segment in Company A with a corresponding company in the same line of business, or with a business segment of another company in the same line of business.

For companies with several distinct lines of business, the segment disclosures allow analysts to determine where growth is occurring and which parts of the business are profitable. Because the required segment information is in summary form only, detailed analyses cannot be made between segment 1 of Company A and Company B in the same line of business. The segment data is useful to look at trends. Furthermore, the information provides a roadmap to investors and analysts when discussing the company with corporate management.

Having said this, two major deficiencies in segment information should be noted. First, companies can and do change segments. So, as an example, a company might report sales and profits by geographical region for several years. Then it may change the reported segments to go to a product orientation, irrespective of the geographical data disclosed previously. While arbitrary changes in segments are not permitted, most companies can usually find a reason to justify that the new segments are better than the old segments.

The second problem with segment information is that strong intra-company business relationships often exist, such as supplier/customer, between and among segments. As a result, somewhat arbitrary splits must be made among revenues and costs to develop the required data. Such arbitrary cost accounting decisions may well weaken the usefulness of the segment data when trying to compare results with other integrated firms.

Nonetheless, segment information has been helpful to shareholders and analysts, and as noted, the SEC monitors these disclosures closely.

Why did the FASB choose not to use the existing segment disclosures as the basis for monitoring the FV of goodwill? After all, companies were already developing the information for GAAP disclosure, and no additional work would have been required.

The FASB, after pretty careful deliberation (reported in ¶ B 101-112 of SFAS 142) in effect said: if segments were too high a level, and companies assigned goodwill to a lower level, then that lower level (the reporting unit) would be the basis of testing goodwill. As a practical matter, many companies do use their segments as reporting units, but in some cases when detailed financial statements are available, the same segment will have two or more reporting units.

Paragraphs 30 and 31 of SFAS 142 state the following, which if somewhat convoluted, nevertheless is what companies have to do:

> *A reporting unit is an operating segment or one level below an operating segment (referred to as a component). A component of an operating segment is a **reporting unit** [emphasis added] if the component constitutes a business for which discrete financial information is available and segment management regularly review the operating result of that component. However, two or more components of an operating segment shall be aggregated and deemed a single reporting unit if the components have similar economic characteristics. An operating segment shall be deemed to be a reporting unit if all of its components are similar, if none of its components is a reporting unit, and if it comprises only a single component. The relevant provisions of Statement 131 and related interpretive literature shall be used to determine the reporting units of an entity.*

The reason for putting this emphasis on reporting units is that once a choice is made, it becomes difficult to change internal allocations and come up with new reporting units. The FASB wanted to discourage games being played; if goodwill in a reporting unit might become impaired, the company could try to rearrange units to avoid the impairment charge.

The critical element in choice of reporting units comes with a new acquisition. Should the acquired business be put into an existing reporting unit, or should it be considered a new and stand-alone reporting unit? After we see how goodwill is actually tested, we will come back to this key point.

Valuing the reporting unit is the first and crucial step in testing for goodwill. By definition the FASB says goodwill is *not* impaired if the

FV of the reporting unit is equal to or higher than the book value of that unit. If the FV is *less* than the book value, then SFAS 142 requires going to Phase 2, discussed as follows, wherein all the assets in the reporting unit must now be valued at current FV.

There are basically two separate approaches to determining the value of a reporting unit. First is the income approach, wherein one prepares a forecast of revenue, expenses, capital expenditures, and cash flow. The resulting cash flows are discounted at the current Weighted Average Cost of Capital (WACC). Most companies doing their own testing utilize the income approach, primarily because they already have projections as part of the annual budgeting and long-range strategic planning process.

The second approach to value a reporting unit is to use the market approach, comparing the subject property with comparable publicly traded firms. While companies are permitted to use this approach, and some do, professional appraisal firms usually perform this analysis.

We strongly recommend that companies use *both* methods in determining the FV of a reporting unit. The reason is twofold. First, unique circumstances may affect the Discounted Cash Flow (DCF) or income approach method, perhaps causing a short-term blip in future results. The way the test works, if the FV is even $1.00 less than book value, then you must go to Phase 2, which involves a lot of work and significant resources. Experience suggests that no operating business is always increasing its sales and profits; even one bad year can cause a reporting unit to fail the Phase 1 test comparing FV with Book Value. Thus the DCF approach is often unduly influenced by the most recent quarter or year's results.

Companies generally are less likely to fail the market comparable test because you are looking at anywhere from four to six or more other companies, not all of which will be having operating results going in the same direction. In other words, using the market approach provides some protection against single-company adverse results from sole use of a DCF analysis.

The question will naturally be raised here: what if the two separate tests, income and market, produce different results? This is why valuation is an art and not a science. Correlating the results of two different valuation approaches requires professional judgment and is the primary reason that most firms use outside valuation specialists to perform the annual Phase 1 testing of reporting units. We have repeatedly seen situations where, by using both approaches, the company does not fail the Phase 1 test, whereas one test alone does show a potential impairment.

This discussion is predicated on the basic assumption that most companies do not want to take an impairment charge. Of course, if the reporting unit holding goodwill is doing poorly, there may be no choice; companies generally believe that today's poor outlook is temporary, that operating results will improve shortly, but because the FASB test in Phase 1 is like a cliff, all or nothing, some means must be found to offset temporary poor results. Using *both* the income and market approaches together represents a very good insurance policy. Companies that have followed this procedure have been pleased with the results. Companies that rely solely on the income approach to value a reporting unit have more than their share of problems.

At this point, if both valuation approaches are followed, then one of two results will occur. The company may find that the FV of the reporting unit is *above* the book value, in which case the exercise is over for the year because by definition there is no impairment of goodwill. Alternatively, the FV of the reporting unit, at the date the test is made, is *below* the book value. In this case there may or may not be an impairment, but the only way to find out is the mandatory requirement to perform the Phase 2 test. This involves valuing *all* the separate assets of the reporting unit, which needless to say, can be a time-consuming and potentially costly exercise.

PHASE 2: IMPLIED GOODWILL

For this discussion, we will assume that the reporting unit being tested is a self-contained manufacturing operation with a single product line, one factory, and a straightforward distribution system. The same procedures are followed for any type of business, but space precludes covering any more detail.

The start of the Phase 2 approach is to obtain a detailed listing of all the assets on the company's books that relate to the specific reporting unit. This may or may not be easy, and there can be unbelievable complexities if common manufacturing or distribution assets are used by more than one reporting unit. Here we assume no such complexities, but we discuss them briefly at the end of this section.

The detailed asset listing will contain all the usual working capital asset categories, PP&E, identifiable intangibles, and goodwill. Depending on when any prior acquisitions were made, there may well be identifiable intangible assets in the reporting unit, such as trade names, customer lists, and patents. By definition there will *always* be goodwill in the reporting unit's books, because if there were no goodwill, there would be no reason to go to the Phase 2 analysis; there may or may not be other identifiable intangible assets on the books.

The first step is to determine the current FV of each component of working capital, specifically inventories and receivables. These usually pose few problems, and as a shortcut many appraisers at least begin the analysis by assuming that FV and book value are close enough that detailed appraisals are not required.

Next is the determination of the current FV of PP&E. The actual determination of these values is discussed in detail in Chapter 9. The basic assumption in valuing PP&E for a Phase 2 impairment study is that the assets will continue in use. Consequently, one would ordinarily not determine values from the used equipment or auction market, which implies a lack of continued use. Values for PP&E typically do not change rapidly, so if fairly recent appraisals were made, or the book values were based on a recent valuation as a result of a business combination, one could apply basic cost indexes to the previous book values and be reasonably close.

Where Phase 2 tests run into difficulty is in the valuation of the reporting unit's identifiable intangibles. Keep in mind that the valuation on the testing date is made irrespective of what is on the books. The reason this is so important, if not critical, is that before the adoption of SFAS 141, many companies lumped all intangibles into goodwill and put nothing against other intangibles.

At the time this was a reasonable approach, inasmuch as there were neither financial reporting nor tax consequences from this simplification. Now, however, the previous shortcut has come home to roost. The worst situation is where there are now large amounts of goodwill and zero shown for, say, trade names. Think through the consequences for a minute. If the trade names have significant value (think Coca-Cola) and are not shown on the books, what happens when the true current FV of the trade name is developed?

The way the arithmetic works out is that the FV of the reporting unit has already been determined. From that is subtracted the current FV of the working capital and the identifiable intangibles. The difference is the implied goodwill. The following example shows this:

Book Value of Reporting Unit:	$11,000,000	
Working Capital	$2,000,000	
PP&E	$4,000,000	
Goodwill	$5,000,000	
	$11,000,000	
Fair Value of Reporting Unit:	$10,000,000	
FV ≤ BV = Go to Phase 2		
Phase 2:		
Fair Value: Working Capital	$2,000,000	
PP&E	$3,500,000	
Trade Name	$1,500,000	
Total Fair Value of Assets:	$7,000,000	$7,000,000
Implied Goodwill:		$3,000,000

In this mini-example the implied goodwill of $3 million is $2 million less than the carrying amount of $5 million; thus, according to SFAS 142, the company must recognize immediately a $2 million impairment charge. Look again at the example. The difference between book value and FV is only $1 million, but the company has to take a $2 million write-down! This is because the company had not recognized on its books any value for the trade name, even though it definitely had substantial value.

The lesson is clear: Errors in the allocation of a purchase price yesterday can cause financial reporting problems today, and any errors today in a new allocation, resulting from a current business combination, have the potential for *future* impairment losses.

Many people believe that the FASB was punitive in its refusal to let companies go back and reallocate prior allocations to correct for the inappropriate lumping in of all intangibles into goodwill. Nonetheless, that is the rule, and in fairness to the FASB, it was fully cognizant of what it required. The author's personal belief is that the FASB wanted to demonstrate to the business community that any inaccuracy in financial reporting had consequences. In this case it certainly made the point, because several firms found out to their dismay in having to report major impairment write-downs.

There is a flip side to this phenomenon. Assume the buyer has a very profitable reporting unit, one where the FV as a business far exceeds the book value. In that situation there is a substantial cushion, the difference between FV and BV. In that situation if a new acquisition is made, and placed in that reporting unit, it will be almost impossible to have an impairment loss. The reason is that the goodwill of the new acquisition is immediately incorporated into the total goodwill, and the FV of the entire reporting unit is the only thing considered in making the Phase 1 impairment test. So unless the whole unit suffers significant losses, any impact from the new acquisition may have little overall impact.

The consequences of this phenomenon are straightforward. To the extent one has a choice of where to place a new acquisition in terms of a reporting unit, it is generally advisable to add it to an existing profitable unit. The reason is to utilize the built-in gains from the existing business to cover any potential problems arising from the new acquisition. The FASB was fully aware of this potential and decided that the true economics were reflected properly. Further supporting this approach is that companies typically try to integrate new acquisitions, and very soon the identity of the new purchase is lost; consequently, the only asset to be tested is the total reporting unit containing the existing plus the new businesses.

It is possible that a new acquisition may not fall neatly into just one existing reporting unit. In such a situation the company and/or its valuation specialist must split the acquired business's assets and liabilities between or among the receiving reporting units. While this exercise sometimes requires professional judgment, as long as it is done in good faith, and not to meet some objective, it is unlikely the allocation will be challenged.

It is even possible for some of the new goodwill to be added to a reporting unit that does not receive any other assets. This will actually be required, if the synergies from acquiring the new business in practice help a product line in another reporting unit. A simple example shows this. Assume the buyer acquires a chemical company, a single plant, and a single product line. The buyer uses some of the product itself, and the remainder of production is sold in the open market at arm's length to third parties. The buyer can now obtain the formerly purchased raw material at a new lower manufacturing cost, not the higher market selling price. This lower production cost immediately transforms into higher operating profits at the unit that buys and uses the newly acquired firm's product. The benefit of acquiring the company, the intangible that is called goodwill, properly has to be split on some rational basis between the new reporting unit representing the acquired business and the old reporting unit that obtains the benefit of lower cost.

One final point in discussing reporting units should be mentioned. You cannot change the makeup of reporting units simply to avoid a goodwill impairment charge. The FASB indicated that if, and only if, the company actually reorganizes its management structure can reporting units be realigned. This follows from the FASB's determination that reporting units have to have their own financial statements. Virtually always following a reorganization, the company will start to prepare current internal financials to provide new management with the tools they need to run the business. Consequently, it only makes sense that the current financial statements now become the basis for measuring and reporting on the new organization structure. Inasmuch as the old statements relating to the old structure will no longer be available (perhaps without substantial what-if effort), the FASB recognized reality.

We have not seen situations where, to avoid a write-down, a company restructured management to be able to report in such a way that there is no longer a need to incur an impairment loss. Certainly, this is theoretically possible, but the costs would in all likelihood outweigh the gains.

Goodwill impairment charges are not necessarily viewed as a major negative by shareholders and analysts. Observations on actual reported impairments suggests that analysts and the market pay less attention to goodwill impairment charges than might be expected. The reason is that the operating problems causing the FV of the reporting unit to decline will already have been disclosed. Then at the testing date, those problems will affect the FV of the reporting unit, which then leads to Phase 2 detailed valuation and final determination. Thus the elapsed time between public disclosure of a business problem and the actual impairment charge taken in a quarterly 10-Q or annual 10-K is such that analysts will have fully taken everything into account.

Finally, most companies when disclosing an impairment charge always preface the announcement with the statement, "Well, it's only an accounting charge with no cash flow consequences, so don't worry about it." It reminds us of *Mad* magazine's Alfred P. Neuman, who used to say, "What, me worry?" Somehow one never sees a company when it buys another firm, which has no impact on earnings but does have a dramatic impact on cash flow, tell shareholders, "Well it's only a cash outflow, but it doesn't affect earnings."

Be that as it may, we have rarely seen market reaction to impairment charges, and in fact the market response is often positive. Actually, in our practice we have had occasions when companies *wanted* to clean up their balance sheet and in fact wanted to write off some goodwill, but the FASB also anticipated this, and the rules were pretty carefully drawn up to make one action as difficult as the other. For practical purposes, if one is on the borderline between having an impairment loss for goodwill and not reporting the impairment, then it is easier to implement the loss than to preclude the loss. Being just a little more conservative in valuing the reporting unit will cause an automatic move to Phase 2, the detailed valuation of all assets. As we have seen elsewhere, it is always possible to be conservative in valuation.

Precluding a goodwill impairment charge, however, demands very close attention to the Phase 1 valuation of the reporting unit. The FASB is pretty explicit that one must use the same approaches and methodology each time; this is one of the reasons we strongly suggest use of two different valuation approaches so that no one factor totally dominates. Even so, with two valuation approaches, there is a limit to how much the comparables can be tweaked or the discount rate adjusted. When a company is on the cusp of having to report a goodwill impairment charge, it is obvious that the independent auditors will be aware of the situation, and with the Sarbanes-Oxley Act threat from the Public Company Accounting Oversight Board (PCAOB) hanging over their head, audit firms are unlikely to be lenient in stretching the valuation.

TESTING IDENTIFIABLE INTANGIBLES WITH AN INDEFINITE LIFE

We have seen that testing goodwill for impairment first requires determining the FV of the reporting unit. Fortunately, the testing for impairment of indefinite lived intangible assets, such as licenses and trade names, does not involve such a two-step process. The impairment testing rule is simple and straightforward: *Determine the FV of the intangible asset every year. If the FV is less than carrying value, write the asset down to FV.* The reverse, of course, does not hold true. If the FV is greater than the carrying value (i.e., higher than when it was acquired), the company cannot write up the value. We often use the analogy of the roach motel, where you cannot get out once you enter; for intangible assets, you can write it down but you cannot ever write it up.

Unlike goodwill, where an unprofitable acquisition's goodwill can be offset by other profitable portions of the reporting unit, thus precluding a write-down, for intangible assets each stands on its own. So if you have three trade names, two of which have increased in value, and one has been discontinued, basically you can *not* net the differences. The discontinued trade name would be written down to FV, and the other two would remain unchanged. About all the company can do with the two remaining trade names is disclose to investors in the company's Management Discussion & Analysis (MD&A) report that the remaining names have an FV above the carrying amount. Presumably one could disclose the amount of such an increase in value, although we are not familiar with anyone who has taken this step.

The actual valuation of individual indefinite lived intangible values follows the procedures discussed in Chapter 6. Basically, in the normal course of events, if licenses are more or less automatically renewed, and the cash flow of the business is equal to or has increased since acquisition, there is no reason to perform a detailed valuation. The company can make the analysis, and probably the independent auditors would not require a valuation specialist be hired. The situation is similar for trade names. If revenues of the product or service have held even or increased, it is unlikely the value has decreased; hence no impairment exists and the review can be cursory.

The problem for indefinite lived intangible assets is that they are not amortized. Consequently, as and when there is a drop in value due to lower sales volume (trade names) or nonrenewal (license), the impairment loss is likely to be steep. It is analogous to falling off a cliff: one minute you are safe at the top and the next you have fallen severely. Put a different way, impairments of indefinite lived intangible assets are rarely gradual. What we see is that things go along well for a period of time, and then a change in circumstances occurs. The new FV determination is substantially below carrying value, and the impairment loss may be both unexpected by investors and larger than expected.

This reason causes many companies to consciously choose a definite life for acquired intangible assets. Because the SEC seems to frown on indefinite lives (which are not amortized), there is not likely to be much push back if a company, on initial acquisition, consciously chooses a definite, albeit long, life. We have seen many firms choose to apply a 40-year life to licenses or trade names, just so they can amortize a little bit each year. A further advantage of choosing a definite life is that the impairment test is different for assets with a specific life. This is discussed in the next section.

TESTING IDENTIFIABLE INTANGIBLES WITH A DEFINITE LIFE

With the possible exception of licenses and trade names, virtually all intangible assets (other than goodwill) have to be assigned a definitive life and amortized over that life. As mentioned elsewhere, while many companies in practice amortize intangibles on a straight-line basis, the rule in SFAS 142 actually requires that the amortization relate to the diminution in value. Thus if a customer relationship base, say magazine subscriptions, is given a ten-year life, it is unlikely that one-tenth of the customers will leave every year. More likely is an accelerated life, whereby more customers fail to renew in the early years, while dedicated customers, fewer in number, will be very loyal.

The reason for bringing up this point is that both the life and the amortization method directly affect how intangibles are tested for impairment. Recall that most intangibles are valued based on the cash flows associated with the asset. So a longer-lived asset will be worth more, but be amortized over a longer period, while if assigned a shorter life the total value will be reduced. In practice, it often makes little difference to the annual charge whether a long life or a shorter life is assigned because the impact on annual earnings over the near term may be quite similar.

The testing requirement for intangible assets with a definite life is *not* based, at least directly, on the current FV! Rather, the FASB in SFAS

144 requires that such assets be tested using "undiscounted future cash flows." Careful readers at this point, particularly those familiar with present value concepts and DCF analysis, will be scratching their heads. Did the FASB, and the author, really mean *un*discounted cash flows? Yes. To our knowledge this is the only place in finance and accounting where future cash flows are added up arithmetically and not discounted back to present value.

The rule in SFAS 144 requires that the future cash flows of an asset to be tested, including both identifiable intangibles as well as PP&E, be added up arithmetically. Then, if the sum of the future cash flows is equal to or greater than the book value (carrying value) of the asset, there is no impairment. If the sum of the future cash flows is *less* than the book value, then by definition an impairment exists.

The rules further require that in case of impairment, the asset then must be written down to FV, not just to the sum of the future cash flows. This means that in effect there is still a two-stage process: first the impairment test and then, if necessary, the FV determination.

Several points come to mind:

- What are the relevant cash flows that have to be measured?
- How far out into the future do you measure the cash flows?
- What do you do if it is difficult to identify or measure the cash flows related to the specific asset being tested?
- What if the true FV of the asset is less than Book Value, but the undiscounted cash flows are still greater than Book Value?
- Do you determine the FV by reference only to the cash flows you used in the test?
- Why does accelerated amortization of an intangible help avoid an impairment?

The *relevant cash flows* of a particular intangible asset, such as a trade name or a patent, may be relatively easy to identify. That is, for example, the royalty income associated with a trade name can be based on anticipated future sales. The cash flows related to a specific unique patent likewise relate to the sales of the patented product or the royalties generated by the patent.

Problems arise when several assets jointly contribute to the cash flows. So, as an example, a major trade name undoubtedly has value in and of itself, but without manufacturing facilities and a distribution system, there would be few if any sales. This problem was discussed in Chapter 6, and the accepted solution in valuing the patent or the trade name is to look at the cash flows from future product sales, but then reduce them by a charge for the use of the manufacturing and distribution resources. Needless to say, the determination of these appropriate contributory charges, and their application in practice, involves significant professional judgment. Because those charges affect the net cash flows, and the sum of the net cash flows determines whether or not there is an impairment, it may well be that whether an asset passes or fails the test is a function of those contributory charges.

For other intangible assets, particularly the customer relationship asset required by SFAS 141 and 142, the identification of the appropriate cash flows is a matter of perhaps even greater judgment. The first step is usually to go back and see how the existing book value was created when the asset was acquired. Keep in mind that at this point almost all intangible assets on a company balance sheet were acquired in a business combination. So the working papers of the original allocation had to have included a methodology.

The real issue is that subsequent to the date of the acquisition, the acquired firm's assets have probably lost their identity. The company now has one sales force calling on all its customers, of which just a portion was incorporated into the "customer relationship intangible" now on the books. Given normal attrition of old customers, and addition of new customers for the acquired firm's product lines, it quickly becomes very difficult, if not impossible, to identify the true cash flows of the *original* customer base.

But the asset being tested is that original customer base, not today's customer base. In practice if the acquired customer base represented 10% of consolidated sales at the acquisition date, then one can reasonably assume that 10% of *today's* total sales can be used for the cash flow test. This is not particularly sound theoretically, but it is the most practical approach to what is essentially an unsolvable problem. In some cases, companies try to identify specific customers that were acquired, and follow those customers in the future for the impairment test. Even this approach presents difficulties if the acquired customers start buy-ing additional products from the consolidated firm.

In our experience, auditors who review impairment tests usually take a pretty realistic approach to these operational problems. That may be because the undiscounted cash flow test is such that it takes a dra-matic drop in volume and profitability to flunk the test. In short, while there are both theoretical and practical problems in identifying the rel-evant cash flows, in practice few companies fail to meet the test and have to impair their intangibles that were given a definitive life.

How far into the future do you *measure the cash flows?* When the predecessor to SFAS 144 came out, it was not totally clear how far into the future one should carry the cash flow analysis. After all, if the item being tested had only $1.00 per year of positive cash flow, but you pro-jected this very far into the future, you could always avoid having an impairment. Many people did have to suspend disbelief in applying a 60-year cash flow analysis when nobody can reasonably project the basic operating environment that far into the future; we did see such analyses, but the support for such assumptions often appeared weak.

Now the FASB has in effect stated that you can only carry the cash flow projection forward for the same period of time as the life of the underlying asset. So if you have assigned a ten-year life to the asset, you cannot project cash flows out further than the remaining life (eight years, if the test is being made two years after acquisition) assigned for account-ing purposes. Again, the undiscounted cash flow test is such that absent major economic or competitive changes, few firms fail to pass the test.

What are the *relevant cash flows?* This question may be the most difficult to answer because it gets involved with serious questions of cost allocation and cost accounting. Most companies have significant Sell-ing General & Administration (SG&A) expenses that are not directly traceable to specific assets, specific customers, or even product lines and associated developments. Yet in projecting future cash flows associated with an intangible asset being tested, it makes a tremendous difference whether one uses a direct costing approach or a full allocation approach. Furthermore, one must realistically put in the cash flow analysis not only the cash inflows expected but also any required cash outflows required to maintain the asset. So assuming a 30-year life for a trade name, but only a 15-year remaining life for the PP&E required to manufacture the product, one has to incorporate the anticipated capital expenditures into the cash flow analysis. Because this is on an *un*discounted basis, the full impact of the projected cash outflows will be felt immediately.

It is difficult to generalize on the cost accounting issues, whether to use a full cost or a direct cost approach. Obviously, a direct cost approach would help pass the test because there would be fewer deductions from expected revenues, but auditors probably would raise serious questions if the client did not at least apportion *some* amount of shared and overhead costs.

Suppose you are certain that the FV of the asset is less than the sum of the undiscounted cash flows. Do you stop there and write down the asset to the newly derived number? The FASB is quite specific that SFAS 144 is a two-step test. The first step determines solely whether or not the asset is impaired. If the carrying value (book value) of the asset is greater than the sum of the undiscounted cash flows, then the company, or usually the independent valuation specialist, must determine the current FV of the asset and book the reduction in value as a current expense.

The determination of the current FV of the asset that is impaired may well be a DCF approach, in which case one would be well advised to use the same cash flows. Put a different way, how could you explain one set of projected cash flows for the impairment test, and then turn around and say that the real FV of the asset has to be determined with a *different* set of cash flow projections? However, there is no requirement that the FV determination be based on a DCF or income approach to value. One can reasonably utilize either the cost approach or the market comparable approach in determining the current FV of the impaired asset.

Once in a while a question comes up when it is obvious that the FV of the asset is less than the carrying value, but the undiscounted cash flow test does not support this assumption. A good example would be a brand name that was acquired, with expectations of long-term continued use, and with an increasing sales volume. Under those circumstances, the FV of the trade name would have been fairly high. Now say five years later the company decides to stop using two different trade names for similar products and determines that all sales of most of the products will be under the older name. It will, however, retain and use the acquired trade name for one specialty product line, accounting say for only 10% of the original anticipated volume.

In such a situation most observers would agree that if the acquired trade name is now being used on only 10% of the anticipated sales, that its value must have gone down. Those observers would be correct. The value of the Oldsmobile trade name to General Motors is decreasing year by year as no new Oldsmobile autos are sold and fewer and fewer customers remember the brand. So, while Oldsmobile was self-developed and not on the GM balance sheet, assuming it had been acquired one would be comfortable in asserting that the value after the discontinuance of new car sales under the Olds trade name was greatly diminished. But in our original example, and in the case of the Oldsmobile name, there are still some sales, and those sales can be quite profitable. Replacement parts for Oldsmobile cars will be sold many years into the future, just as Ford Model A and even Model T car parts are still produced and sold.

The point is that even though the value of the trade name is obviously reduced, the brand may still pass the undiscounted cash flow test merely from a reduced, but long-lived, level of profitable sales. You can ask whether the people who wrote SFAS 121, now SFAS 144, were unaware of this issue. The answer is that the FASB and staff were fully aware of this issue. What happened was that to make a formal impairment test work in practice, and be accepted by the FASB's constituency of financial statement preparers, the undiscounted test was a conscious compromise. Effectively, by putting in the undiscounted cash flow test, the FASB knowingly set things up so there would be fewer impairment write-downs, and those assets that failed the undiscounted test would be impaired beyond a reasonable doubt.

But they were unwilling to go to the theoretically correct approach and make companies determine the true FV of all assets every year. The cost of such FV determination would have been too high; this author among others said at the time there were not enough appraisers in the world to value all assets every year. The undiscounted cash flow test incorporated into SFAS 144 is absolutely unjustified on any theoretical grounds, other than that it is a practical compromise. As such, it has serious flaws that many people have pointed out. What those critics fail to ask, however, is "What is the alternative?" The answer to that question, effectively determining FV of all assets using approved valuation techniques, is not going to be accepted by companies and their auditors, neither of whom are ready to embrace full FV accounting and reporting. While many academic theoreticians have eloquently and convincingly made the argument for FV accounting, those with the responsibility for implementing such a notion have resisted it totally.

Hence SFAS 144, with all its theoretical flaws, seems to work in practice. If an asset fails the undiscounted cash flow test, it definitely should be written down. If an asset with a definite life, whether tangible or intangible, still passes the undiscounted cash flow test, but its real value is impaired, then under current GAAP the answer (if material) should be disclosure, not an accounting entry.

Avoiding an impairment charge through accelerated amortization was discussed briefly in a previous section. Most financial officers do not, at first glance, like the idea of accelerated amortization of intangible assets. It makes current earnings lower, albeit future earnings will be increased proportionately. That theory, that the charge is only a matter of timing, has little appeal for a CFO or CEO who has to explain *this quarter's* lower earnings, and who could care less about potentially higher reported earnings three years from now.

The issue might be looked at a little differently if a different choice is presented. Instead of looking at straight-line versus accelerated amortization of an initial value for a specific intangible, compare amortization with an unexpected impairment charge. The faster the amortization of an intangible, the less is the chance for an impairment charge ever to occur.

We have seen instances where business plans regarding the use of a trade name change and the company faces an impairment charge because of a sound business decision. Alternatively, we have seen cases where a company wanted to discontinue an acquired trade name and sell its entire product under one name. In that instance, to avoid an impairment charge, the company retained the name for a period of time, which may have been uneconomic in terms of marketing expenditures but avoided a sudden charge to earnings, albeit a noncash charge.

In this book we cannot provide management consulting advice, tempting as that might be. Our professional judgment, and experience with clients, however, suggests that following the accelerated amortization requirement of SFAS 142 may, in practice, be a sound approach. While few auditors so far seem to have focused on this requirement, given the

SEC and PCAOB emphasis on auditors following GAAP, it is only a matter of time before the amortization pattern of intangibles achieves a much higher level of scrutiny.

IMPAIRMENT OF PROPERTY, PLANT, AND EQUIPMENT

While we cover the valuation of PP&E in the next chapter, in this chapter we are discussing the measurement of impairment to current book values, irrespective of whether those values came through a business combination or were on the company's books all along.

SFAS 144 deals with impairment of PP&E in the same way as with identifiable intangible assets. It is a two-step approach, with step 1 being the undiscounted cash flow analysis discussed previously and step 2 being a write-down to FV if the asset group fails the step 1 test. Unlike the testing of specific identifiable intangible assets, each of which presumably stands on its own, the basic valuation problem with PP&E consists of one issue: "What is the appropriate grouping of fixed assets to be tested, valued, and written down?"

Think of an integrated production facility (e.g., a machining operation in a construction equipment factory). There will be numerous individual pieces of equipment, and if it is a production line, there will also be some sort of conveyor system. Now assume there is one grinding machine that is obsolete and should be replaced before being fully depreciated. The book value of the grinding machine is in excess of its FV, no matter how it is determined. Should an impairment charge be taken? The answer is no.

The reason is that it is virtually impossible to determine a stream of future cash flows directly related to the single grinding machine contained within the total production line. SFAS 144 states that you have to test for impairment, assuming there are impairment indicators, the smallest grouping of assets for which there is an identifiable cash flow stream. In this example, one could presumably determine a cash flow stream for the production line, based on current and projected production over the next few years, but any reasonable assumption of the total cash flow would probably be in excess of the book value of the total line. So, in such a case, SFAS 144 precludes anything other than looking at the total production line.

In our experience there are relatively few situations where actively utilized PP&E turns out to be impaired, as long as the test covers a production unit. Now when a company ceases production, say by outsourcing to China, and the equipment will be idled, then there is no question that SFAS 144 comes into play and the step 1 test is easy: zero cash flows. The assets are then valued on the basis of value in-exchange, sale to a dealer or scrap.

As long as production is planned to continue, and the company is not selling at a loss, then it is unlikely there will be an impairment charge. Some auto parts manufacturers, such as Visteon or Delphi, with labor costs that significantly exceed foreign competition, may well have the type of economic situation envisioned when SFAS 144 was developed. But for most competitive businesses, it is very easy to pass the Phase 1 test.

CONCLUSION

In exchange for giving up pooling of interest accounting, and not having to write off or amortize goodwill, the FASB required companies to test goodwill, and other intangibles, for possible impairment. If the FV is less than book value, then an impairment charge must be taken. However, the calculations are not quite so straightforward.

For goodwill, the FASB developed a new concept of reporting units, similar to business segments. It is necessary to determine every year the FV of every reporting unit that has goodwill in it. We strongly recommend using both the income approach (DCF) and the market comparable approach. Providing two separate tests of value provides a lot more flexibility, and sudden short-term fluctuations can be precluded from mandating a premature write-down. In addition to goodwill, other identifiable intangibles must also be tested for impairment each year. There are two separate categories: those assets that were assigned an indefinite life and those assigned a definite life.

Intangible assets with an indefinite life are not amortized each year, but a direct valuation is necessary. That means an FV determination, on a separate basis, of every indefinite lived asset is required every year. While companies can, and do, perform this test by themselves, practice seems to be that accounting firms, and the SEC, much prefer having those tests performed independently by valuation specialists.

For intangible assets assigned a definite life, and amortized over that life, the impairment test is quite different. Instead of looking at the FV of each asset, a company only has to look at all the future cash flows associated with each of the assets. As long as the sum of the (undiscounted) future cash flows is greater than the carrying value of the asset(s), then by definition there is no impairment charge, either permitted or required.

While many companies amortize intangibles with a definite life on a straight-line basis over that life, the FASB actually requires that amortization follow the loss in utility of that asset. As a practical matter, while few companies do this, virtually all intangibles decline in value on an accelerated basis. Amortization, therefore, *should* be accelerated. Until the SEC and PCAOB make this a high priority, it is unlikely that companies will want to take higher charges earlier. The one advantage of doing so, however, is that if more of the value is written off earlier, then the chance of any future impairment charge is dramatically reduced.

The major idea to be taken from this chapter is that before putting a life on an intangible asset, whether indefinite or definite, thought should be given to the future amortization pattern. Thought should also be given to possible changes in use or value of the intangible asset so as to anticipate and therefore preclude the need for a future impairment charge. While experience so far suggests that the market does not penalize companies for impairment charges, because they are "not a cash cost," any impairment charge reflects on prior management decisions. No management wants to be in the position of having to justify a past acquisition. In effect, an impairment charge suggests that the purchase price was too high or that subsequent events were not properly anticipated.

For PP&E we rarely find that impairment is likely because most businesses with positive cash flow do not flunk the Phase 1 test. Only if the underlying economics have changed dramatically does the future cash flow, on an undiscounted basis, become less than the current book value. Keep in mind that the book value of most PP&E usually has been written down from original cost because of depreciation charges taken over the years.

CHAPTER 9

Valuation of Hard Assets and Real Estate

At present companies reflect the Fair Value (FV) of hard assets and real estate when they are acquired, whether through direct purchase or as part of a business combination. Unlike financial instruments, which are marked-to-market daily or monthly, machinery, equipment, land, and buildings continue to sit on the balance sheet at their original cost less accounting depreciation, irrespective of any increase in value. Because all assets, other than land, are depreciated for accounting purposes, write-downs of such assets because of impairment are rare, as discussed in Chapter 8.

So, while the current FV of hard assets is not regularly determined as part of preparing normal financial statements, the determination of FV has two areas of interest:

1. The FV of machinery, equipment, buildings, and land (hard assets) must be determined at the time of a business combination.

2. Many companies are sitting on substantially undervalued assets, which has two consequences:

    Reported gains can be recorded on the profit and loss (P&L) statement if such assets are sold.

    In a few cases, such undervalued assets may attract unwanted attention from potential acquirers.

In this chapter we will discuss just how appraisers determine the FV of machinery and equipment, as well as real property. Keep in mind that the origin of appraisals was in the 1890s, where insurance companies and their insured agreed in advance to accept as proof of loss the value of machinery, equipment, and building as determined by an appraisal.

HIGHEST AND BEST USE

Highest and best use is often defined by real estate professionals as:

> *The reasonably probable and legal use of vacant land or an improved property that is physically possible, appropriately supported and financially feasible and that results in the highest value.*[1]

Conceptually, the highest and best use relates strictly to land, where various alternative uses are possible. In the context of this book, we deal with so-called improved properties where there will be improvements on the land, with improvements being basically structures. An example of the concept would be the FV of a parking garage downtown in a major city. The property has value based on the income stream from the garage. The underlying land has a separate value if the parking structure were demolished and the land was vacant and available for construction of an office tower or an apartment complex; this assumes that there is economic demand for additional offices and/or apartments.

In valuing the property for a purchase price allocation, the appraiser would consider the intended use by the owner (i.e., will the parking structure continue to be used for its intended purpose?). But even if the new owner says, "I will continue to use the property as a parking garage because my employees need it every day," the appraiser would be obliged to see what, say, ten acres of a downtown block is worth on the open market. Then the appraiser would subtract the cost of demolition to arrive at an *alternate* value for the land.

So we would end up with two values: one for continued use as a parking garage and a second if the land were offered on the market for a different use (e.g., office tower or apartments). If the vacant land value is higher, that is the amount that should be determined as the FV for financial reporting purposes, even though the owner says he is not going to tear down the garage. The Financial Accounting Standards Board's (FASB's) concept of market participants comes into play here because if the owner *would* put the garage on the market, some developer would pay the vacant land price and demolish the structure. Another parking garage operator would not be able to match the developer's offer and still obtain an appropriate return on investment (ROI).

If a parking garage owner paid the market price for the structure, what an experienced real estate developer would and could offer, he would have paid so much that the rental income from parking would be insufficient to provide a profit on the purchase price. Thus the concept of a free market suggests that sooner or later land, and associated structures, will be utilized at their highest and best use.

We had an example of a hospital that was vacant because a new facility had been built nearby. Under state law, the structure could no longer be used as a hospital, in an effort to reduce the oversupply of hospital beds with a consequent increase in costs to patients. The valuation issue then became, what is the highest and best use of a hospital building (with all its ancillary features such as oxygen hoses, operating rooms, electrical connections for X-ray units, etc.) that was designed and built as a hospital but could no longer be used for that purpose. In this case the facility was in a college town, and the answer was that the facility, with moderate incremental expenditures, could be turned into a student dormitory. Obviously there would be inefficiencies in the subject building, relative to a newly constructed dormitory, and those differences affected the value of the existing hospital shell. Nonetheless, use as a dormitory, and the cost to convert it to that use, had a higher value than the cost of total demolition and building a new dormitory from scratch. So, in this instance the FV of the hospital that could not be used as a hospital was developed from the value of a new dormitory, less the cost of conversion.

This approach to questioning whether the current use is the highest and best use is actually used in virtually every real estate valuation. The appraiser mentally asks the highest and best use question, and in virtually all cases the current use is the highest and best use. But while alternate valuable uses are relatively infrequent, nonetheless the appraiser will have asked the question.

An additional example is a major professional organization that was moving from New York City and a committee from the organization's board was looking at alternate sites for new construction. One desirable property was offered, but right next door was a very unattractive skating rink. The real estate agent assured the committee, "Trust me, the highest and best use of that skating rink is another office building, so you don't have to worry, it will be torn down soon." The committee ultimately chose a different location, but a funny thing has happened. Twenty years later, the skating rink is still there! And the property still has not been redeveloped! Just because there is a higher and best use does not automatically require the present owner to sell or convert.

Property rights still permit an owner to make uneconomic decisions, and there is little that others can do about it.

VALUE IN-USE VERSUS VALUE IN-EXCHANGE

Although the concept is sometimes difficult for accountants to grasp, the truth is that the same asset can have quite different values depending on its intended use. Before starting any appraisal assignment, a valuation specialist will determine the purpose for which the client needs, and will utilize, the values to be developed. If the client says, "How much can I sell this milling machine for on the used equipment market?" we derive an answer that is referred to as *value in-exchange*. The concept, consistent with the definition of FV, is what a willing buyer, in this case a dealer, would pay for this specific asset at this point in time.

However, the client could ask the appraiser, "How much could I sell the entire production facility for, knowing it contains this very special milling machine?" In this case we are talking about a prospective buyer who would operate the assembly line and utilize the milling machine, along with the other assets, to produce the output that customers are buying. The value of the milling machine as part of an ongoing production process is going to be higher than if it is offered for sale to a used equipment dealer. A few of the differences are:

- The milling machine has already been delivered and installed, hence the new buyer is saving freight and shipping expense.

- The item has been debugged and presumably is working.

- The milling machine's tooling is available, so there will be no start-up delay.

- The freight and shipping expense to the dealer will not be incurred.

- The dealer requires a normal markup and has operating expenses in running his business. He subtracts his expected operating costs and profit from what he thinks he could sell the milling machine for to another buyer some time in the future to arrive at the amount he is willing to pay. Hence the value to the seller, if he pursues a second-hand market, incorporates those costs and profit the dealer requires.

In valuing any asset, whether real estate, machinery, equipment, or even intangible assets, both the client and the valuation specialist have to obtain in advance a clear understanding of the purpose of the appraisal. We call this the premise of value, and every valuation report should clearly delineate the premise of value being used. If a client wants both values, in-use and in-exchange, then effectively there are going to be two separate reports, or at least two separate sections of one report.

Ordinarily, for allocation of purchase price, the FV of acquired hard assets is assumed to be in-use, unless specifically identified otherwise. SFAS 141 explicitly allows for these two separate valuation concepts, and it is up to the acquirer to identify for the appraiser which assets will be retained and which disposed of. This determination will probably be made as a result of the due diligence effort performed before the acquisition.

PHYSICAL INSPECTION AND THE CONDITION OF ASSETS

The very essence of the appraisal process is physical inspection of the assets being valued. The author has testified in court several times, and if he had not seen the assets under consideration, the following inquiry from the opposing counsel would have been devastating, "Tell me, Mr. King, how could you determine the condition of the assets if you did not see them?" Perhaps the answer would have been, "Well, I took so-and-so's word for it." That is not very persuasive, particularly in a court of law, and because most appraisers prepare their reports as though they will have to testify, it simply is ingrained in the DNA of every appraiser to see the assets being valued.

Now, it must be stated clearly that appraisers are *not* auditors. Thus in valuing inventory, we would want to see a representative sample, in order to determine the condition. But appraisers do not and should not count inventory or verify the count of others. Appraisers clearly state in their report that they rely on the client's financial statements. So if the auditor has signed off on a value of $1 million for inventory, that presupposes that the counts are correct. The appraiser may develop his own values but will not independently verify that all the items are there. Similarly, the appraiser will utilize the fixed asset register and will inspect all the major items and a sample of the minor items, but will not usually independently count, for example, every PC. The appraiser would rely on the quantity of PCs reported and value that quantity based on today's market conditions.

However, appraisers who specialize in machinery and equipment (M&E) do have to utilize specialized knowledge to determine the condition of the assets being appraised. That is why it can take several years for an appraiser to fully reach his potential. The basic valuation concepts and skills are relatively easy to learn; the application of those concepts and skills to *specific* businesses requires experience.

Now nobody can be expert in all production areas, in all types of construction, or in all types of transportation equipment. Rather, an experienced M&E appraiser knows what to look for, who to ask, and what questions to ask. In most production operations, there will be a plant engineer, or other comparable manager, who is currently responsible for maintenance of existing equipment and replacement as needed with new equipment. Such an individual is the go-to individual at the start of every inspection performed by an appraiser.

A skilled appraiser will inquire about current performance relative to new equipment, physical deterioration of the assets, excessive maintenance expense, and so forth. An experienced eye can quickly determine the current overall condition of assets, since some companies have a policy of very high preventive maintenance, whereas other firms wait until something breaks down before fixing it. Neither approach is right or wrong, but what is being done will significantly affect the appraiser's judgment.

At times an appraiser will be asked to determine the approximate value, on a quick guess basis, where the client perhaps does not have the time, or does not want to pay the time and expense, to have a physical inspection. Appraisers, while reluctant to do so, will on occasion provide such an estimate of FV. They will clearly state in any report that such asset values were determined without a physical inspection. Such answers may be good enough for certain purposes, but probably would not stand up in court.

Why do appraisers have to see the assets being appraised? The answer can be summed up in one word: Depreciation. As will be discussed in the next section, depreciation for an appraiser is *not* the same as depreciation for financial statements. Accountants have developed a convention over the years that the original cost of assets capitalized should be written off over the useful life of the asset, with an allowance for salvage value if appropriate. Conceptually this sounds good, and very few accountants ever challenge the underlying rationale for depreciation charges.

There are two major flaws with depreciation accounting, at least as practiced in the United States. First is that the useful life is usually far less than the actual expected life for most assets. This comes about because of a desire to obtain the maximum tax benefits. Many, if not most, companies use the same life for book purposes as for tax; the consequence is that the short tax lives granted by Congress to encourage investment do not necessarily reflect the actual economics of most equipment and production processes. Anyone who questions this assertion need only go out on the shop floor and see how many assets that have been fully depreciated for tax and financial purposes are still productively employed.

The second reason book and tax depreciation is erroneous revolves around changing price levels. While land is not depreciated at all, over time most land has appreciated in value, but Generally Accepted Accounting Principles (GAAP) accounting does not permit write-ups of increased values, at least until the asset is sold at arm's length to a third party. Just as land usually appreciates in value, so do buildings. Most buildings are assigned a 40-year life for purposes of calculating depreciation, based on permissible tax accounting.

If buildings truly lost most of their value in 40 years, one would not expect to see many buildings in use today that were built before 1970. The truth is that the effective life of most buildings ranges from 60 to 70 years up to literally hundreds of years. One astute observer pointed out that medieval cathedrals are still being used today, after some 600 years, for their original purpose.

Rather than being reduced in value over time, which depreciation accounting inherently assumes, many buildings actually appreciate over that time. How many times has the Empire State Building in New York City (built in the early 1930s) been sold? Each of those sales has been at a progressively *higher* price. Had financial and tax depreciation been accurate, one would expect subsequent sales of the Empire State Building to have been at progressively *lower* prices, to reflect a diminution in value.

So, if land appreciates, albeit not ever depreciated, and buildings tend to increase in value despite depreciation charges, what about machinery and equipment (i.e., production equipment)? While it is true that virtually all computer and electronic-related assets do diminish in value quite rapidly, most equipment (e.g., process equipment—think chemical plants and refineries), office furniture, and machine tools do not lose value at anywhere near the level assumed by accountants in their depreciation calculations. When appraisers are hired to determine the FV of hard assets, they cannot go to the financial statements and simply tweak the numbers shown. Rather, appraisers have to determine the current FV by looking at, and evaluating, each significant asset individually.

ACCOUNTING DEPRECIATION VERSUS APPRAISAL DEPRECIATION

We have discussed accounting depreciation, but what is depreciation as determined by an appraiser? The major professional group for appraisers of machinery and equipment is the American Society of Appraisers. In their major publication *Valuing Machinery and Equipment,* they state:[2]

> *Using the cost approach the appraiser starts with the current replacement cost of the property being appraised and then deducts for the loss in value caused by physical deterioration, functional obsolescence, and economic obsolescence. The logic behind the cost approach is the principle of substitution: a prudent buyer will not pay more for a property than the cost of acquiring a substitute property of equivalent utility. The principle can be applied either to an individual asset or to an entire facility.*

As shown in this definition, for an appraiser depreciation is the "loss in value" from today's replacement cost that must be identified and quantified. So, in effect, today's true FV is related neither to the original cost nor to the accumulated depreciation applied to that original cost as calculated by accountants, even though the latter has been verified and certified by the independent auditor.

This difference between depreciated original cost, as calculated for financial statements, and FV as determined by an appraiser represents a hurdle that must be overcome in discussing valuation. Financial managers, and security analysts for that matter, are comfortable with what they are familiar with: original cost less accumulated depreciation expense charges. The fact that this information is truly irrelevant to an appraiser is sometimes hard to grasp.

So let us start out with the fundamental bedrock of valuation theory. With the exception of unique works of fine art and a few similar items, most assets have been acquired to perform a specific function. The principle of substitution mentioned in the quote really sums it up. People acquire assets to accomplish something, not for the sake of acquisition.

If a machine shop needs a milling machine, there will undoubtedly be differences among various models from different manufacturers, but what is important is to be able to mill a piece of steel, not have a specific Milacron model to show off to prospective customers. Thus the appraiser looks at function and performance, not outward appearances or brand names.

So if we are determining the FV today of a Milacron milling machine acquired in 2001, we first determine if the same or a similar machine is available new from the manufacturer. For many types of equipment, gradual improvements in performance and productivity are made over the years. So if today's equivalent model has certain features not on the subject piece of equipment, we have to recognize these differences.

Let's use an example, as shown in Exhibit 9.1. We are determining the FV today of a Milacron milling machine that cost $45,000 in 2001 and has had $18,000 of depreciation expense charged, so the net book value is now $27,000. The appraiser would determine that the nearest replacement, in 2006, is a new model with a price of $50,000 set by the manufacturer, but the new machine runs 10% faster and is in perfect condition.

If we were performing a value in-use valuation, we would start with the replacement cost new (RCN). Then we would determine the physical, functional, and economic losses in value to arrive at today's FV. We discuss each of these three potential loss areas in the following sections.

Physical Depreciation

The determination of physical depreciation can only be performed by a physical inspection of the asset(s). It should be understood that determination of physical depreciation through inspection represents professional judgment. There is no ruler or yardstick one can take out onto the factory floor and measure depreciation from wear and tear.

Appraisers who specialize in M&E have been in many facilities with all types of assets. A skilled appraiser can estimate physical depreciation quite closely after a walk-through of the facility and discussions with production, engineering, and maintenance personnel. Some companies have a strong preventive maintenance policy, trading current expense dollars

Exhibit 9.1 Determining the Fair Value of a Milacron Milling Machine

Subject Asset:		
Date Acquired	2001	
Cost New	$ 45,000	
Accumulated Dep'n	$ 18,000	
Net Book Value	$ 27,000	
Replacement Asset:		
Current Date	2006	
Cost New	$ 50,000	
Physical Depreciation:	10%	Based on Observation
Amount	$ 5,000	
Functional Obsolescence:		
Potential Output of New Machine	$500,000	
Performance Penalty of Old Machine	10%	Based on New Machine Specifications
Loss in Output	$ 50,000	
Operating Margin	7%	Assumed
Pretax Loss	$ 3,500	
Less Tax at 40%	$ 1,400	
Capitalization Rate	14%	Assumed
Functional Obsolescence	$ 10,000	
Economic Obsolescence:	$ 5,000	See Text
FAIR VALUE:	$ 30,000	

for longer asset lives. Others try to keep current expense to an absolute minimum, at the cost of shorter effective lives. Some firms will go to the time and expense of periodic overhauls on major pieces of equipment that can result in almost like-new condition. Others make do by fixing problems only as they come up. In short, maintenance policy, as observed by the appraiser, is a good indication of physical depreciation.

Some assets may have a capacity over their lifetime to produce "x" output, so if good production records are available, one can estimate physical depreciation as the ratio between total expected output and remaining output. A copy machine may be able to produce 2 million copies; if total production to date is 800,000 units, one would estimate

40% depreciation or 60% remaining useful life. Similarly, a tractor may be designed for 8,000 hours of continuous use; if the meter shows 5,000 hours of use to date, this suggests 63% depreciation or 37% remaining useful life.

It cannot be stressed too much that inspection of the assets, combined with an appraiser's experience, is required to determine actual physical depreciation. As mentioned earlier, accounting and tax lives are usually significantly shorter than the physical lives of most assets.

An astute reader, looking at Exhibit 9.1, will realize that one of the key elements in determining the FV of an existing asset is proper assessment of what the cost today of a new replacement asset would be. In some cases this is easy, so a new half-ton truck is an excellent replacement for a six-year-old half-ton truck, or a new laptop PC is a good replacement for a four-year-old unit. But technology changes quickly. Then there are manufacturers who go out of business and no longer make a particular asset. The list of problems in determining RCN is never-ending. Again, while it appears repetitive, the only answer is the judgment and experience of an M&E specialist.

When determining physical depreciation, particularly related to less than perfect maintenance, one aspect should be noted. Appraisers distinguish between curable and noncurable depreciation. Curable depreciation would be as simple as replacing a balky clutch on a truck. The appraiser, if he finds curable depreciation, determines the cost to cure and subtracts that from the value of the asset, assuming it is back in good condition. However, many types of physical depreciation simply cannot be cured, or at least it is totally uneconomic to do so. In that case the subject asset is simply valued in its current condition. No subtraction is made for current outlays, but by the same token the asset value is effectively permanently impaired.

Functional Obsolescence

The American Society of Appraisers defines functional obsolescence as:

> [It] is the loss in value or usefulness of a property caused by inefficiencies or inadequacies of the property itself, when compared to a more efficient or less costly replacement property that new technology has developed. Symptoms suggesting the presence of functional obsolescence are excess operating cost, excess construction

(excess capital cost) over-capacity, inadequacy, lack of utility or similar conditions.[3]

As will be discussed later, where economic obsolescence is considered to be *outside* the asset, the essence of functional obsolescence is that the asset simply does not, or cannot, perform as well as a new replacement asset. In other words, within the asset itself is the problem. An existing 50,000 barrel-per-day (bpd) refinery is going to have higher operating costs per barrel than a new 150,000 bpd state-of-the-art refinery, if one was to be built. The present value of that differential is a measure of the functional obsolescence.

In Exhibit 9.1 we calculate, in a much simplified manner, the penalty because the new milling machine perhaps has computer numerical controls. The penalty in this case is measured in terms of annual output, 10% in the example. The present value of the future cash flows represented by that 10% reduction in output is shown as $10,000. Put a different way, the new machine, if it were to be acquired, would produce $10,000 more total output over its life, but because we are valuing the existing machine, not the new one, we subtract that $10,000 penalty from the RCN of the replacement asset.

Again, as with physical depreciation, we can have curable or noncurable functional loss in value. A curable functional loss might be to add, or replace, a new computer-controlled device that would bring the old machine up to the capacity of the new machine. However, if the cost to install the new computer were $15,000, but the increase in value would only be $10,000, then we would consider the functional obsolescence to be noncurable.

Reading this description, there is a mention of "excess construction." Appraisers frequently run into this problem, particularly in real estate. We, and others, are often called in to determine the value of a corporate headquarters complex, perhaps for sale and leaseback. Some such buildings have jokingly been referred to by employees and others as the "CEO's Taj Mahal." Construction costs could have originally been upward of $250 per square foot depending on how much marble was used and how much unused open space exists. In some cases there is also what can best be described as grandiose landscaping.

What is the current FV of such a facility? Using just the cost approach to replicate the existing facility, it might even be as high as $300 per square foot. The trouble is that there are few, if any, buyers for such magnificent structures. Shareholder complaints alone would preclude most companies from buying someone else's opulent palace. In determining the FV, therefore, while we would quickly estimate the cost to reproduce the existing building, the more reasonable approach is to look at the cost today to construct a normal Class A office building with the same number of square feet. So there would be a functional penalty for loss of value because other buyers would not be interested in taking on such a project.

To carry this example further, the high ceilings in the open spaces would incur excess heating, ventilating, and air conditioning (HVAC) costs, and all the marble would have to be maintained. Thus there would be a *second* functional penalty related to future maintenance and operating expenses that a new buyer would have to incur. The essential principle here is that there may not be a market—willing buyers—for assets that were custom-designed or custom-built. Many readers will be familiar with this concept in the private residential market where unique homes are often on the market, and unsold, for a long time because few individuals happen to share the taste of the current owner.

In valuing M&E, functional obsolescence is easier to quantify and easier for prospective buyers to deal with. Exhibit 9.1 shows a very simplified calculation of functional obsolescence in a standard machine tool. The same concept would hold true in a process facility, for example, where a 10,000-barrel brewery would simply have higher unit costs than a 50,000-barrel operation. If new breweries being built are all in the 50,000 range, then the owner of an existing 10,000-barrel facility cannot compete on a price or cost basis. (This disregards the opportunity to specialize in low-volume specialty beers, for which a small unit might be adequate.)

From the appraiser's perspective, then, valuing the smaller operation would involve determining the present value, on a Discounted Cash Flow (DCF) basis of the cost penalty per barrel. The essential idea, again getting back to the principal of substitution, is that a buyer would be essentially indifferent between paying a low price for the capital equipment and absorbing higher operating expenses, as contrasted with originally paying more for capacity and enjoying lower operating expenses. While this theory may sound overly simplistic in the case of the brewery, the concept nonetheless is valid.

The fact is that virtually any piece of production equipment can be sold—at the right price. Ask any used-car dealer or machine tool auction house. Everything sells, albeit at times for scrap value. But the fact remains that at a small number above scrap value, there are, and will be, buyers who are short of capital but make up for it with the ability to get stuff to work. The thought process that goes through the mind of a restaurant owner—whether to buy a used deep fryer at an auction or a new one from the manufacturer—is identical to what we have described. The buyer calculates, maybe only on the basis of rules of thumb, as to how long the used equipment will last and how much higher the operating expenses will be, in determining how much to bid for the used asset or to meet the seller's price on the new asset.

An appraiser cannot just look at a piece of equipment and determine the amount of functional obsolescence. An experienced appraiser can probably estimate quite closely the physical depreciation by physical inspection of current condition and maintenance policy. But determining the cost penalty of a specific asset on the shop floor, in comparison to new equipment, involves significant discussion with plant personnel and perhaps manufacturers' representatives. This level of detail, and the cost and time to accomplish it, is usually only applied to significant assets where the concept of materiality applies.

The concept of the cost to cure applies in functional obsolescence just as it does in evaluating physical depreciation, wear and tear. A new television set has a built-in high definition tuner, while last year's model does not. In evaluating last year's television model, the appraiser would simply subtract the cost of an external high-definition tuner to compensate for the functional difference between the old and new sets.

At the other extreme would be a coal-fired generating plant that was built before current environmental regulations were established. Here the cost to cure, retrofitting a current scrubber system to a plant that was not designed for such use, may well cost more than the depreciated value of the existing plant. Yet if the choice is between operating the plant or paying for the scrubber system, one might make a calculation that it is either cheaper to shut down the existing facility and start over or to pay for the scrubber.

It is difficult to generalize about functional obsolescence because each situation is unique, but the concept is readily understood, and the calculations are straightforward. The thought process that the reader goes through in evaluating whether to buy a used car or a new car is identical to that of an appraiser evaluating productive assets, whether buildings or machinery and equipment.

Economic Obsolescence

While the concepts of physical depreciation and functional obsolescence are easy to grasp, and in line with common everyday thought processes, the appraiser's concept of economic obsolescence is sometimes hard to explain. The American Society of Appraisers defines it as:

> Economic obsolescence *(sometimes called "external obsolescence")* is the loss in value or usefulness of a property caused by factors external to the property, such as increased cost of raw materials, labor, or utilities (without an offsetting increase in product price); reduced demand for the product; increased competition; environmental or other regulations; inflation or high interest rates; or similar factors.[4]

Perhaps the easiest example is to refer to the proverbial buggy whip factory. The idea is that you can have the most modern production facility for producing buggy whips, with no physical depreciation and state-of-the-art equipment for which there is no functional obsolescence. Yet, because there is virtually zero demand for buggy whips, the factory has very little value. About all that could be done is to dispose of the assets individually in the used equipment market and sell the land and building for its next highest and best use.

A real-life example we ran into once involved a large amusement park with a very expensive, absolutely modern, and up-to-date roller coaster ride. Such rides are exceedingly expensive and can generate a lot of traffic for an amusement park—if there are enough people in the market area who wish to go to an amusement park. In this instance the total attendance at the park, despite excellent marketing efforts, was such that a satisfactory ROI could not be achieved. Consequently, the FV, what a willing buyer would pay, would be less than the current purchase cost of the ride. This is what economic obsolescence is all about. Can the subject property produce a satisfactory rate of return to the owner or to a market participant? If so, then the FV, on an in-use basis, is the RCN less physical depreciation and functional obsolescence. If not, then a calculation must be made of the economic penalty.

A second instance was a large chemical plant whose raw material was primarily natural gas. The market price of natural gas has been volatile and at levels substantially above those assumed when the plant was constructed. Even worse, an island in the Caribbean had virtually unlimited supplies of natural gas at essentially no cost. A comparable chemical plant was built there, and the U.S. facility continually struggled to make any sort of net profit. We were called in to help lower the property tax because the local assessor's formulas did not take economic obsolescence into account. We pointed out in our report that the country was supposed to assess on the basis of Fair Market Value (the same as FV for financial reporting) and that the true value of the facility was affected adversely by the natural gas pricing situation, over which our client had no control. Our valuation of the facility was a small fraction of the cost of replacement less physical and functional depreciation because of these market conditions.

If the assemblage of assets does not produce the level of ROI that investors demand, we must reduce the value of the assets to a level where market participants would be interested in buying. In other words, economic obsolescence is determined by the market, not the assets themselves, which is why the term "factors external to the property" is used in the previous definition.

In almost every valuation, it is incumbent on the appraiser to determine whether the FV of the fixed assets, using the cost approach, can be supported by the underlying income. If the income-generating potential is low, no rational investor will pay to buy assets, no matter how much they might cost to replicate. In other words, a seeming bargain may be no bargain at all. As the old saying has it, "if it is too good to be true, it probably is not worth buying."

NEGATIVE GOODWILL

Goodwill is an accounting concept that is a residual amount between the purchase price of a business and the sum of the FV of all the identifiable assets. So if you buy a business for $10 million, and the appraiser says the FV of all the assets he can find is only $9.2 million, then by definition the buyer will put $800,000 on the books as goodwill simply to keep the debits and credits equal.

Another way to look at goodwill is to say that it is the amount paid for a going concern business, the costs involved in setting up a business, hiring the staff, obtaining all the facilities, and so forth. Under this definition of goodwill or going concern, one could make a valiant effort to quantify the intangible asset on a direct basis, rather than simply as an accounting residual. As a specific example, many observers believe that an assembled workforce has significant value to any business, particularly when virtually every Chairman's letter tells shareholders, "Our employees are our single greatest asset."

In its infinite wisdom, the FASB refused to believe that appraisers had long been able to measure the value of the workforce in place; the FASB consciously chose in SFAS 141 *not* to permit this asset to be quantified, rather requiring any value properly assignable to the workforce to show up in the goodwill residual. Consequently, while many people believe that the elements of goodwill can be identified and quantified, under today's rules it is not worthwhile making any effort along those lines. Simply accept the fact that goodwill is the difference between what you paid and what you received.

But, someone will ask, "what if we received more than we paid for?" One can easily see that in the give and take of negotiating the purchase and sale of a business, that the buyer may have obtained a bargain purchase. One could obtain, in other words, $1 million of assets by paying only $950,000. Or could you? The definition of FV talks about a willing buyer and willing seller, both of whom are knowledgeable. Why would a knowledgeable and willing seller, not under compulsion (e.g., under threat of bankruptcy), sell $1 million of assets for $50,000 less than they are worth?

One could hypothesize endlessly about the possible circumstances that would account for a prospective seller accepting less than assets are really worth, but in the real world if both parties are equally skilled in negotiation, one would not expect to see very many bargain purchases. In this case the term bargain purchase simply means the buyer paid less than the assets were worth.

Yet, in the process of performing appraisals for purchase price allocation, there often are situations where at least the preliminary FVs of the identified tangible assets are in *excess* of the amount paid by the buyer. At first glance, in such situations, it appears the buyer got a bargain and/or the seller left some money on the table.

At this point we have to interject an observation regarding the sale of businesses. The following thought should be foremost in the mind of any prospective buyer: "There is always a reason why a business is for sale." If a business is going along well, making a good profit, with a strong customer base, powerful and competitive products/services, and with a deep management bench, why should the owners sell? What is wrong with making a good profit from a business with growth potential? There are a lot of prospective buyers who would love to acquire such a business, but then what will the sellers do with the money they receive from selling the business?

It is sort of like a home owner in San Diego who suddenly finds that his house has gone from the $300,000 he paid for it to a mind-boggling $1 million, which certainly has happened. But if he sells, to try and cash in on the appreciation, where does he move to? All the other houses in town have had similar price increases. The only way he can truly cash in is to move to some other location and start over. Many individuals, with family and friends, do not want to tear up roots, which is what is required to enjoy the cash windfall.

Similarly with a business, what will the sellers do? This is not to suggest that sellers are not motivated to move on. Obviously, they are, and that is why businesses are sold, *but,* if the sellers are moving on, what does this imply about future management of the firm? In such a situation the buyer will now have to put in its own management team, and while most buyers are confident of their own ability to step in and run the business, often it is not as easy as they thought.

So, if a business is for sale, one question has to be, "Why are you selling, and if you leave, how hard will it be for someone else to take over?" Besides management getting tired, there are many other reasons for a business to be put on the market. Often there are problems with products, customers, or competitive conditions. Sometimes there are significant potential liabilities.

Given the flexibility inherent in financial reporting, many companies have been burnished in the two or three years before going up for sale. Advertising and research and development (R&D) can be reduced, fewer new products introduced, prices raised, extra collection efforts made, and inventories reduced to enhance cash flow. The list of stratagems is long, and the imagination of sellers is unlimited.

Many times a buyer will find unexpected problems, no matter how much due diligence has been performed before closing. While specifics change with each situation, the generalization seems to be true that buyers should beware. In fact, this concept goes back 2,000 years to the Romans, who cautioned caveat emptor. In short, there *always* is a reason why someone is selling the business, and usually the reason is going to cost the buyer money.

Now, we get back to the FV of the assets acquired. Start with the assumption that the transaction price probably was fair and that there are few if any true bargain purchases. If the preliminary FVs of the acquired assets *exceed* the purchase price, then by definition the FASB says this business combination has negative goodwill. But if we are correct that there are very few true bargain purchases, then both the buyer and the valuation specialists should ask some more penetrating questions.

The issue then revolves around the *real* reason(s) the sellers are selling. To be specific, what does the seller know about the business's future that the buyer may not totally have taken into account? As mentioned earlier, there are an almost infinite number of reasons why the seller would perceive trouble ahead, and it is unrealistic to think the seller will volunteer this belief. After all, if the seller started off by saying, "By the way, here is my list of potential problem areas . . . ," the buyer would either walk away or bargain for a much lower price. It is totally unrealistic to think the seller will provide a roadmap to the problems, which is why due diligence is performed.

Having said that, due diligence comes in many flavors. Because every business has actual or potential problems, if the due diligence process is too rigorous, no deal would ever get done. But far more common is the other end of the spectrum, where due diligence turns out to be little more than a *pro forma* sprinkling on of holy water to confirm a deal that the buyer's CEO has already decided on! It is not until the valuation specialist starts looking at the specifics of the assets acquired, adds up the preliminary FVs, and sees that there is an imbalance, that really serious questions get asked, such as "What are we overlooking that made the seller so generous in selling us $100 worth of assets for $85?"

While each business combination is unique, the circumstances here are fairly common. Often it turns out that at least the seller expects some discontinuities in future sales and/or expenses. Most financial projections start out with the past three to five years and then project them forward for the next five, ten, or more years. The seller perceives that past trends are unlikely to be continued, whereas the buyer probably assumes not only past trends continuing but also major improvement arising from both synergies and better management.

Obviously, both sides are unlikely to be correct, which ultimately explains why the seller accepts a price that on first glance by the buyer seems to be a bargain purchase. Many commentators have observed that perhaps a majority of business combinations do not meet expectations; after the fact it turns out that buyers simply paid too much. Our analysis here suggests a reason for this occurrence. Past trends do not continue indefinitely into the future, and this can be exacerbated if the seller has spent the previous couple of years putting the company in shape to be sold (i.e., adding window dressing).

Now, let us get back to the topic of economic obsolescence. As we saw, the term denotes reductions in value from outside the business (i.e., external market and economic conditions affecting many businesses). Suppose the first pass of valuing the assets suggests that a bargain purchase occurred. Perhaps the sellers anticipated some softening in the market, stronger competitors with new products, a disaffected workforce, or any of the factors that can adversely affect a business. That perception would explain why the seller seemingly sold for too low an amount. But at this point the buyer must stop and ask, "What if the seller was correct, that there are some potential landmines?" What now has to be tested is the economic underpinning supporting the asset values.

We saw that the most perfect factory for making buggy whips would be worth little because there would be insufficient cash flow to support the values. Exactly the same thought process must be undertaken at the first sign that the buyer obtained a bargain purchase. "What are we possibly overlooking? What did the seller see that we do not? What could go wrong, and how would it affect the asset values?" In short, it is our belief that whenever there is an apparent bargain purchase, with negative goodwill as a potential result, the buyer should re-examine the financial projections: "Are there contingent liabilities? How sure are we that sales growth will continue? Are there going to be actual Selling, General & Administrative (SG&A) increases, as opposed to cost saving synergies? What personnel losses will occur, causing us to hire more employees?" Put a different way, the financial projections should be reworked with a far more conservative underpinning.

A re-evaluation of future economic outcomes will probably lead to the conclusion that, in one form or another, economic obsolescence should be applied to the asset values. Every dollar of reduction in value caused by economic obsolescence reduces, dollar for dollar, negative goodwill. We suggest that in the interests of conservatism, to avoid unpleasant surprises, that extra effort be put into evaluating economic obsolescence.

Inasmuch as nobody can foretell the future with accuracy, a conservative assessment of future revenue and income trends can lead to supportable reductions in FV. Such reductions will reduce, if not eliminate, the apparent bargain purchase and prevent the occurrence of negative goodwill that is almost an oxymoron. Looked at from a slightly different perspective, whenever a business combination does not work out as well as expected, there is a high degree of likelihood that there was economic obsolescence related to some or all of the acquired assets.

Now, few buyers like to admit soon after a transaction is consummated that perhaps they paid too much. As appraisers, we have seen this frequently, but invariably the client is reluctant to hear it. To be specific, the financial staff, which we as appraisers are dealing with on a day-to-day basis, probably shares our outlook, but once the CEO has made up his mind to "complete the deal," few employees are courageous enough to continue to make adverse comments. We, as appraisers, will develop our values on a professional basis, and in the short-term the existence of negative goodwill will be perceived favorably by the client. That the negative goodwill is probably a harbinger of problems to come is a very unwelcome message.

HIERARCHY OF EARNINGS

Recall that in Chapter 7 we discussed the subject of intangible assets. One of the major identifiable intangible assets that the FASB and the Securities and Exchange Commission (SEC) are very interested in is customer relationships. Essentially this is the fact that the target company has ongoing relationships with customers that provide immediate income.

Looked at another way, by buying the target company, the buyer avoids the time required to acquire customers doing business at the same volume. Most companies that are bought bring the following to the buyer:

- Products
- Workforce
- Customers and distribution network
- Supplier relationships (if applicable)
- R&D activities (if applicable)
- Production facilities, office facilities
- Production know-how, patents, and so on

Now at this point we have to see the inter-relationship between the customer relationships and the assets acquired. The simplest example we can come up with is the acquisition of an office building that is being rented out to tenants.

This example is of an office building in Washington, D.C., with three major tenants (including the stable federal government) that is 95% occupied. The real estate is valued three different ways, using the cost, income, and market approaches. All three approaches provide preliminary value indications of about $60 million. In other words, it would cost approximately that amount to build a similar structure, comparable buildings are selling for $55 million to $65 million, and the building throws off income of $5 million per year, which provides an investor with a market return of more than 8%. Now the issue is the accounting entries if the office building is one of the assets acquired in a business combination.

Assuming we have used all three approaches to value, this is what the preliminary worksheets would look like:

Cost to replicate the building, less physical and functional depreciation, including land value:	$60,000,000
Market price for similarly sized and located buildings:	$62,000,000
Income approach: Net Cash Flow of $5,300,000 with investors looking for 9% cash on cash return:	$58,888,000

Most appraisers would correlate those three answers and figure the Fair Market Value of the building was ±$60 million. So, if the building is worth $60 million, fully (95% equals fully) leased, what is the value of the tenant contracts by themselves? In this example, the answer has to be zero. There are normal rents being charged for the area, and a willing buyer would be satisfied that at lease expirations, the existing tenants will either renew or new tenants will be found at the same rents with only normal absorption delays.

However, if someone argues that the tenant contracts have value in and of themselves, then the value of those contracts, however figured, has to be *subtracted* from the indicated income approach, making that approach much lower than the other two. Certainly the cost approach is the same irrespective of whether or not the building is leased, and *the market approach automatically incorporates a normal occupancy* as long as the market is reasonably strong with no anticipated problems—in this case Washington, D.C., where the market is now and probably will continue to be strong. Under this scenario, even a long-term contract, as long as it was at market rates, with the federal government would not have excess value.

The accounting question dealing with the FV of assets is this: How do the proponents of carving out a separate customer contract value handle this situation? They cannot change the cost approach, the market approach can be supported with any number of comparable sales, and the income approach already implicitly assumes normal occupancy and current rates, which are present. Only if there were *above-market* rental rates on existing leases would there be any value to the customer lease agreements by this analysis. Analyzed this way, the income from the property is just sufficient to support the value, with no excess value available for customer contracts or customer relationships.

What this demonstrates, at least to the author's satisfaction, is that there may be relatively few cases where the true FV of the acquired assets, particularly Property, Plant, and Equipment (PP&E), is really more than the acquisition price of the business combination. What happens is that the FV of the PP&E is determined in accordance with sound valuation practice, but then any intangible assets cannot be supported by the underlying economics. In that situation one either has to reduce the value of the PP&E to allow dollars for intangibles such as customer relationships or one has to state that the acquired business simply does not have any intangible assets separate from the PP&E.

The total thrust of this concept is that a "normal" return must be generated by hard assets, such as land, buildings, and M&E. Only if there are then excess earnings, over and above what is normally expected by an investor, will there be any amount to support valuation of intangible assets.

Look at our example, where the true FV of the building is $60 million. If an appraiser then assigned some figure such as $15 million to the customer contracts for long-term rental of the building, the total of identified assets of the building plus the intangibles would be $75 million. If the building had been the only major asset of the target company, and the purchase price had been $61 million, it would have appeared that the buyer obtained $75 million of assets ($60 million for building and $15 million for intangibles) for the bargain price of $61 million. While every circumstance is different, our experience suggests that most sellers are knowledgeable, while few buyers obtain bargain purchases. Thus, if this analysis is correct, there should rarely, if ever, be negative goodwill, which is the accounting result of a bargain purchase.

The lesson to be learned is simple: The true FV of an asset assumes that it is being appropriately utilized for the purpose for which it was acquired. A normal return on that investment is assumed by the buyer as well as the seller. Thus for acquisitions where tangible assets are an important ingredient in the company's operations (this leaves out service firms and consulting businesses where there are few real tangible assets other than furniture, fixtures, and computers), there probably should be relatively low amounts of intangible assets and virtually never negative goodwill.

ASSETS HELD FOR SALE

In a business combination, the buyer will often know ahead of time, probably as a result of its own due diligence efforts, that certain of the assets are going to be disposed of as soon as possible. In other words, the buyer does not plan to use the assets and will turn them into cash as soon as possible.

The accounting treatment is very straightforward and totally correct. The appraiser is required to determine the FV of the asset on the premise that it will be sold (i.e., this is a value in-exchange). The basic methodology is for the appraiser to contact used-equipment dealers specializing in that particular type of asset and obtain an indication of value. Alternatively, appraisers have access to listings of prices realized at machinery and equipment auctions. Certainly, it is difficult to observe physical and functional depreciation from an auction price list, but often the price itself, in relation to the original date of acquisition (based on serial number), gives a good indication.

Dealers and auctions are the two primary sources of information about what market participants are paying for comparable assets. It should be kept in mind that in a value in-exchange valuation, all costs associated with bringing the asset into the client's facility will be lost. Given the relatively slow turnover in the used equipment market, it should not surprise anyone if the FV determination of assets to be sold is but a small percentage of the book value, not to mention the original cost or the replacement cost new (RCN).

For buildings and/or land, real estate, at least in theory the FV of assets held for sale, should be little different from assets valued on the assumption of continued use. This is because appraisers typically use all three approaches to value (i.e., cost, income, market) in every real estate valuation assignment, so there should be similar results independent of the purpose of the valuation.

WHAT TO DO ABOUT UNDERVALUED ASSETS

The history of U.S. business is rife with stories about assets that had significant value, but were on the books for very nominal, in many cases even zero, value. The most commonly cited example is the Coca-Cola trade name, but Microsoft's Windows software would be equally as applicable. The issue is what, if anything, companies can do about letting investors know the value of the assets if they are either not on the books at all, or more commonly shown only at historical cost, which can be very low.

The accounting and financial reporting issue is caused by the fact that we do not have Fair Value Accounting, and consequently assets can never be written up to true FV. This is not a plea for Fair Value Accounting, because in our opinion the cure might well be worse than the disease. Nonetheless, the inability of companies to show the true current FV of their assets on the face of their financial statements can have adverse consequences. The best recent example is K-Mart, where a corporate raider took over Sears at what, in this case, was a true bargain purchase. He saw value in Sears' real estate that was not reflected on the financial statements and that other analysts had overlooked. (So much for the efficient market hypothesis.) Here Sears' management lost its company to a raider because the FV of the real estate (i.e., owned and leased buildings and land) was perceived by at least one investor as greater than shown on the balance sheet.

What could Sears' management have done, to use this unfortunate company as an example, which might have precluded the takeover? The SEC for years has pleaded with companies to "tell it like it is" in the Management Discussion and Analysis (MD&A). There was nothing precluding Sears' management from providing estimates to shareholders about the FV of the real estate. The only downside would have been the potential criticism that if the real estate was worth significantly more than it was on the books for, then current management might not be achieving a satisfactory ROI, but this is what happened. A new owner came in anyhow to take advantage of the undervalued assets.

While companies must disclose the FV of all financial instruments, there is still room for voluntary disclosure is in the area of real estate and significantly undervalued productive equipment. We only mention intangibles that are not reflected on the balance sheet here because they are the subject of separate analysis in Chapters 7 and 8.

How can PP&E assets be undervalued? One of the major ways we have seen is in relation to fully depreciated assets. There is little correlation between the physical and functional life of assets and the period over which financial accounting depreciates those assets. Companies tend to use the shortest possible lives for tax accounting, and typically utilize the *same* lives for books, even though conformity is not a requirement. Nevertheless, many assets are fully depreciated on the books but still in excellent condition and *still being used*. Most companies, right or wrong, do not use expected salvage values in computing depreciation expense. Hence fully depreciated assets typically have zero book value. However, they do have real economic value and ideally should be reflected on the books of account.

The subject of internal controls over PP&E, and the impact of the Sarbanes-Oxley Act on PP&E, are outside the scope of this book on fair value for financial reporting. They do impact the matter we are discussing. Just as many companies are still using fully depreciated assets (which implies too rapid prior depreciation charges), so do most companies have difficulty locating assets that are in the fixed asset record.

Exhibit 9.2 Portion of Fixed Asset Register of Sample Company

Asset No.	Install Date	Description	Cost	Net Book Value
133	1994	Construction Consultation	700	261
569	1994	Telephone System	168,800	-0-
885	2001	J. Smith Travel Exp. Reim.	1,271	297
948	2002	Prof. Services	285,010	123,504
980	2002	Ultrium Clean Cart	175	10
983	2002	Credit on Maint. Agreement	−1,600	−89
1075	2002	CRM Training	8,156	906
1177	2003	Perf. Tiles for Data Ctr.	260	123
1276	2004	Exchange 2003 Upgrade	10,380	7,785
1313	2005	Keyboard	36	32

Source: Used with permission. Copyright © Montgomery Investment Technology, Inc.

So we have the very common situation of assets in use that are not on the books and assets on the books that cannot be found or identified.

Exhibit 9.2 is a representative sample copied from the Fixed Asset Listing of a $1 billion client.

Undoubtedly, the telephone system is still in use and has significant value, but it would be difficult, if not impossible, to locate and verify most of the remaining assets. Besides what appears to be an *improper* capitalization policy, the company does not appear to have a *minimum* capitalization policy. One approach to fixing this set of problems would be to revalue the telephone system upward to the same amount (as long as it did not exceed current FV) that the remaining assets were being written off. It would then be possible to control the one large asset and not pay attention as part of corporate assets to such items as a $175 cleaning cart or a $36 keyboard.

The 80/20 rule, that 80% of the value of all the items is represented by 20% of the number of items, definitely holds true for PP&E. The basic thrust of internal control, as required by Sarbanes-Oxley, and as recently enunciated by the Public Company Accounting Oversight Board (PCAOB) and the SEC, is that resources should be devoted to major items that can affect financial statements. By the same token, resources should *not* be placed on immaterial items. This particular company's fixed asset record might not pass close PCAOB or auditor scrutiny, but the problem is not insoluble.

SARBANES-OXLEY REQUIRED CONTROLS ON PP&E

Your auditor is addressing a meeting of your Audit Committee and starts off the presentation with the following chilling announcement: "You have a material weakness in your internal controls!" These words likely would cause palpitations in the hearts of Audit Committee members, as well as CFOs and Controllers. True material weaknesses in internal controls represent a major problem for everyone involved.

Companies have annually been spending up to $10 million to $15 million in efforts to comply with the Sarbanes-Oxley (S-Ox) requirements. The majority of efforts by financial managers to comply with S-Ox has been placed in such areas of a company as revenue recognition and other seemingly substantive areas. Many companies may believe that, as a result of these efforts, they are on top of internal control problems. Do not be too sure, however.

Over the years, one area has proven to be difficult to control— PP&E. Almost every year in the past, and for almost every company, when auditors prepared their annual management letter, the subject of PP&E has been brought up. Often there is a recommendation that the client perform a physical inventory of its PP&E, reconcile it to the books, and makes necessary adjustments to the books of account. If this recommendation has been made for several years, and little done to comply, what is the impact in the era of S-Ox? Is there, in fact, a material weakness in a company's PP&E—and what are the consequences?

A reading of PCAOB Auditing Standard 2 is instructive. Paragraphs 65 and 66 read, in part:

> ¶ 65 *"When deciding whether an account is significant, it is important for the auditor to evaluate both quantitative and qualitative factors, including the:*
>
> - *Size and composition of the account;*
> - *Susceptibility of loss due to errors or fraud;*
> - *Accounting and reporting complexities associated with the account*
> - *Exposure to losses represented by the account*
>
> ¶ 66 *"For example, in a financial statement audit, the auditor might not consider the fixed asset accounts significant when there is a low*

> *volume of transactions and when inherent risk is assessed as low, even though the balances are material to the financial statements. Accordingly, he or she might decide to perform only substantive procedures on such balances. In an audit of internal control over financial reporting, however, such accounts are significant accounts because of their materiality to the financial statements."*

The PCAOB makes it clear that internal controls over PP&E *must* be considered by management and reviewed by the auditor, if material to the financial statements, and, for most companies, PP&E *is* material.

SIZE OF THE PP&E PROBLEM

An analysis of 27 of the 30 nonfinancial companies in the Dow Jones Industrial Average shows that gross PP&E represents 36% of total assets, while even net PP&E is almost 20% of total assets. In our judgment the gross figure is the more important for evaluating internal controls, because it represents the actual items on hand, at essentially original cost that approximates current FV. Financial depreciation is not based directly on any diminution of true loss in value and often is overly rapid because of income tax considerations. In practice, given the offsetting factors of declines in real value as a result of physical and functional depreciation, offset by inflation, gross PP&E may be in practice pretty close to true FV. Thus, if our analysis is correct, more than one-third of the FV of all assets of nonfinancial firms is in PP&E.

An even more instructive analysis is to look at depreciation expense. For the same 27 Dow Jones companies, depreciation expense is 4.6% of revenues; this may be below the magical 5% materiality threshold sometimes utilized by management accountants and auditors, but looking at depreciation expense as a percentage of pretax income, which is the real measure of its importance, for the average Dow Jones company, depreciation is 34% of pretax income. By any standard of materiality, 36% of assets and 34% of income are material. This may be why the PCAOB explicitly refers to PP&E in Auditing Standard 2 as quoted previously.

CONTROLLING PP&E

Our professional experience suggests that internal controls over PP&E are deficient in many companies. Yet up to now these deficiencies have largely been ignored. The reason(s) for continued noncompliance with internal controls, discussed in this section, will no longer stand up in the S-Ox era.

Here is why poor controls have been allowed in the past. As paragraph 66 (referenced above) of the PCAOB Standard shows, for *financial statements*, present controls on PP&E are "good enough." If assets are lost, missing, or stolen, annual depreciation charges sooner or later will write off the balances. Comparing this year's depreciation to last year's depreciation, the two will be comparable, even if both are wrong. Finally, the cost of implementing and enforcing internal controls on PP&E is a messy job that is easily ignored.

Without meaning to demean any individual's performance, our experience suggests that in many companies, fixed asset accounting usually receives a low priority. Often the most junior accountant is put in charge of this function; alternatively, an accountant nearing retirement is given this job as a good way to keep him busy until he leaves the company. Very few accountants coming out of school view fixed asset accounting as a good career path. Far better to develop a career path, and become expert, in cost accounting, budgeting, or FASB and SEC external reporting requirements. Finally, many companies give PP&E a low priority because fixed asset accounting systems are inexpensive and can be run from a PC. The software spits out all the necessary reports for financial reporting, insurance, and property taxes. Controlling PP&E appears to be automatic.

The problem is that the PC-based reports are usually wrong! Every time we, as appraisers, do a detailed study of fixed assets, we invariably determine that up to 15% or more of the assets on the books cannot be found. Where did they go? Some were traded in on new equipment. Some were scrapped. Some were modified to perform a different function. Some, such as PCs, are truly missing.

Offsetting this loss, we often will find *assets* on the floor that are *not* on the books. Where did they come from? When companies have strict capital expenditure policies, managers will often work around this by placing five Purchase Orders for $4,900 each instead of requesting one $25,000 machine. Maintenance and plant engineering are skilled at crafting equipment that is needed now, rather than waiting for the Purchasing Department to obtain quotes, and so on. At times it is almost impossible to determine where assets came from.

In most merger and acquisition (M&A) transactions, companies carry forward the fixed asset records without verification. So to the extent that there were errors in the target's records, these now continue to be wrong on the new owner's books.

In the final analysis, irrespective of the causes, most fixed asset records are likely to be wrong. How far wrong are they? How significant is the lack of control? As S-Ox and the PCAOB have now made clear, this perfunctory approach to controls will no longer suffice. It takes only a brief look at the history of HealthSouth and WorldCom, where asset values were deliberately overstated and not caught by auditors, to see why these errors have been a primary cause for the new emphasis on controlling PP&E.

A PERFECT SOLUTION

In an ideal world, there would be one solution to the problem. A company would periodically take a complete physical inventory of PP&E, just as it does of merchandise inventories. The company would reconcile the inventory to the books, making all needed adjustments. The balance of PP&E on the books would then correctly reflect the assets owned. Subsequent depreciation expense would be both accurate and reliable. Information for insurance placement and proof of loss would be accurate and available. Filings for property tax assessments would be readily performed, and to the extent missing assets were removed from the record, property tax and insurance payments could probably be reduced.

What is wrong with this picture of a perfect world? The phrase "take a complete physical inventory of PP&E and reconcile the inventory to the books" is infinitely easier to say than to do. Several questions have to be answered. Should we start with a printout of what the fixed asset ledger shows and go looking for the assets? Or should we take a new physical inventory of what is actually out there on the floor and try to find the assets in the ledger? Having had experience with both methods, the author can confidently express the opinion that each approach will show large numbers of assets that cannot be matched. Assets are physically there that cannot be found on the records, and assets on the records will not be found physically.

Now what do we do? While "two wrongs don't make one right," as the saying goes, our experience suggests that in the absence of massive theft or fraud (again, think WorldCom and HealthSouth), there may well be a rough correspondence between missing assets presently on the ledger and the value of assets on the floor that cannot be identified in the property record. This potential offset might be of little comfort to CFOs and CEOs who have to certify the quality of their internal controls or to auditors who have to express an opinion on those assertions. Nonetheless, fixing the records may not entail a big net dollar adjustment.

Depending on the size of the company, and the resources available, taking a complete physical inventory and reconciling it to the books is a large undertaking, both time-consuming and expensive. If undertaken, the company will start out with a clean slate and then can implement and follow better controls in the future, but this is an expensive proposition.

It is difficult to estimate the cost of performing such an inventory and reconciliation, but it could be as low as $5.00 or as high as $12.00 per line item of existing property record. Whether the exercise will result in a net write-off, or a net write-up, is difficult to determine in advance; hence it is also hard to determine whether depreciation expense will go up or come down. Certainly, any net write-down would be a noncash charge, with subsequent lower depreciation expense each year. The opposite phenomenon, a write-up, would show a pickup this year to income, offset by higher depreciation charges in the future, does not fall within current Generally Accepted Accounting Principles (GAAP). Whether any such write-ups or write-downs would have to be classed as an accounting error is best left up to the company and its auditor, or perhaps to the SEC and PCAOB.

In the context of S-Ox, and the PCAOB's emphasis on internal controls over PP&E, this solution of a complete inventory, and any concomitant accounting entries, may be a requirement imposed by the company's Audit Committee, irrespective of the cost or consequences. However, there may be a lower- cost alternative to a full-scale inventory.

A WORKABLE SOLUTION

In our professional experience, it is possible to break the total job of reconciling the property record into manageable pieces. A low-cost approach can provide at least initial comfort to CFOs, CEOs, and Audit

Committees. The methodology involves performing a complete reconciliation, but initially only on a statistically significant portion of the asset records.

Most asset records have a location for each line item. One sorts the record by physical location and then in descending dollar amount. You then take the largest 20% of the items by dollar amount and try to find them, either in the expected location or elsewhere in the company. At the same time, go to the department(s) or floor(s) that are the test area, and physically list all the large dollar items. Then comes the difficult part, going back to the company's existing records to try to find the individual items somewhere within the overall property record system. As mentioned previously, in real life some of the items on the records cannot be found, and some of the items physically there cannot be identified on the asset ledger.

The procedure then involves totaling up the two groups (i.e., those not found and those found but not recorded) and comparing the totals. Because we are likely dealing with 80% of the dollar values, it is realistic to simply disregard the numerous small items. This approach, while practical, may not appear elegant, but it does work. Often the two groups will offset each other in approximate dollar terms. The company then makes the correcting entries so that for the representative plant, department, or floor, the company knows the record is reasonably accurate, at least for 80% of the value, and that depreciation expense from here forward will be at least 80% correct.

The process can be carried out sequentially over a period of months until the entire company has been reconciled, missing items written off, and items physically there now carried on the books. The advantage of this approach is twofold. The time and cost to complete it is reduced, compared to a total-company approach. If, as we expect, the overall magnitude of the net dollar change is minimal, then there can be some comfort that the financial statements are not materially in error. In addition, with new and accurate property records, a sound *control system* can be implemented, thus assuring compliance in the future.

This still leaves one major task to be accomplished. That is, rigorous controls must be placed on managers and supervisors, holding them personally responsible for the accuracy of the fixed asset records compared to the actual PP&E present. In subsequent inventories, any errors will be charged to their department's operations, thus affecting performance reporting. Absent personal responsibility, assets are still going to go missing or appear unannounced. Assets will be transferred, sold, or traded in without the necessary accounting entries. Maintenance expenditures will continue to be used for PP&E, capital expenditure controls applied improperly, and so forth. Personal responsibility for assets is ingrained in the military. There is no reason it will not work in the private sector.

MINIMUM CAPITALIZATION AMOUNTS SHOULD BE RAISED

We further recommend strongly that companies significantly *increase* the minimum capitalization amount. Many of the errors and difficulties in controlling PP&E can be traced to overwhelming, but insignificant, detail. A recent survey conducted for Financial Executives International found that the median minimum capitalization amount is approximately $1,500. In our professional judgment this is way too low for the early 21st century. Twenty years ago, companies generally used $1,000, so as prices have increased, the minimum capitalization amount has barely moved for most firms.

For most companies, adopting a minimum of $10,000 (even $25,000 for major multinational firms) would cut down the number of entries and in exchange allow true control over the assets with real value. How much effort is expended today trying to control PCs with an average value of significantly less than $1,000? (Note to the reader: "It's midnight; do you know where *your* PCs are?") Charge small items to expense when purchased. Existing capital expenditure controls over acquisitions can be retained; it is just the subsequent accounting entry that changes.

An argument will be made that, in the year of change, overall expense will go up as formerly capitalized PCs (and other low-dollar-amount items) keep on being depreciated while new acquisitions are also charged to expense. The answer is simple: The old system did not work, it does not work, and it will not work in the future. Sarbanes-Oxley demands that internal controls work; S-Ox does not require capitalization of any particular amount, only that whatever the policy is be followed. The cost in the year of changeover cannot be avoided, and if the cost of changing to a new capitalization policy is material, then this should simply be considered part of the S-Ox adoption. The way to look at it is: There is no free lunch; getting a fixed asset control policy, one that will work, is going to require company resources, including possibly a one-time increase in expenses compared to the prior periods. Once the change is adopted, then year-to-year comparisons will be back to normal.

CONCLUSION

Sarbanes-Oxley, and the resulting PCAOB requirement for testing internal controls, is mandating a totally new attitude toward PP&E. What could be sloughed off in the past because financial statements may not have been affected materially is no longer permitted. Companies *must* have a policy on the control of PP&E, and that policy *must* be followed. Results have to be tested and reported. For the first time, Audit Committees are going to be involved in fixed asset accounting. No longer can PP&E be given to the most junior accountant with the hope that things will work out. Corporate Controllers and CFOs now have to be personally involved and take responsibility for the results. No longer can the annual management letter from the auditors just talk about fixed assets. Now, under S-Ox, it will be *results* that count.

The solution we recommend is as follows:

1. Perform a physical reconciliation on a sequential basis.

2. Do not try to do the entire organization at one time.

3. Limit the analysis to the top 80% of the dollar items, probably only 20% of the line items.

4. In taking the physical inventory, for items on the floor not found on the ledger, develop current Fair Market Values based on appraisal methodology.

5. Using the test as a sample, estimate the dollar amount of any net change (net write-up or write-down), which will lead to prioritization of the subsequent pieces of the reconciliation.

6. Adjust the capitalization policy to reflect economic reality. In this day and age a $500, $1,000, or even $2,000 minimum capitalization only results in extra work and *less* control.

7. Once the assets and the books are in agreement, hold the individual managers personally responsible for subsequent results. If the Army can do it, so can U.S. Industry.

With respect to the Fair Value of PP&E, the most important aspect is that in a business combination, the buyer must make sure that the economic support for the PP&E is sufficient before any intangible assets are valued. The hierarchy of earnings concept suggests that before value can be assigned to customer relationships or goodwill, the assets must be returning the usual rate of return required by investors. The market participant approach of the FASB surely supports that a buyer would pay less for an office building that was not rented than for one that had normal occupancy. Because the valuation approaches generally assume that assets are being utilized for the purpose for which they were acquired, only if such a normal return is present will the FV of the asset be realized. Only if there are *excess* earnings will there be such intangibles as trade names, customer relationships, and goodwill. By the same token, there should hardly ever be negative goodwill as a result of what is initially perceived as a bargain purchase.

ENDNOTES

1. *The Appraisal of Real Estate,* 12th ed. Appraisal Institute. Chicago, 2001, p. 305.
2. *Valuing Machinery and Equipment,* Machinery and Technical Specialties Committee of the American Society of Appraisers. Washington, D.C., 2000, p. 108.
3. *Valuing Machinery and Equipment,* op. cit., p. 69.
4. *Valuing Machinery and Equipment,* op. cit., p. 70.

CHAPTER 10

In-Process Research and Development

L ess than a year after its formation, in its first substantive pronouncement (Statement of Financial Accounting Standard 2 [SFAS2] issued
in 1974), the Financial Accounting Standards Board (FASB) determined
that all research and development (R&D) expenditures should be charged
to expense. The opposing view, that R&D expenditures had value and
benefited future periods (thus meeting the test of an asset), was not accepted at that time. Because of a diversity of practice (some companies
capitalized R&D while other comparable firms expensed it), the FASB
wanted to eliminate alternative accounting approaches to similar transactions. Right or wrong, the then-current FASB chose to expense all R&D.

In effect, the FASB used three arguments to support its position:

1. For any specific project there is uncertainty as to whether or not
   there will be future benefits.

2. There is a perceived lack of causal relationship between expenditures for any specific R&D project and subsequent benefits.

3. R&D benefits, as contrasted with costs of R&D, are difficult to
   measure at any point in time.

These are all valid points, and the FASB has only recently even been
willing to acknowledge that R&D does have value to an enterprise. The
basic conundrum, as seen in Norwalk, Connecticut (home to the FASB),
is that the FASB members have put total priority on the balance sheet
and view the income statement as having secondary importance.

Because it was believed to be difficult to value R&D at a point in
time, and because of the uncertainties involved in any valuation, it was
simply easier to mandate immediate expensing of all R&D expenditures;

consequently, nothing appeared on the balance sheet. If companies were allowed to capitalize all R&D expenditures, the immediate question is whether the cost incurred to date bears any relation to the true Fair Value (FV).

While estimates vary, certainly less than 50% of all corporate R&D ultimately arrives at a position where positive cash flows can be attributed to the specific project. Pharmaceutical companies are a perfect example. For every blockbuster drug that sells hundreds of millions or billions of dollars of product, there probably are at least ten false starts that have to be abandoned. This is why pharmaceutical companies say it costs perhaps $600 million to develop a single successful drug. What they are really saying is that this drug cost perhaps $200 million, but an additional $400 million was spent on other projects that had to be abandoned. Yet at the time each of those failed projects was begun, there was an expectation of possible success. Put a different way, no rational management deliberately incurs costs on projects that are expected to fail right from the beginning. The issue in R&D valuation is twofold:

1. *How does one determine definitively when a project is a total failure?* Companies that want to avoid a hit to current quarter earnings for previously capitalized R&D would have a great incentive to assert to the auditor that *perhaps* things will turn out better next quarter! The truth is that there is never a good time to report a loss. Thus expensing R&D has the benefit of smoothing out earnings and avoiding major write-offs.

2. *How does one determine the value of R&D?* There is virtually no correlation between cost incurred to date and the FV today based on future cash flow expectations. A similar phenomenon holds true in oil exploration. There is no correlation between the amount spent on a well and the total value of the oil discovered. A cheap well can uncover a giant deposit. A very expensive deep well drilled in 10,000 feet of water can come up empty.

COST VERSUS VALUE

A recurring theme of this book is that cost and value are not necessarily related. It is true that a new home that *costs* $300,000 from a builder probably has a *value* at the date of purchase of $300,000. Several months later, depending on many factors, the value of the house may well be higher than the cost. While homes can appreciate in value, recent model automobiles almost invariably depreciate in value from their original cost. Cost is higher than value for a one-year-old car and lower than value for the one-year-old house.

Many people have wanted to use the *cost* of R&D as a proxy for the *value* of R&D. This would be a simple and cost-effective measurement tool. The numbers could easily be audited. By capitalizing on the balance sheet amounts expended for R&D, companies would be encouraged to perform R&D work, because reported earnings would be higher. Shareholders and creditors who used the financial statements would gain because they could see the value of what the company had done. Many people have proposed such an approach, using the arguments pointed out here.

Such proposals to capitalize the *cost* of R&D, in the expectation that both the company and outsiders would now know the *value*, have always floundered. The reason is simple. As stated previously, the cost of R&D provides virtually no clue as to its real value. Historically, well over half of R&D ends up not accomplishing its original objective, the project is discontinued, and any amounts capitalized would ultimately have to be written off. Meanwhile, before the final determination of success or failure, readers of financial statements would have been misled into thinking they were receiving information about the future value of the R&D when in practice there was little or no correlation between the cost incurred and the value today.

The FASB in 1974 probably got it right. Expensing R&D avoided one type of misleading information (i.e., that accumulated cost somehow equaled FV), but it did not solve the second half, telling the true FV of R&D performed. A compromise was for companies to show in the footnotes the dollar amount of R&D performed during the year that was charged to expense. This way, analysts could compare R&D expenditures for the company from year to year and compare one firm's R&D with its peers, both in absolute amount and as a percentage of revenue. In short, SFAS 2 has been in place for 30 years and has worked.

DEVELOPMENT OF IN-PROCESS RESEARCH AND DEVELOPMENT

The issuance of SFASs 141 and 142 stopped goodwill from being amortized. As a consequence, companies no longer feared that goodwill amortization would adversely impact reported earnings. Before SFASs 141 and 142, however, companies very much wanted to minimize goodwill on their books. Several creative ways were found to accomplish this goal, one way being to treat a merger and acquisition (M&A) transaction as a pooling of interest. Pooling was subsequently outlawed by SFASs141 and 142. Another way of minimizing goodwill was to allocate a portion of the purchase price to in-process research and development (IPR&D).

The logic was that the acquirer was buying an asset (i.e., the R&D in process, not yet complete); such IPR&D must have some true economic value, and therefore such expenditures met the definition of an asset. Otherwise, the target company would not have been working on the project(s). Under SFAS 2, R&D had to be expensed, so if a company bought R&D that was in process, it was an asset but then must immediately be written off.

One of the earliest such transactions, which was widely reported, was when IBM acquired Lotus Development. Lotus had been performing a lot of work to develop and introduce *new* products, as well as working on future upgrades of *existing* products. IBM and its accountants and appraisers determined that a major portion of the Lotus purchase price was, in fact, paid to acquire the IPR&D; thus the only allowed accounting treatment was immediate expensing. This then dramatically lowered the amount of goodwill that would have to be charged off each year for the next 40 years.

By reporting the huge IPR&D amount as a one-time write-off, security analysts in effect discounted the one-time charge to expense in evaluating IBM. But by the same token, IBM was going to have substantially lower charges in future years for amortization of goodwill. Put a different way, it was the best of both worlds for IBM. People disregarded the one-time IPR&D expense charge, but paid attention to subsequent higher reported income. It does not get better than that.

IBM's experience was evaluated by many other companies, with the result that IPR&D became a hot topic in the M&A world. Appraisal companies were hired to see how much of the purchase price could be allocated to IPR&D, based on the then-current valuation techniques being used. Some truly remarkable analyses were performed, purporting to show that 50%, 60%, and even 80% of the purchase price of many acquisitions was in fact IPR&D. Whether companies and their appraisers and auditors truly believed this cannot be determined at this late date. Nonetheless, the assertions were made and reported in the financial statements of acquirers.

No good deed goes unpunished. This creative application of accounting principles and Generally Accepted Accounting Principles (GAAP) was too good to be true. The Securities and Exchange Commission (SEC) weighed in on two tracks. First, it more or less adopted an unofficial standard that no more than 30% of a total purchase price could be assigned to IPR&D and thus written off immediately. Second, it urged the American Institute of Certified Public Accountants (AICPA) to undertake a study to recommend just how companies should determine the value of IPR&D.

As will be discussed later, while the AICPA Practice Guide standardized the *calculation* of IPR&D, the issuance of SFASs 141 and 142, which removed the amortization of goodwill, completely removed the pressure on companies to maximize IPR&D. At the time this book is being written, purchased IPR&D must still be written off immediately, but companies, if anything, are trying to *minimize* the amount to reduce the charge to expense. As an aside, one must have a small degree of sympathy for those who write accounting standards and rules. Companies seem capable of using existing rules, no matter how written, to their own benefit.

The FASB has announced that as part of its purchase price procedures, which will result in the issuance of SFAS 141R, acquired IPR&D will *not* have to be expensed in the future. Instead, the acquired IPR&D will be capitalized as an intangible asset and tested at least annually for impairment. (See Chapter 8 on Impairment Testing.)

At this point the International Accounting Standards Board (IASB) seems to have taken a slightly different approach and requires capitalization of development expenditures, but not research expenditures. It deals only with the cost of such development expenditures, not FV. IASB requirements, in detail, are outside the scope of this book.

VALUATION OF IPR&D

In 2001, just as SFASs 141 and 142 were being issued, the AICPA issued a Practice Aid titled "Assets Acquired in a Business Combination to Be Used in Research and Development Activities: A Focus on Software,

Electronic Devices, and Pharmaceutical Industries." This report was the consequence of the SEC's request to the AICPA to standardize the calculation of IPR&D.

While an AICPA Practice Aid is not a formal part of GAAP, nonetheless the recommendations of the Practice Aid are followed virtually 100% of the time. This is because, as the only authoritative guidance, accountants are expected by their auditors to follow the recommendations, and auditors know that, in turn, the SEC will ask questions if the Practice Aid guidelines are not followed. Put a different way, the only approved methodology for valuing IPR&D today is provided by the Practice Aid. The following section is directly based on the recommendations of the Practice Aid. We explain what is required and why the information has to be gathered. However, anyone actually calculating IPR&D in a specific situation would be well advised to go directly to the Practice Aid, and to follow it like a recipe in a cookbook.

In Chapter 5.3 of the Practice Aid, the authors recommend that IPR&D be valued using the "Multi-period excess earnings method." The remainder of Chapter 5.3 then discusses the method, and we follow the recommendations here, step by step.

The Practice Aid lists 10 steps to be followed:

Step 1.   Select the Prospective Financial Information (PFI) that best reflects the final purchase price.

Step 2.   Evaluate and document the key assumptions relating to the elements that make up the PFI and ascertain that the PFI reflects management's good-faith best estimates.

Step 3.   Eliminate synergies (i.e., acquiring company and acquired company assumptions that are not consistent with assumptions used by market participants) from the selected PFI resulting in the "adjusted PFI."

Step 4.   Identify assets acquired, including assets to be used in R&D activities.

Step 5.   Confirm the existence of assets acquired to be used in R&D activities, including specific IPR&D projects.

Step 6.   Eliminate effects of non-IPR&D activities from the PFI resulting in the "final PFI."

Step 7. Apply contributory asset charge for assets that contribute to the generation of the cash flows (i.e., apply contributory asset charges to the cash flows).

Step 8. Calculate the present value of the cash flows using a discount rate appropriate for the specific asset acquired being valued.

Step 9. Compute the related income tax benefits resulting from the amortization of the asset acquired for income tax purposes.

Step 10. Evaluate the overall reasonableness of the asset's FV relative to the other assets acquired and the overall purchase price.

We discuss each of these in turn.

1. Select the prospective financial information that best reflects the final purchase price. Step 1 sounds innocuous, but it may be the single most important aspect of the total exercise. The issue is simple: whose projections do you use? The budget process at most companies involves a lot of politics and trade-offs. For R&D, not only are there political issues (i.e., whose project is going to be funded?), but there are also real issues regarding the outcome and cost of each specific project currently being worked on. Essentially, R&D budgets are a zero-sum game. Add a new project, or add a budget to an existing project, and some other project is not going to be adopted or will have to be cut back.

Thus there is a human tendency to be optimistic about the chances for success and the stringent cost limits that any one project is going to achieve. The National Aeronautics and Space Administration (NASA) has experienced this with regard to the Space Shuttle and the Department of Defense with regard to the Star Wars interceptor project. Seemingly, success is always just around the corner, and cost projections invariably are exceeded. The same phenomenon exists with corporate R&D.

Thus the question, in valuing IPR&D, is: "whose projections do you use?" The more conservative the cost outlook, and the more optimistic the chances of success, the greater will be the likelihood of a large IPR&D value for the project. *Increasing* the value may be considered desirable; alternatively, the company may wish to *minimize* the value. In short, the company can control the final IPR&D value through the choice of forecasts or projections.

The AICPA Practice Aid attempts to resolve this issue by requiring the projection that "Best reflects the final purchase price." Unfortunately, this is no advice at all. First, we have never seen a purchase transaction for a company as a whole where the buyer, in the due diligence phase, had gotten down to the detailed level of looking at *each* specific IPR&D project. Second, if the financial staff projects the costs and outcome, the answer will usually be significantly different from the project manager; the division sponsoring the research project will have a third outlook, while the company's research director will probably have a fourth set of ideas. The solution has to be practical. We recommend talking to the project director to get a feel for the potential success of the project and to the financial staff for a cost projection. This will probably balance an optimistic viewpoint (project director) with a conservative viewpoint (corporate controller).

The Practice Aid then goes on to make a point that is valid for all valuation assignments. They say that "management should take responsibility for the completeness and accuracy of the PFI alternative selected for use in the valuation." They continue, however, that "The valuation specialist is responsible for evaluating the methodology and assumptions used by management in preparing the PFI and concluding whether the PFI is appropriate for use in valuing the assets acquired."

The bottom line seems to be that in a perfect world, management would make a good projection and the appraiser would be comfortable with that projection. The discussion in Chapter 13 should be referred to here regarding what appraisers should do if they *do not* believe in management's projections. Suffice it to say here that in the case of IPR&D, it will be difficult for an appraiser to substitute his judgment for that of management with regard to the potential outcome of the project, but one can review critically the financials, based primarily on the accuracy of prior projections. So, for example, if one were evaluating the Star Wars project of the Department of Defense, it would be a rash appraiser who would try to determine the ultimate ability to shoot down a missile in flight; by the same token, skeptical questions about future cost outlays based on past performance would certainly be in line.

2. Evaluate and document the key assumptions relating to the elements that make up the PFI and ascertain that the PFI reflects management's good-faith best estimates. In an R&D project for the pharmaceutical industry, hopefully the outcome is going to be a new drug that will sell to patients. The question here revolves around revenue and cost of sales projections if the drug turns out to be successful and passes muster with the Federal Drug Administration (FDA). The Practice Aid, in effect, suggests treating skeptically management's projections, putting the burden on them to support the critical variable affecting future cash flows, including anticipated additional R&D expense to complete the project.

One can see from these recommendations the word "document." We do not believe the role of the appraiser is that of an auditor. As valuation specialists, we can and should use our professional judgment in evaluating what we are told, but unless one believes management is deliberately misleading (in which case one should abandon the project), appraisers should accept in good faith management's statements that are not at odds with the world at large.

Thus we do not feel it necessary to collect a vast documentation file supporting every line of a projection. If management gives you a one-page projection for a project, and upon questioning things this appears to be reasonable, it is our recommendation that you would only have to file that page in the working papers. It would be excessive to require written support for each of the ten elements called for in the Practice Aid for each research project in process. Appraisers have limited time for each element of a valuation assignment, and companies will not pay for the appraiser to waste time on nonessential tasks. Leave it up to auditors to build massive working paper files.

Note: In case of a litigation assignment, this recommendation should not be followed, but very few FV assignments for financial reporting, the subject of this book, ever get to the stage of litigation.

3. Eliminate synergies (i.e., acquiring company and acquired company assumptions that are not consistent with assumptions used by market participants) from the selected PFI resulting in the "adjusted PFI." Experience shows that with regard to IPR&D, there would be relatively few synergies. Certainly, the completion of the project would in all likelihood be performed by the target company personnel. Ultimate sales and profitability of the product(s) involved in the project might be enhanced by the buyer, but the solution to this problem is to use the target company's own projections made before the acquisition. There are very few R&D projects approved without the proposal having at least some indication of hoped-for results, assuming successful completion. So while the subject of synergies is important elsewhere in FV for financial reporting, in the specific case of IPR&D, it is pretty much a nonissue.

4. Identify assets acquired, including assets to be used in R&D activities.

5. Confirm the existence of assets acquired to be used in R&D activities, including specific IPR&D projects. These steps, 4 and 5, in the Practice Aid really relate to the valuation specialist's overall approach in beginning a valuation for allocation of purchase price. Before you can start valuing individual assets, it is necessary to identify all the assets that have to be valued. Therefore, as part of the IPR&D methodology, the Practice Aid reminds that many intangible assets are probably not on the target company's books. See Chapter 7 for a discussion of identifying intangible assets.

A second requirement within this step is verifying that the specific R&D projects are still in-process, because if completed they do not qualify for the treatment discussed here. By the same token, one has to determine that the project(s) are sufficiently advanced that they have substance and have the potential, if successful, to generate future cash flows. Thus while many large companies have literally hundreds of projects under way at any point in time, for valuation purposes one need only consider those with material future cash flow potential. The traditional 80/20 rule makes sense here, where only 20% of the total projects (at most) will have at least 80% of the cash flow and income potential for the future. The truth is that numerous small projects in total may not be material to the overall allocation, and undue effort should not be wasted on these.

6. Eliminate effects of non-IPR&D activities from the PFI resulting in the "final PFI." Often a company will have two or more projects under development that depend on each other, or a research product is going to be sold in conjunction with existing products, thus enhancing sales volume or profitability. Put a different way, a stand-alone project that will develop its own unique revenue stream is much easier to analyze than a project that is going to be intimately tied up with other aspects of the acquirer's business.

The analysis of what revenues, and costs, should and should not be included in an IPR&D valuation is going to be directly a function of the specific facts and circumstances. It is easy to generalize what to do, and hard to generalize how to do it.

Essentially what is required, if the IPR&D amounts are material, is to discuss with the relevant management how the company will proceed to bring the project to completion, what additional or incremental costs will be incurred. These costs must include not only direct project costs but a proportionate share of overhead, particularly R&D management. The allocation of overhead is essentially an exercise in cost accounting, and if help is required, the target company's accounting staff can provide the necessary judgments.

What is required is, to the extent possible, to treat the specific IPR&D project as a stand-alone business. To the extent that the R&D project will require the use of resources also used in other activities, it is essential to provide for the *cost* of those resources. The Practice Aid provides a methodology that has since then become standard practice in valuation. This is discussed in the following section.

7. Apply contributory asset charge for assets that contribute to the generation of the cash flows (i.e., apply contributory asset charges to the cash flows). The concept of "contributory charges" received a boost upon issuance of the Practice Aid; while previously developed, it had not been in wide use. The easiest way to explain it is to use the example of working capital.

If a new drug is successful, then the sales, cost of sales, and Selling, General, and Administrative (SG&A) expenses can be estimated directly. But one cannot sell a product without having inventory and accounts receivable in the normal course of business. Obviously, carrying these assets on the balance sheet has a cost, at a minimum an opportunity cost. Absent the new drug, and its related required working capital, the company's cash resources can be invested in the money market. Assuming the IPR&D project is successful, upon commencing sales, inventories and receivables will start to increase and the firm's cash balances will go down. In turn, interest income from money market investments will drop.

However, the cost of carrying receivables and inventory should be recognized not as the lost interest income, but more realistically at the company's borrowing rates, perhaps prime rate, plus or minus a premium depending on the financial strength of the company. Some appraisers feel it appropriate to put in an additional risk premium on the grounds that there is business risk in holding inventory and receivables. While the Practice Aid recommends using only the short-term borrowing rates, it would appear more realistic to require a rate of return on working capital somewhat above that level. By putting into the cash flow projection an interest charge for working capital, the project in effect bears its share of the cost of working capital for the company.

A similar contributory charge is made for fixed assets, workforce, patents, technology, and any other identifiable intangible assets, such as the quality management system used in Exhibit 10.1.

Exhibit 10.1 shows how these contributory charges affect cash flow projections. The contributory charges *reduce* the future cash flows and thus reduce the value of the IPR&D. As noted earlier in the chapter, when the SEC first got involved in the calculation of IPR&D, the focus was made to *reduce* the dollar amounts attributable to IPR&D. Thus, mandating the inclusion of contributory charges had the twofold effect of providing a theoretically better answer and practically providing a much smaller value. Now, most companies want *low* values for IPR&D, as well as other identifiable intangibles, so the contributory charge concept is warmly welcomed by management.

8. Calculate the present value of the cash flows using a discount rate appropriate for the specific asset acquired being valued. The calculation of present value is simple and straightforward using an Excel spreadsheet; the book assumes that readers are familiar and comfortable with performing present value calculations. The key point here in step 8 is "using a discount rate appropriate for the specific asset acquired being valued." The choice of an appropriate discount rate is one of the recurring themes in valuation.

The Practice Aid refers to several studies that look at historical rates of return, as well as calculations of the Weighted Average Cost of Capital

(WACC). It is tempting to say that in valuing IPR&D, one can use a discount rate between 20% and 30%, because that is probably where the answer will come out. Unfortunately, auditors, and the Public Company Accounting Oversight Board (PCAOB) in reviewing auditor work papers, are unwilling to accept unsupported assertions by a professional valuation consultant—even if the answer is right.

Note: The author tells clients that it is relatively easy for an experienced appraiser to develop the proper FV. What takes time, and costs professional fees, is the written report that *supports* the answer.

One approach that the author uses, and is supported by the Practice Aid, is to look at the rates of returns that venture capital investors typically look for. In many ways an in-process R&D project is similar to a start-up venture of a newly formed company. In true start-up situations, after friends and family put in the initial capital, and chances of success appear, then venture capital investors typically look for, say, 25% to 35% returns. It is not that they achieve those results; rather, to offset the anticipated losses, they require 30% or more on the *successful* ventures to provide a reasonable return on the overall fund.

One can make an argument that an IPR&D project developed by a target company and acquired in an M&A transaction should have lower risk, and hence a lower required rate of return, than a true start-up business venture. The IPR&D project has already been scrutinized several times by executives of a successful company who know the market and the technology. In short, there are fewer unknowns; consequently, we believe that a rate of return below 30% is likely to be appropriate in many if not most cases. Put a different way, if an IPR&D project requires a greater than 30% rate of return, it has to have a very big payoff very quickly because discount rates at or above 30% put very low value on positive cash flows five years out; for cash flow that is ten years out, there is virtually no value today. FASB Concepts Statement 7 (Con 7) is starting to be used in these situations of uncertainty as to future outcome (see Chapter 7). Basically, the expected value approach eliminates the need for a choice of a discount rate, because it requires use of a risk-free (i.e., U. S. Treasury) rate.

Offsetting this simplification is the requirement in Con 7 that the analyst evaluate the various probabilities. Specifically, one has to come up with reasonable alternative outcomes, develop cash flow for each, and

Exhibit 10.1 Sample Company: Determination of Intangible Asset Values for Allocation

Determination of Intangible Asset Values for Allocation
IPR&D

Valuation Date: January 3, 2006.

Pre-Tax Profit Rate: 17.8%

($000s omitted)

	2005	2006	2007	2008	2009	2010	2011	2012	2013	2014
Sales Projection for New Product	5,362	5,630	5,912	6,207	6,518	6,843	7,186	7,545	7,922	8,318
Pre-Tax Profit [17.8%]	954	1,002	1,052	1,105	1,160	1,218	1,279	1,343	1,410	1,481
Less Return on Working Capital [1.336% of Sales]	72	75	79	83	87	91	96	101	106	111
Less Return on Workforce [1.73% of Sales]	93	97	102	107	113	118	124	131	137	144
Less Return on Quality Mgmt Sys. [3.75%]	201	211	222	233	244	257	269	283	297	312
Available:	589	618	649	682	716	752	789	829	870	914
Less Taxes at 40%	353	371	390	409	430	451	474	497	522	548
After-Tax Cash Flow	236	247	260	273	286	301	316	331	348	365
Discount Rate: 22%										
Discount Factor	0.81967	0.67186	0.55071	0.45140	0.37000	0.30328	0.24859	0.20376	0.16702	0.13690
Present Value:	193	166	143	123	106	91	78	68	58	50

Value Indication: $1,077 Tax Benefit: = Value Indication/(1−((tax rate × annuity factor)/tax life))

Tax Benefit $ 140   FV $1,217

FAIR VALUE $1,217

Annuity Factor: PV(Discount rate, tax life, −1) $4.32

(*continues*)

Exhibit 10.1 Sample Company: Determination of Intangible Asset Values for Allocation (*Continued*)

Employee Workforce		Weight	Working Capital Charge
Method A:	Annual Payroll		Accounts Receivable + Inventory = 2 months or .1667 of Sales
	$1,997,000		8% Return Required on Working Capital
	½ year for hiring and training:		Percent = .16 × .08 0.01336
	$ 998,500	0.6667	
Method B:	Cost to hire employee:		
	$10,000 per employee		
	80 employees		
	$ 800,000	0.3333	
	Fair Value of Workforce		
	$ 932,340	10-year Life	
	Absorption Rate = $93,240/$5,400,000	1.73%	

then assign expected probabilities to each possible outcome. Many analysts believe it is harder to assign probabilities to a range of possible outcomes than it is to develop and support a single risk-adjusted discount rate. There is one strong advantage of using a Con 7 approach. Someone who reviews a valuation report can always question the choice of and support for a single discount rate.

Using a probability approach, as long as the range of alternatives are reasonable, and the assigned probabilities appear to be basically correct, it is difficult for an auditor to challenge the answer. She can say, "I disagree with your probabilities. Instead of a 10% chance of the project being a success, I think it is 15%. Instead of a 20% chance of the project failing, I think it is 10%." Anyone and everyone can challenge the probabilities. By the same token, the auditor has no more supportable basis for challenging the appraiser than the appraiser had in the first place.

When one is dealing with one-time occurrences, such as a single R&D project, one cannot develop statistical probabilities mathematically. It is going to be one person's judgment call against another, and the appraiser has the advantage in that his numbers are on the report. So all of a sudden, the burden of proof shifts to the reviewer to demonstrate that her probabilities are better or more supportable.

Although it requires a little more work, we believe that the FASB's expected value approach, as laid out in Con 7, provides more support and less basis for challenge. Certainly this approach is required in any FIN 46 analysis, so it is difficult for an auditor to challenge an expected value approach. All he can do is apply a reasonableness test, and if the appraiser has truly tried to play it straight, the valuation report will stand up to scrutiny.

9. Compute the related income tax benefits resulting from the amortization of the asset acquired for income tax purposes. "The valuation of an intangible asset would include (a) the expected tax payments resulting from the cash flows attributable to the intangible asset and (b) the tax benefits resulting from the amortization of that intangible asset for income tax purposes."[1] The overall subject of accounting for income taxes is covered in SFAS 109 and is beyond the scope of this book.

Suffice it to say that appraisers are currently required to calculate a "tax benefit" for intangible assets, whether or not one agrees with the underlying theory. So, if the true FV (what a willing buyer and willing seller would agree upon) is $1,000, then for purposes of SFAS 141 an additional amount is added to cover this tax benefit. In Exhibit 10.1 we show the tax benefit and the formula we have used in the calculation.

An additional tax problem must be discussed briefly here. If the target company has a net operating loss carryforward, we believe that the discounted cash flow (DCF) analysis should reflect the actual projected tax situation. An alternative view, dealing with market participants, might suggest that provisions for taxes on income should be provided irrespective of the specific company tax situation. The argument goes that most companies pay taxes, and leaving out income taxes, which are somewhat uncertain in the future anyhow, may misstate the value of the asset(s).

Inasmuch as the allocation deals with a specific company, at a specific point in time, we believe the stronger argument is to look at the facts and circumstances existing at that point in time. A little more troubling is in valuing a Subchapter S or limited liability partnership firm that does not pay taxes at the corporate level. Appraisers are not in full agreement on this topic. The way we look at it, if the Subchapter S company is to continue in its existing tax form, then no tax provision need be made. If, however, the valuation is made for possible sale of the company, and the most likely prospective buyer would be a Subchapter C corporation, then a charge for income taxes should be included in the valuation, because that is the way a prospective acquirer would make a determination.

10. Evaluate the overall reasonableness of the asset's fair value relative to the other assets acquired and the overall purchase price. Step 10 is both the easiest and the hardest aspect of any valuation, whether for allocation of purchase price to IPR&D or any other purpose. As an appraiser dealing with complex transactions involving a lot of computations, there is a normal sense of relief when one finishes the last Excel spreadsheet. Consequently, it is all too easy to sit back and congratulate oneself on a job well done.

The tug back to reality comes when the report is sent first to the client for review and then to the client's auditors. Questions will be asked, assumptions challenged, the source of data reviewed, and usually it will turn out that the appraisal function is only about 60% over upon completion of the worksheets and written draft.

Significant time savings can be realized if the appraiser steps back when the value conclusions are first reached. In the case of IPR&D, the client has some ideas about the value(s) of the purchased IPR&D, the target's R&D staff has some ideas (which may or may not be similar to the acquirer), and the appraiser should have formed at least a preliminary viewpoint after conducting the interviews and doing the detailed analysis and writing the report. We strongly recommend that in this, as in most other valuation cases dealing with financial reporting, the appraiser put himself in the shoes of the client: "What answer would the client *like* to have? What answer will solve the client's problem(s)?"

This does *not* mean that the appraiser should follow the old "M-A-I, Made as Instructed" rule. Given auditor, SEC, and PCAOB oversight, true and total independence on the part of the appraiser is mandatory. But this does not preclude understanding the client's perspective and desires. In turn, this means that when the appraiser has developed the preliminary value indications, the results should be tested against known client desires. Undoubtedly there will be differences, often large differences, but the very exercise of trying to understand the valuation from the client's perspective will do two things.

First, the analysis may turn up some errors in the valuation, such as erroneous assumptions about future sales, or a discount rate that may be too high or too low. Better for the appraiser to catch those errors than have them pointed out by the client or the auditor. But even if the assumptions and methodology are supportable and totally in accordance with professional appraisal standards, the answer(s) may not be what the client is looking for. We have seen two different responses at this point:

1. Tell the client "That's the way it is. I am the professional, I have used my best professional judgment, and if you don't like it, just pay me for my time and don't use my work." Obviously, nobody actually would use those words, but the author has heard these sentiments expressed in virtually the exact tone. In effect the client is told, "Take it or leave it, I am out of here." In this situation, professional pride triumphs, the appraiser thinks to himself how well he stood up to client pressure, and unfortunately never hears from that client again.

2. Tell the client that valuation is an art, not a science. "Two different appraisers should be within 10% of each other, but will never

hit the same exact number." Therefore, since there is some relevant range within which the appraiser can work, perhaps the work effort can be reviewed to see whether one or two assumptions may be on the high or low side.

A good-faith effort on the part of the appraiser to meet the client's needs, even if not totally successful, will retain the client, because the appraiser will be able to go over every crucial assumption in the valuation and point out that most of them came from the client. Telling the client, "the only way to get a materially different answer is for you, the client, to change your projections, but you have already given me your best estimate. So tell me what is now going to change your forecast." This second approach usually retains the client.

It is easier to apply the second approach if the appraiser does some homework first, *before* sending the draft report to the client. If it looks like there will be a discrepancy, it is better to nip it in the bud by supplementing the report with an analysis of the key variables driving the answer. There is never going to be 100% correlation between a client's desires and an appraiser's best professional judgment. At a minimum, the appraiser should be prepared to discuss why his professional opinion may differ from the client's expectations.

CONCLUSION

The proper accounting for R&D has gone from some companies expensing and some companies capitalizing to SFAS 2, which requires all companies to expense all R&D activities. The FASB, at the SEC's urging, changed the rules in SFAS 141 and required valuation of IPR&D, with immediate expensing in accordance with SFAS 2.

Now with issuance of SFAS 141R, the rules are changing once again, and the IPR&D FV will now be capitalized and tested for impairment periodically. Continuing R&D expenditures will be expensed, except for multinational firms subject to the IASB. For those firms, expensing of research and capitalization of the cost of development is required.

If this issue appears complicated, it is. Both FASB and IASB have promised to re-address all aspects of R&D, including in-process amounts, in the goal of converging the two accounting systems.

ENDNOTE

1. *Assets Acquired in a Business Combination to Be Used in Research and Development Activities,* AICPA Practice Aid Series, AICPA, New York, 2001, ¶5.3.98.

CHAPTER 11

Valuation of Inventories and Receivables

The owner of a small gift store had made arrangements to sell her store. The buyer was going to acquire the inventory, assume the lease, and retain the existing employees. At the closing the seller presented the buyer with a complete inventory listing showing the retail selling price of every item. The buyer indicated that was interesting but she could not buy the inventory at retail, turn around and sell the same items at the same price, and ever hope to cover her salary, rent, and utility expenses. The seller demurred, saying, "But that is what they are worth, that is what they sell for."

At that point, with the deal on the point of collapse, the seller's lawyer interjected and confirmed that there was no way that the buyer, any buyer, could acquire the inventory at the retail selling price. In that industry, inventory was usually purchased at a 50% discount from retail selling price, and the deal finally closed when the seller realized that it was 50% or nothing.

This is a stark example of the problems in placing a value on inventory. What is the value, to whom, and for what purpose? For the seller it was retail, but for the buyer it had to be wholesale.

For most businesses, as discussed in the following section, inventory is almost 10% of total assets, and for retail and other merchandise firms, inventory can account for up to 40% of all assets. One would think that assets of this magnitude would have received a lot of professional attention from standard setters over the years.

An examination of the output of the Financial Accounting Standards Board (FASB) over its first 30-plus years would show that a disproportionate amount of time and effort has been expended on leasing, income taxes, and financial instruments. Virtually *no* time or resources have been spent by the FASB on two of the largest categories of assets owned by businesses. We refer to inventories as well as Property, Plant, and Equipment (PP&E). We have covered many of the elements of valuing PP&E in Chapter 9, and this chapter discusses the valuation of inventories and receivables.

Interestingly, given the magnitude of corporate assets that inventories comprise, the FASB has been virtually silent on accounting and valuation issues. Exhibit 11.1 shows that for the 15 largest Fortune 500 industrial firms, inventories represent 8.5% of total assets. Most observers would conclude that this is material and deserves more attention than has been given.

In fact, as will be shown later, the rules governing the accounting for inventories date back to 1953, when Accounting Research Bulletin 43 was issued. Put a different way, there has been no practical change in accounting for inventories for over a half century. But that is about to change, in at least one way.

The FASB's issuance of the revised Standard on Business Combinations (SFAS 141R) calls for buyers to account for the seller's inventory at Fair Value (FV), not at the seller's cost. Let us see what the prevailing rule has been for more than 50 years. The valuation of inventories for financial accounting and reporting has historically been based on what is referred to as LOCOM (Lower of Cost or Market), with the assumption that only rarely will the market value for inventory be *below* cost. In short, in more than 99% of all financial statements, inventory is shown at its cost, not its true FV.

Usually, the cost of inventory is lower than its FV, if you assume that it will be processed and sold in the ordinary course of business. If the inventory is obsolete or surplus, or the customer base has disappeared, then the FV will be below cost, and a write-down is mandatory. But up until now, inventory has *never* been written up to FV. This goes back to the principle of conservatism, which everyone learned in the first week of Accounting 101. Losses are recognized immediately, whereas gains can be recognized only after they have been realized by an actual sale. In short, inventories have rarely been valued at FV, and all accounting

Exhibit 11.1 Inventories

Based on 2005 Fortune 500 Listing of the 15 Largest Industrial Companies by Revenue

($ millions)

Company	Revenues	Assets	Inventory	Inventory as % of Assets
1 Wal-Mart Stores	$ 288,189.0	$ 120,624.0	$ 29,497.0	24.5%
2 Exxon Mobil	$ 270,772.0	$ 195,256.0	$ 10,462.0	5.4%
3 General Motors	$ 193,517.0	$ 479,603.0	$ 12,247.0	2.6%
4 Ford Motor	$ 172,233.0	$ 292,654.0	$ 10,766.0	3.7%
5 General Electric	$ 152,363.0	$ 750,330.0	$ 9,778.0	1.3%
6 ChevronTexaco	$ 147,967.0	$ 93,208.0	$ 2,983.0	3.2%
7 ConocoPhillips	$ 121,663.0	$ 92,861.0	$ 3,666.0	3.9%
8 IBM	$ 96,293.0	$ 109,183.0	$ 3,316.0	3.0%
9 Hewlett Packard	$ 79,905.0	$ 76,138.0	$ 6,464.0	8.5%
10 Home Depot	$ 73,094.0	$ 38,097.0	$ 10,076.0	26.4%
11 McKesson	$ 69,506.0	$ 16,240.2	$ 7,495.0	46.2%
12 Cardinal Health	$ 65,130.6	$ 21,369.1	$ 7,471.0	35.0%
13 Altria	$ 64,440.0	$ 101,648.0	$ 10,041.0	9.9%
14 Kroger	$ 56,434.4	$ 21,091.0	$ 4,729.0	22.4%
15 Valero Energy	$ 53,918.6	$ 19,391.6	$ 2,317.0	11.9%
	$1,905,425.6	$2,427,693.9	$131,308.0	8.5% median

emphasis has been on determining the true cost of the inventory. What then is the true cost of inventory?

TRUE COST OF INVENTORY

ARB43 states, regarding accounting for inventories[1]:

> *The primary basis of accounting for inventories is cost, which has been defined generally as the price paid or consideration given to acquire an asset. As applied to inventories, cost means in principle the sum of the applicable expenditures and charges directly or indirectly incurred in bringing an article to its existing condition and location.*
>
> *In keeping with the principle that accounting is primarily based on cost, there is a presumption that inventories should be stated at cost. The definition of cost as applied to inventories is understood*

to mean acquisition and production cost, and its determination involves many problems. Although principles for the determination of inventory costs may be easily stated, their application, particularly to such inventory items as work in process and finished goods, is difficult because of the variety of problems encountered in the allocation of costs and charges. For example, under some circumstances, items such as idle facility expense, excessive spoilage, double freight, and rehandling costs may be so abnormal as to require treatment as current period charges rather than as a portion of the inventory cost. Also, general and administrative expenses should be included as period charges, except for the portion of such expenses that may be clearly related to production and thus constitute a part of inventory costs (product charges). Selling expenses constitute no part of inventory costs. It should also be recognized that the exclusion of all overheads from inventory costs does not constitute an accepted accounting procedure. The exercise of judgment in an individual situation involves a consideration of the adequacy of the procedures of the cost accounting system in use, the soundness of the principles thereof, and their consistent application.

For practical purposes, this quote from the Generally Accepted Accounting Principles (GAAP), written at least 50 years ago, is the latest thinking on the subject of valuing inventories! Put in simple English, inventories should be valued at cost, while GAAP admits that the determination of cost involves a lot of judgment. Many management accountants, often called cost accountants, spend their entire careers trying to determine the cost of the inventories at the company for which they work. Additional time is spent by independent auditors verifying company determination of cost. Auditors also check that the *quantities* of inventory are correct, ever since the infamous McKesson & Robins scandal of the 1930s. In that situation, the company had falsely claimed inventory as present and showed it on the financial statements. There was no inventory, but because the auditors did not attempt to directly view the inventory, which in fact was nonexistent, the financial statements had been certified as correct even though they were wrong. Ever since then, auditors physically inspect inventories, both in terms of quantity and in terms of cost. But assuming that companies can count what is on hand, the accounting issues always revolve around cost.

This book deals with FV, so in this chapter we have to look at what the differences are, if any, between FV and "cost." We have put cost in quotation marks because the proper costing of inventory is way beyond the scope of this book. There are several cost accounting textbooks each with literally 1,000 pages; every one of these textbooks attempts to teach the fundamentals of cost accounting. Then in practice every company has its own unique costing system. Virtually every cost accounting system has an implicit assumption, virtually never made explicit, that the cost of inventories is always *below* its value.

It is obvious that in this book we must focus on valuation, not cost, since the subject of cost accounting has been beaten into the ground. The truth is that cost and value, whether for inventories or any other asset, are *not* the same. At times they may be similar and at other times quite at variance with each other.

However, a few words on how cost accounting techniques are being used to value inventories for financial reports are still in order. The basic problem in inventory cost accounting revolves around overhead, inasmuch as the labor and material costs of inventory are usually pretty straightforward.[2] The fundamental issue with which cost accountants wrestle is how much overhead is appropriate to be assigned to specific cost objects. Theorists have argued that no overhead should be charged to inventory, and this approach is sometimes referred to as direct costing. GAAP, as we saw, does not permit this approach for financial reporting, but many companies feel that better decisions can be made for pricing, and outsourcing, if overhead is disregarded.

Other management accountants argue, equally vehemently, that *all* overhead has to be associated with products in order to fully price out products for sale. The assumption is that managers will not charge customers enough to fully cover all costs of doing business. Although it is obvious that a correlation exists between product costs and selling prices, the author has rarely seen management of a company fooled by an inaccurate cost system, although relative profitability of products, or services, can be somewhat misleading if an inappropriate cost system is in place.

The reason for this brief discussion is that valuing inventories for financial statements can actually affect cash flow. Contrast this with allocating part of a purchase price to customer relationships while the remainder is assigned to goodwill. What decisions about the business are ever going to be affected by having $5 million for customer relationships and $15 million for goodwill, as contrasted with the reverse, of $15 million for customer relationships and $5 million for goodwill?

The tax impact is the same in either situation (15-year amortization for taxes for all intangibles), and while goodwill does not have to be amortized, and customer relationships do have to be amortized, there is zero impact on cash flow, albeit a slight difference in reported earnings per share. A case might be made that if all inventories were to be carried on the balance sheet at FV, then management might be able to make better decisions regarding both production and customer pricing.

The FV of inventories is sometimes described with the term Net Realizable Value (NRV). This amount is assumed to be the expected selling price, less cost to complete, less selling expenses, and plus a reasonable profit. Thus the only cost element in the FV calculation is the cost remaining to be incurred to complete the product. However, until the advent of SFAS 141R, the concept of NRV was not considered part of GAAP. Here is what the *Wiley GAAP* guide says:

> *Inventories valued at selling price. In exceptional cases, inventories may be reported at sales price less disposal costs. Such treatment is justified when cost is difficult to determine, quoted market prices are available, marketability is assured, and units are interchangeable. Precious metals, certain agricultural products, and meat are examples of inventories valued in this manner. When inventory is valued above cost, revenue is recognized before the point of sale. Full disclosure in the financial statements is required.*[3]

LIFO: HALF OF FAIR VALUE

Raw materials, such as sheet steel or a barrel of petroleum, are usually valued at what the company paid to acquire the asset, including inbound freight but without any overhead allocation. If there is the basic assumption in valuing inventory, that the highest and best use for the specific inventory item is continued use in the business (as contrasted with a liquidation sale to some third party at a distress price), then the cost to replace the item today is probably the best indication of value.

LIFO (last in, first out) inventory is a method of inventory valuation that was developed during and after World War II to minimize tax payments in a period of rising costs and prices. For tax purposes, the Cost of Goods Sold (CGS) calculation is computed *as though* the most recent purchases (at presumably the highest cost) were the first item(s) sold. Thus in a period of rising prices, the CGS is higher, and the reported profit (and taxes!) is lower. In terms of cash flow, LIFO is considered highly desirable, at least as long as incoming purchase prices are rising.

LIFO, as with many other things in life, is not a totally free lunch. Congress provided the LIFO inventory method to help companies struggling with ever-increasing input prices, perhaps at a time when firms were less able to pass along those raw material costs to their customers. After all, commodity prices tend to fluctuate more than processed items. So in a period of inflation, with perhaps speculative influences over selling prices, being able to pay less tax was, and still is, quite a benefit. But what Congress giveth, a later Congress taketh away. In one of the few examples of Congress getting directly involved with GAAP and financial reporting, there is a conformity requirement in the Internal Revenue Code. This states that if companies use LIFO for their tax returns, they *must* then use LIFO for financial statements.

While saving taxes is considered desirable, the effect of LIFO on the balance sheet can be counterproductive. The balance sheet entry for inventories valued under the LIFO method is generally understated, at least in terms of current replacement cost. The newer (higher priced) inventory purchases were charged directly to CGS, leaving the older (lower priced) inventory on hand. The amount of this understatement grows over time as inventory balances increase and as purchase costs rise.

The dollar amount of this understatement is usually disclosed in a footnote to the financial statements that provides information on the firm's accounting policies. Interestingly enough, while this undervaluation can be substantial,[4] few security analysts seem to pay attention to it, because analysts focus on the income statement, and in LIFO accounting the income statement does have what may be the rough equivalent of FV. This "correct" income effect is offset by the "incorrect" balance sheet amount. One reason analysts do not often focus on the understatement of inventory values is that there is only one way to realize, in cash, the benefits of the lower-cost inventory.

There is one way to take the LIFO reserve into income, thus boosting net income, albeit at the expense of paying more in income taxes. A company can deliberately lower its physical inventories, either by shrinking the overall volume of business or by simply letting existing balances run down. At that point the physical reduction immediately translates into putting the older, lower-cost inventory into CGS that results in higher reported profits.

Sometimes a company will implement a new inventory control system that has the effect of letting it carry lower inventories. The reduction triggers the LIFO recapture, and some analysts then are stymied. Is it better for the company to be on top of its inventories, permanently reducing working capital requirements, or is it worse because of the one-time boost to that period's profits? Occasionally a company will deliberately try to trigger a LIFO recapture simply to meet that period's earnings target, but as with other machinations the company will usually be caught out and lose any benefits of meeting the numbers.

The FASB's decision to require buyers to revalue the target's inventories at FV will have a short-term impact equivalent to LIFO. If the newly acquired inventory is stated at the FASB's FV, which we believe is close to NRV, then there will be lower gross profit.

NET REALIZABLE VALUE

To review, FASB Concepts Statement 6 defines NRV as follows:

Statement 6

ARB43, Ch. 4, Par. 9

As used in the phrase "lower of cost or market", the term market means current replacement cost (by purchase or by reproduction, as the case may be) except that:

(1) Market should not exceed the "net realizable value" (i.e., estimated selling price in the ordinary course of business less reasonably predictable costs of completion and disposal); and

(2) Market should not be less than net realizable value reduced by an allowance for an approximately normal profit margin.

What this means is that in determining NRV for finished goods, the amount on the balance sheet will be the estimated selling price less selling expenses and an "approximately normal profit margin." Take a simple example.

An auto parts manufacturer as a target company has a replacement brake shoe that retails for $100 and has a manufacturing cost of $30. The target has an inventory cost of $30 and a gross profit margin of $70, which includes all Selling General & Administrative (SG&A) expenses, which can be substantial. The Net Operating Income, after all operating expenses, is 10% or $10 for the brake shoe. Under the NRV approach to valuing inventory, the inventory would have to be valued at probably $80, representing the $100 selling price less $9 for selling expense, $1 for interest during the carrying period, and $10 for the required profit margin.

That all sounds reasonable except from the buyer's perspective. For the first few months after the deal closes, and the initial inventory flows into CGS, gross profit will be only $20 as opposed to the "normal" $70. Operating profits will be drastically reduced for the first inventory turn. In a retail environment (assume a 12 times turn for inventory), perhaps this means the first month's operating results will show a loss. In a manufacturing environment (assume a four times turn), the newly acquired business will likely show a loss for the first quarter.

The impact of the FASB's rule has probably not been fully appreciated because in the past, inventory values on the seller's books were usually carried forward. This took place even though the then existing rules did call for revaluation of inventories. The fact that inventory was often not revalued was not considered a problem by the buyer (who gained from higher income) and may not have been high on the priority list of auditing firms. Now, with the new scrutiny on FV, it is certain that inventories will have to be revalued, with potentially severe consequences for buyers.

SELLING EXPENSES

The only hope for buyers is to make a strong case that the allowance for selling expenses and the cost to complete for work-in-process will be measured generously. How do cost accountants, and hence appraisers, look at something like selling expenses?

Initially one would go to the profit and loss (P&L) statement and look up the line for selling expenses in total, relate that to total sales volume, and derive a selling percentage. This, however, should be the absolute minimum. It would be reasonable to assess part of the general management of the company, including Human Resources, Purchasing, Finance, Warehousing, and Shipping, as well as any other cost elements unique to that business. In other words, what does it take to support the sales and marketing operation? Essentially, in cost accounting terms, in calculating the appropriate amount for selling expenses allowed in NRV, one should use a fully allocated base, not a direct cost approach.

The more costs that can be justified, the lower will be the inventory value and the higher the future gross profit and hence net income. Candidly, a truly creative approach to this subject will pay dividends, keeping always in mind that whatever is done will ultimately be scrutinized by skeptical auditors and possibly government auditors. As someone once observed, only do that which you would be willing to have seen on the front page of *The Wall Street Journal*.

WHAT IS A "REASONABLE PROFIT"?

The other element allowed in the NRV calculation is an allowance for a reasonable profit. What is "reasonable"? At an absolute minimum the profit, before tax, should be the company's historical operating profit, sometimes referred to as EBITDA (Earnings Before Interest, Taxes, Depreciation, and Amortization).

This should be a minimum because two other factors must be considered. First, we have to look at the profit generated by other market participants; if the target's profit rate is *lower* than that of its competitors, or of other prospective acquirers, then it would appear that the FASB guidance, in its Fair Value Standard, would require one to look at the broader universe. If the target's profit rate is *higher* (perhaps this would not be as common), then that should be used because it obviously would have been taken into account by market participant buyers!

The second factor that should affect the profit rate used in the NRV calculation for valuing the acquired inventories is a profit requirement on the *other assets* required to sell the inventory. Just as we picked up expenses from HR and Finance in figuring out the selling expense, so should we provide a return on the investment in the infrastructure necessary to sell the inventory. The asset base could include a proportionate amount for receivable balances until the sold inventory is paid. It would also include a return for the warehousing assets, and if the parts were manufactured (as compared to purchased as finished goods) then there is an asset base for the manufacturing facilities.

Having said this about increasing the cost and profit elements, there will still be a higher amount allocated to inventories than was on the books of the target. Consequently, in figuring out the very short-term impact of an acquisition, for the first month or the first quarter, this increased inventory value must be taken into consideration.

WORK-IN-PROCESS AND RAW MATERIALS

Determining the FV of finished goods inventories involves only an analysis of selling price, selling expense, and reasonable profit. For work-in-process (WIP), one also has to calculate the "cost to complete," that is, to finish the production cycle so you have product that can be sold.

If a company were being liquidated, and our FV calculation does not involve a liquidation scenario, you would find that finished goods inventories might sell at 40% to 60% of the inventory carrying cost. Raw materials might sell at 60% to 70% of cost, with the assumption that suppliers might take back some of the items at a discount. Many raw materials (e.g., steel or copper) can easily be disposed of. Rough castings, however, probably have little more than scrap value if the company went out of business.

The FV calculations for allocation of purchase price assume continued use, so let us take the example of the rough castings and see how they should be valued. There would be machining required, plus inspection. If the parts then were sold to buyers at that stage, the only difference from before is adding in the straight manufacturing cost. If the castings are then part of a larger assembly that goes into a major product, then things become far more complex. A rough casting for an engine block first must be completed and then assembled into a larger product, perhaps a tractor. If the target company had 275 castings on hand, representing requirements for the next month's total factory production, should you determine the cost to manufacture 275 tractors? The answer would be yes, but only if all the other parts requirements were on hand on the date the M&A transaction closed.

Given modern scheduling processes, it is unlikely that all of the parts would ever be on hand to fully complete the manufacture and assembly related to the actual number of castings, valuing the castings on a stand-alone basis. Before falling into a never-ending trap that would be a bottomless pit, another approach has to be found. Valuing all raw materials and most WIP inventory cannot be accomplished through a cost to complete analysis. There are simply too many what-if scenarios that could be employed.

Instead we recommend cutting the Gordian knot. Simply take a single percentage of the raw materials and a separate percentage of WIP and apply those percentages to the book values on the target's financial statements. The decrease in precision will not be that great, and the saving in management, valuation, and auditing time will be significant.

The only question then is to arrive at approximate percentage rates for raw materials and WIP. It would be difficult to assign a *premium* to book value in developing an FV for raw materials and WIP. In effect the entire earnings cycle has to be completed, with all the uncertainties that involves. By the same token, while a discount to book is probably justified, it is unlikely that auditors or the Securities and Exchange Commission (SEC) would be comfortable with a large "haircut," to use a Wall Street term.

Obviously, the facts and circumstances will ultimately determine the valuation of raw materials and WIP, but it would seem that a 5% to 15% discount from book value is not inappropriate. Recognizing that the finished goods inventory in all likelihood will be written up, a small write-down on the other part of the inventory does not seem out of line.

INVENTORY OBSOLESCENCE

Few generalizations seem safer than to assert that almost every company has worthless inventory on its books. Virtually every company of any size has a computerized system. Sort it by age, dollar amount, or location and you will find a lot of strange entries. If it is at all possible to sort it by dividing the number of items on hand by the usage for the past 12 months (annual turnover), you will find items where it would take 50 years or more to use up. If you sort it by recent usage, you will find items for which there has been zero demand, and so forth.

There are three reasons companies do not clean up their inventories. First, it takes time and manpower, and most firms do not have knowledgeable inventory control managers or staff with nothing else to do with their time. Cleaning up inventory takes a degree of knowledge of the company and the items, such that this cannot be done mechanically. In theory you could write a program that said "List all items with more than five years' stock on hand" or "List all items with zero demand in the last year." You could then give that list to someone, tell them to pick out the items from the shelves, and throw them away. The company would save on space, property taxes, insurance, and would get a tax deduction. With all of these benefits, why do companies not do this, even if available staff is busy?

This leads to the second reason inventories are rarely purged or cleaned up. Somebody remembers a time when an item that had virtually zero demand suddenly was needed by a customer, it was found, and people said, "Thank God we didn't ever get rid of that part." It takes only one or two experiences of this sort before everyone believes that the old adage applies, "Better safe (having the part still on hand) than sorry (having cleared out the part last year)." Nobody can guarantee that any particular part will *never* be needed or sold. From there it is a short leap of logic (and faith) that *nothing* should be thrown out, "just in case."

Finally, the third reason why inventories are not cleaned out is a simple one. Despite the benefits (i.e., tax deduction, reduced taxes and insurance, and the availability of additional space), physically getting rid of inventory requires a journal entry. And the entry reads:

Dr. Cost of Goods Sold (Inventory *Expense*)	$xxx.xx
Cr. Inventory	$xxx.xx

Now a debit to expense, no matter how beneficial to future operations, is going to affect this period's reported net income. Few companies want to take the charge, and it is always easy to rationalize *not* cleaning up the inventory (and taking the expense) by assuming, "Well, you never know, we *might* need that inventory, so better safe than sorry. We will just keep it on hand, avoid the expense charge, and be better able to provide service to our customers."

Whether it is good management policy or not, the fact remains that for most companies a certain amount of dollars are tied up in physical inventory that is highly unlikely ever to be converted into cash. Companies are often reluctant to take necessary write-downs.

A business combination, however, provides the perfect opportunity to get such items off the book. Keep in mind that the requirements of SFAS 141R call for the Fair Value of acquired assets to be put on the buyer's books. If the FV of surplus and obsolete inventory is essentially zero (scrap value may equal the cost to dispose of the assets), then the buyer should insist on a thorough scrubbing of the inventory records and the inventory. As long as good items are not valued at zero, just to boost future income, there can be no complaints if old inventory is not carried forward at the seller's historical cost. There should be no unfavorable tax consequences.

If the business combination is a stock purchase, then the selling corporation will obtain a tax deduction when the worthless inventory is scrapped. And if the scrapping is simultaneous with the purchase accounting, then the seller's tax return will show the benefit of the disposal, while the buyer's books will never have had the bad inventory in its financial statements. If the business combination is a purchase of assets, then placing zero value on worthless inventory will simply place more of the purchase price into intangible assets that are amortizable over a 15-year period.

The critical aspect is that the Internal Revenue Service (IRS) will not let a company take a tax deduction for worthless inventory unless the items are physically disposed of. While financial reporting *requires* asset write-downs for worthless assets, tax reporting *precludes* a "valuation allowance" unless the items are no longer under the control of the entity. Harsh as this tax treatment may appear, it does make sense, because otherwise companies would be tempted to take large reserves for taxes on worthless inventory, keep the items on hand, and hopefully sell some or all of the items later. In other words, deductions would be accelerated and income recognition delayed. The audit problems for the IRS would be monumental. So the rule is easy to understand and apply. If you want a tax deduction for worthless inventory, physically dispose of the items. It is that simple. Companies ordinarily do not do this very often because of the hit to the P&L. A business combination provides perfect timing for both tax and physical inventory reporting to be in sync, without any P&L penalty. Here is a situation where application of the stringent FASB rules on FV of inventories will be a positive help.

SUMMARY OF FAIR VALUE OF INVENTORIES

Companies now have to make an explicit determination of inventory values in every business combination. Past practice, although not necessarily correct, was usually to carry forward the seller's inventory values. The assumption often was that since inventories are audited every year, the buyer could rely on the seller's books in this important area.

As we have seen, however, while auditors may review the physical inventory, and the pricing policies and procedures, they rarely go into detail, line item by line item. Companies know this should be done periodically to save shelf space, reduce property taxes, reduce insurance premiums, and obtain a higher degree of accuracy in their production control records, but knowing what *should* be done, and doing it, are not the same thing.

Because cleaning out and discarding surplus and obsolete inventory has a negative impact on reported income, companies do not do this as often as they should. From the perspective of the buyer in a business combination, the new emphasis on determining the true FV of inventory is going to have mixed consequences on whether earnings are accretive or not.

For finished goods inventory, the new FV will probably be higher than the seller's carrying value. The concept of NRV, established in GAAP for years, essentially is the methodology for determining the FV of inventories. The elements that make up NRV are clear, although their exact determination in practice provides some flexibility.

For WIP and most raw materials, the most practical approach to determining FV is not to try to estimate an NRV, which has to assume virtually the entire production cycle. Rather, we recommend, solely as a practical alternative, applying a percentage factor to each of the categories based on the seller's carrying values. Admittedly not theoretically pure, there is a limit as to how much incremental cost a buyer can be expected to incur in order to make the resulting answers only slightly more accurate.

Finally, the timing of any business combination suggests that is the moment to purge all bad inventory items that are never going to be sold but are simply taking up space. There is no P&L penalty, and there will be savings in taxes, insurance, and storage.

VALUATION OF RECEIVABLES

Under the new SFAS 141R rules, accounts receivable will have to be entered on the books of the acquirer at FV, which the FASB indicates should not be the face amount less an overall reserve for bad debts. Common practice for at least the last 50 years has been for companies to set up a bad debt reserve, a charge to bad debt expense and a credit to the reserve. Then, when a specific receivable is written off as uncollectible, it is charged in total (assuming a 100% loss) to the reserve. At the end of the period, the reserve is restored through a further charge to bad debt expense; the amount of the closing balance of the reserve is a function of historical experience (a loss rate) applied to the period-end balance. Thus as receivables go up and down with sales level, the reserve is adjusted so that it can absorb normal or expected losses, even though no specific identification of possible losses has been made.

The major argument in favor of this approach is essentially statistical: We know a certain percentage of our customers will not pay, but we do not know in advance which they will be. A similar analysis is made by a casino: they know that certain players will win the jackpot at the slot machines. They do not know which customer, and they do not care because the machines are set to provide an *overall* return (say 95%) to the customers, with the balance kept as the house's gross profit.

The FASB has chosen, in its FV pronouncements on receivables, *not* to use or rely on a statistical approach to the collectibility of receivables. They now require that a separate determination be made of each receivable on a stand-alone basis. How practical is this? The answer is that it can be done. How reliable will the answers be on any specific receivable? Probably not very reliable.

The assumption that the buyer, or its valuation specialist, can predict in advance which receivables will be collectible 100 cents on the dollar, which at 50 cents on the dollar, and which will be written off is fallacious. If someone *knew* that Company XYZ's receivable was going to be written off as uncollectible, no rational credit manager or sales manager would have approved the credit in the first place. Banks do not deliberately make loans to deadbeats. U.S. Steel does not deliberately deliver steel to a customer that will not pay.

Yet the FASB Standard in effect assumes that buyers of the target company, or their representatives, can do what the target firm's own staff could not do—pick out *in advance* the winners from the losers. Now let us give the FASB credit for some intelligence. They cannot realistically expect a buyer to do a better job than the seller was able to do. If the buyer is to determine the true FV of each receivable balance, some sort of probability has to be applied to each individual account. In other words, nobody can be expected to go down a list of 100 receivables and correctly pick in advance which exact three will pay 50 cents on the dollar and which two specific customers will be a total write-off. The only realistic methodology will be to apply some sort of overall expected loss percentage to the majority of receivables that are current. For receivables that are past due, and aged by due date, decreasing percentages of recovery can be applied, starting with those 30 days past due down to the oldest on the books.

The issue, undoubtedly to be raised by an auditor reviewing the analysis, is whether the FV determination is too conservative. If you apply an overall discount to the current rates, and more or less specific discounts to the past due accounts, are you in effect over-reserving? The answer will depend on who did the analysis and how realistic they tried to be. The acquirer will want the most conservative set of assumptions that can be supported. If one looks at the FV determination of receivables from the perspective of market participants, then there are, in fact, many market participants who are in business to buy receivables.

Such firms are often referred to as factors. Particularly in the furniture and clothing business models, factors are an integral part of the business cycle. The same retail store is buying clothing (or furniture) from many different manufacturers. The factor, working with the manufacturer, sees the same retail customer many times, whereas for any one manufacturer they will have limited experience with any particular retailer.

With this concentration of customers, the factor is in a position to evaluate the credit-worthiness of specific customers before buying the receivables. Now there is no single model that all factors use with all manufacturers, but the basic principle is that the factor actually buys the receivables. The price paid, some fraction of the face amount, has three elements. First is the time value of money. If a manufacturer provides "net 60" terms, under the best of circumstances it will not receive payment in less than 60 days. So the factor, buying the receivable on day 1, has to discount the balance for the time value of money. The second cost element, charged by the factor to the customer, is an allowance for bad debts, while the third element is the factor's actual cost of doing business plus profit.

It would not be realistic in a business combination for the buyer actually to contract with a factor to buy the target's receivables, because it would end up being a one-off transaction. Nonetheless, the factoring companies have some broad ranges for the discounts they utilize in buying receivables, and an appraiser, or the company, will be able to obtain supportable amounts with a little research.

In determining the FV of receivables, it would appear that looking at the factoring marketplace, as being composed of true market participants, is supportable under SFAS 141R. Another source of information, albeit limited to very large customer receivable bases, is the securitization market. Many firms, such as auto companies, mortgage bankers, and credit card companies, in effect bundle up pools of receivables and sell securities, whose ultimate payment will come from the cash proceeds of the individual retail customers.

The major Wall Street firms are active in this market and can provide supportable discounts, which the buyers of such securities demand. So if securitizations occur at 97% of face value, a good case can be made for valuing all current receivables at that 97% level. In effect this treats the receivables valuation as though one truly went to the market and offered them for sale to a third party.

SUMMARY OF FAIR VALUE OF RECEIVABLES

No longer can companies simply transfer over the book value of receivables, less a single global reserve for uncollectible accounts. Some approach must be found to value individually each receivable balance. We have presented three approaches, each of which is probably going to provide an appropriate FV; if one can apply more than one approach, and arrive at more or less similar results, so much the better.

The first approach is to analyze individual balances by aging the receivables. One can apply a small percentage discount to current receivables, with larger discounts for increasingly older accounts. The beginning percentage can be based on the target's historical experience, the acquirer's historical percentage, or industry-wide experience. The second approach is to look at what a factoring company would pay. Because factoring companies actually buy receivables for cash, that would provide excellent market participant information. The final approach is to arrive at a percentage discount that would be applied if the receivables were securitized. Again, this would represent what market participants are actually doing and would reflect both the time value of money and the risk of bad debt loss.

Any or all of these approaches in our judgment meet both the rule and the spirit of SFAS 141R. A business combination provides the acquirer the opportunity to truly purge the target's receivables, just as one gets a fresh start on inventories by cleaning out all surplus and obsolete items.

CONCLUSION

The FASB is changing the way companies will have to value inventory and receivables in a business combination. Rather than just carrying forward the amounts of working capital from the target company's book to their own, buyers will now have to value both inventories and receivables directly. The valuation principles inherent in the new approach, particularly for inventories, are going to have a negative short-term impact on reported earnings. The true FV of the inventory, effectively its Net Realizable Value, is likely to be higher than the cost amount on the target's books. Because inventory turns over quickly, a higher beginning inventory will almost immediately translate into a higher cost of goods sold and hence lower operating profits. This will be a one-time impact, albeit not a pleasant one for companies that want a new acquisition to be accretive as quickly as possible.

There will be fewer problems in arriving at the FV of receivables. Effectively, the buyer will start out with zero reserve for bad debts, but the individual receivable balances will be carried at something less than face value. Then as they are paid, assuming 100 cents on the dollar, the company will have a pickup in earnings. It would only be coincidence, however, if the gain on receivables offset the loss on the higher required inventory values.

ENDNOTES

1. ARB43, Ch. 4, Par. 5.
2. The author has had many years of cost accounting experience, and many of the generalizations are just that, generalizations. Certainly in practice there are innumerable issues in determining the correct amount of labor and material that should appropriately be applied to a cost object. Nonetheless, overhead is almost always a much greater issue.
3. Patrick R. Delaney, Barry Epstein, and Ralph Nach, *Wiley GAAP 2005*, John Wiley & Sons, Hoboken, NJ, 2004, p. 244.
4. Rite Aid Corporation's 2005 10-K showed a LIFO reserve of $470 million against total inventories of $2.3 billion and a net worth of $322 million. The LIFO reserve actually would have more than doubled the company's equity.

CHAPTER 12

Valuing Stock Options*

One of the most contentious issues in financial reporting over the past ten or more years has been employee stock options (ESOs). Many companies have used ESOs as a means of compensating employees through the ownership of shares of company stock. The basic theory has been to try and align the self-interest of the employee(s) with that of the company. A shareholder employee is more likely to treat company resources as his own, and work harder for less money, than a nonshareholder employee would. At least that has been the theory.

There has been no controversy that, at least in moderation, grants of stock options to executives, managers, and even ordinary employees can have a positive effect for all nonemployee shareholders. This is why ESO plans are routinely approved by overwhelming votes of shareholders.

There are, however, three areas of controversy. The first is beyond the scope of this book, and deals with the amount of options granted, particularly to the very top officers, usually the CEO. Many experts in corporate governance have argued that too many options have been granted to CEOs and that they have been overpaid for their effort. This is particularly true if a rise in the stock price is more closely correlated with outside economic forces than with individual executive performance. This type of argument will not—and in fact cannot—ever be resolved. How much compensation is too much compensation is a judgment call, with different people arriving at different answers.

The second controversy, slightly more substantive, has dealt with the fundamental issue of whether the granting of ESOs is in fact compensation. Many executives have argued that granting options represents

---

* We are indebted to George L. Montgomery, President of Montgomery Investment Technology, Inc. developer of FinTools® software [www.fintools.com], for aid with this chapter.

some sort of free-will gift; under that theory the option is not an expense to the company or to existing shareholders. Sometimes, although less often in recent periods, such executives argued that ESOs have *no* value because they are hard to value. This argument, while made loudly and repeatedly by many in the high-tech industry, has had little traction with most outside objective observers.

More than ten years ago, one of the then Financial Accounting Standards Board (FASB) members, at a public hearing, responded to that argument, "Well, if options really have no value, then why don't you just give them to me? I think they are valuable, and if you don't want them, then I will take them off your hands and save you any effort in dealing with them!" Needless to say, at least that individual stopped making the case for zero value to the FASB, which has been dealing with the ESO-valuation controversy for many years and has heard all the arguments many times.

The third argument against charging options to expense was frequently made but again gathered little traction. Proponents argued that while ESOs might well represent compensation, the problems in valuing those options were so great, and so intractable, that not charging them to expense was far more reliable than coming up with some arbitrary value. The FASB did not buy the argument that options could not be valued, and while acknowledging that option valuation may not be totally precise, the problem was no more severe than in valuing intangible assets or a bad-debt reserve.

When the original SFAS 123 was issued over ten years ago, the FASB in effect compromised. The arguments against expensing options were vocal, and the opponents were threatening to go to Congress to overturn mandatory expensing. So, instead of requiring expensing, FASB ordered companies to compute the expense of options that had been granted, but companies only had to show the results in the footnotes. The belief was that disclosure alone would allow analysts to make their own adjustments. The FASB for years, however, has argued that disclosure is *not* a substitute for recognition, putting an item into the audited financial statements. With the issuance of SFAS 123R, and with Congress no longer as interested in overturning the FASB's position, companies that issue options must now determine their value at the date of issuance and charge that value to current expense.

One word here about "grant date" accounting versus "exercise date" accounting. Many observers have felt that the most reliable measure of the expense of ESOs is to compare the exercise price with the actual stock price at the date the option is exercised. So if an option had been granted five years ago at $22, and the stock was selling at $72 when the executive exercised, there was a $50 expense representing the amount that existing shareholders lost by having the company sell stock at the then below-market price. A second benefit of exercise date option expensing is that many options that have been granted never are exercised — the executive does not fulfill the vesting requirements or the stock price never rises above the grant price. In this case charging an amount to expense at the grant date, when nothing untoward happens in the future, appears to be unfair.

The FASB's argument in favor of grant date accounting is that the cost of the options is incurred when granted, not when exercised. And, if you wait until exercise, you are understating expense during the period the individual is earning the compensation represented by the option. Irrespective of the merits of the two positions, SFAS 123R calls for grant date valuation, and that is what will be covered in this chapter.

VALUATION OF OPTIONS UNDER SFAS 123R

Readers will recall that an option is the right to acquire another asset, at a specific price for a specified period of time. You could go into the marketplace in October 2005 when Microsoft was selling at $25, and buy an option on Microsoft stock at $25, exercisable at any time prior to January 2008, for a price of $3.70. The value of a 27-month Microsoft option at $25 was established clearly by marketplace participants at $3.70. Similar options are available, and priced, for many if not most NYSE companies and many NASDAQ-quoted firms.

For publicly traded options, prices and hence values are readily available on any Web site dealing with security prices. In fact, a company, OptionsXpress, began by dealing only with options, although it has since expanded its offerings to more normal brokerage. Information on options prices, and values, is now readily available. How do the investors determine that it is worth *selling* a Microsoft option at no more or less than $3.70? How do prospective buyers decide whether it is worth paying this premium to *buy* the option, obtaining the right to acquire the stock at $25 for the next 27 months?

Many readers will have heard of the Black-Scholes-Merton (BSM) option-pricing model. Three financial economists, with the names coincidentally of Messrs. Black, Scholes, and Merton, developed an option-pricing methodology many years ago; they were attempting to understand how market traders actually determined the bid and asked prices for options. Their seminal work boiled down to six variables that could explain the price at which options *should* sell if they were to be fairly valued, with fairness being equally applicable to the buyer and the seller. These six variables are discussed as follows because they are involved in every option valuation:

1. Current stock price
2. Option strike price
3. Period of time during which the option can be exercised
4. Current interest rate
5. Expected dividends to be paid on the underlying stock
6. Expected volatility

   The FASB then introduced a modification to the third variable:

   3a. Expected probability that options will vest and/or will be exercised early

It should be understood that while the BSM option valuation methodology is the most commonly used, there are in fact more than 50 other formulas attempting to develop a value for options. Interestingly, and for this chapter of paramount importance, all of the option valuation methods utilize the aforementioned six variables, although many utilize additional assumptions. Readers should keep one additional factor clearly in mind: Publicly traded options are freely marketed and price quotes widely available, and most of the option valuation models have been developed for such options, where there is a market of buyers and sellers.

An ESO, in contrast, is *not* marketable or transferable. It cannot be bought and sold. In most cases only the original grantee (or the estate in case of death) can exercise the option. It cannot be exercised until the vesting period has been completed with the grantee still on the payroll.[1] Most ESOs go out for periods up to ten years, while publicly traded options typically expire in less than three years. In short there are several differences between marketable options and ESOs. So, while option valuation models were developed for short-term marketable options, ESOs in contrast are long term and not marketable. Applying the *same* option pricing models to two *different* products requires a degree of faith that methodologies developed for the public market can appropriately be applied to the restricted ESO arena. Many of the critics of the FASB's option expensing proposal made this exact point, and came to the conclusion that the differences were too substantial to permit accurate valuation, and hence the FASB should have dropped the whole issue.

Right or wrong, the FASB did decide that the ESO valuation issues were susceptible to resolution. The remainder of this chapter deals with SFAS 123R as it was issued, and as it has been interpreted by the Securities and Exchange Commission (SEC).

SEVEN VARIABLES OF OPTION VALUATION

Because every option valuation model considers the original six variables, we will first discuss what they are. Then we will deal with the two variables that are hardest to estimate. The other four variables are, in practice, pretty much noncontroversial. We start with the easiest two, current stock price and exercise price.

Current stock price represents what the underlying common stock is selling for on the date the options are issued to the recipients. For publicly traded companies, it will be the closing price or the average of the bid and asked price, as shown in *The Wall Street Journal* or another authoritative publication. The reason the current stock price is important in valuing an option is clearly apparent.

Most options are granted, that is, the exercise price is established, at today's quoted price. If Microsoft is at $25 and an option were granted at $22, then the holder (grantee) would instantly have a built-in $3 profit.[2] However, if the stock is at $25 and the option can only be exercised at $30, then the option is worth less because the first $5 of gain can not be captured by the option holder. For the rest of this chapter, we assume that options are granted at the current stock price and that the *exercise price* is the *same* amount.

Period of time during which the option can be exercised is important because the longer the time, the higher is the current value of the option. An option that expires in one month has to be worth less than one that has 12 months until expiration. A one-year option is worth less than a ten-year option. The reason is simple: An option only has real or intrinsic value if the market price is above the exercise price. An option exercisable at $25 will not be exercised if you can go out in the open market and buy the identical security today for $20. Similarly, if the option is exercisable at $25 and the current market price is $32, then one would realize an immediate $7 profit by exercising, and if the option expired tomorrow, you would have no alternative but to exercise or lose the entire $7 gain.

But if the option still had a further year during which it could continue to be exercised, most financial theorists argue that one should hold on to the option in the expectation that the underlying stock price could rise. After all, in the example, the optionee can always exercise at $25, so the gain would be larger if the stock price were to appreciate above $32. Furthermore, the cash outlay to exercise would be delayed, if the option were held until maturity. This logic holds true, however, only if one anticipates that future price changes can go either way.

If you feel that the stock price is almost certain to go down, then it pays to exercise, buy the stock, and sell it on the open market at once, capturing permanently the intrinsic gain. But in the absence of such knowledge, every finance textbook supports the argument that holding the option is preferable to exercise before expiration. The theory is that the stock essentially has an equal chance of going up, or going down, from today's price. With the exercise price fixed, then early exercise involves both a cash outlay and the loss of the potential increase in the value of the option over its remaining life. Whether or not the reader subscribes to this analysis, the fact remains that professionals who live by trading options all agree that longer options have greater value than shorter-term options. This is why companies typically grant ten-year options to employees, trying to maximize the compensation element.

Current interest rate affects the value of an option because by acquiring the option, one does not have to put out the cash required to own the share(s) outright. The higher the interest rate, the more an option is worth because of this time value of money. Because there is nothing that a company issuing an ESO, or the employee, can do about the interest rate, the impact of interest rates on options is outside the control of both parties. The FASB's Standard requires use of the risk-free U.S.

Treasury rate with the same time horizon as the option. So if it is a five-year option, then one uses the five-year zero coupon Treasury rate in the formula. In theory if interest rates change during the life of the option, then its current value will similarly fluctuate. But the FASB explicitly prohibited revaluation of options once they were granted. Consequently, changes in interest rate are in practice immaterial in subsequent analysis by the company or decision making by the employee. Certainly if the price of the stock rises above the exercise price, employees will be tempted to exercise; a similar rise in interest rates, however, will not likely affect the decisions of option holders.

Expected dividends, according to the BSM theory, affect the current valuation of an option. An option holder does *not* receive dividends that are declared and paid by the company, whereas current shareholders do receive the cash dividend. Receipt of dividends, representing a cash return to the shareholder, is considered desirable (disregarding tax consequences). The price of a stock typically goes down by the same amount as the dividend paid, which is why *The Wall Street Journal* shows when a stock goes "ex-dividend." Recall that at one point Microsoft paid a special dividend of $3 to all shareholders. The following day, after the dividend had been paid, the stock declined by the same $3.

Put a different way, all other things being equal, one would rather own stock on the ex-dividend date than a comparable option. The stockholder gets cash, but the option holder receives nothing. Thus the BSM formula for valuing options in effect *subtracts expected future* dividends in determining the value of an option today. The FASB in SFAS 123R tells companies to utilize the past dividend history as the basis for estimating future dividends. This requires a degree of judgment—if companies assume future dividend increases, this will lower the current value of the options granted.

However, one can reasonably expect auditors, and the SEC and the Public Company Accounting Oversight Board (PCAOB), to review and verify that assumption. If the company has consistently raised its dividend every year by $.05, then projecting that into the future will be unlikely to raise questions. But if the same $.80 dividend had been in effect, and unchanged, for ten consecutive years, it might be difficult to justify an assertion today that dividends are expected to increase 10% per year for each of the next ten years. Such an assertion, if true, would dramatically lower the value of today's option grants. A healthy dose of realism is required in both making assumptions and in an outsider reviewing those same assumptions.

It should be recalled that the valuation of an option represents the best thinking at the time of the initial valuation. Changes in subsequent events neither change the value of the option for financial reporting purposes, nor necessarily prove that a mistake had been made. Good faith in making the original estimate is the proper standard. Assertions by management that can be supported will be accepted in any BSM valuation and should not be the basis for subsequent second guessing by any auditors or unhappy shareholders.

The subject of *expected volatility,* one of the key variables in option valuation, is complex, and we can only cover the highlights here. For the record, the estimate of volatility is the single greatest factor affecting the value of any option. Change the volatility assumption and you can dramatically change the value of the option.

Without getting overly technical, the FASB defines volatility as follows:

> *A measure of the amount by which a financial variable such as a share price has fluctuated (historical volatility) or is expected to fluctuate (expected volatility) during a period. Volatility also may be defined as a probability-weighted measure of the dispersion of returns about the mean. The volatility of a share price is the standard deviation of the continuously compounded rates of return on the share over a specified period. That is the same as the standard deviation of the differences in the natural logarithms of the stock prices plus dividends, if any, over the period. The higher the volatility, the more the returns on the shares can be expected to vary — up or down. Volatility is typically expressed in annualized terms.*[3]

In practice, what this means is that the more volatile a stock's price has been (or is going to be), the more valuable is an option on that stock at a particular price. The reason is simple: If a stock is essentially flat, trades in a very narrow range, why pay a premium to obtain an option on that security? If a stock has only moved between $26 and $28 over the last three years, there is a high degree of likelihood that it is unlikely to break out above $30 or below $24. The chances are that over the next three years it will stay between, say, $25 and $29. So how much would one pay to get an option on the stock at $27? You would not pay very much because you could probably buy the stock at that price just by going into the market—without having paid a premium for an option. Put another way, the price of such an option would be very low.

On the contrary, if a stock had fluctuated between $10 and $50 over the last three years, and the stock was today at $27, you could reasonably assume that during the next three years it could be both above $39 and below $15. Certainly, if you expected the stock to go down to $15, you would not buy an option at $27, but if you were uncertain as to the future price, there is probably an equal chance that the stock will be at both extremes over the next three years. One only has to look at the 52-week high and low for any stock in *The Wall Street Journal* to see that almost every stock fluctuates quite a lot, and some stocks fluctuate wildly. Thus for a volatile stock, an option at $27 has a good chance of being valuable if there is any reasonable possibility that the stock will be at or above $39 in the next three years.

As will be discussed later, inasmuch as expected volatility is the single biggest determination of option value, all other things being held constant, companies should spend as much time as necessary to provide a supportable estimate of this all-important variable. Keep in mind once again that the lower the estimate of volatility, the lower will be the value assigned to the option.

The final variable affecting option values is the *expected probability that options will vest and/or may be exercised early.* If 100 executives were to be given options tomorrow, with a four-year required vesting period (the employee must be working at the end of the fourth year to be able to exercise the options), it is highly likely that at least some of the individuals will no longer be with the company for the full four years. The FASB, in requiring options to be valued and expensed at grant date, permits companies to provide an allowance for the expected options that will never be exercised. The theory of expensing is that the cost of the options is spread over the vesting period to reflect the continuing employment, and related employment expense, of the option grantees. If a certain number of employees will not remain at the company long enough to exercise, then it is only fair not to charge that portion of the option grant to expense.

Furthermore, while financial theory suggests that individuals should hold their options and not exercise them until the termination (often ten years), in practice many people tend to exercise them early. An example would be where historical experience shows that when the market price today equals double the original exercise price, most holders choose to exercise. In practice this means that if options were granted at $27, exercise would be anticipated if the stock reached $54, even if the options still had several years to run. This combination of employees leaving before being vested and exercising at a suboptimal time can affect the determination of option values at grant date. The FASB clearly recognized this phenomenon and allowed for it.

SFAS 123R, in paragraph A16, states: "an entity shall develop reasonable and supportable estimates for the employee share option's expected term, taking into account both the contractual term of the option and the effects of employees' expected exercise and post-vesting employment termination behavior." It then goes on in paragraph A 21 to state:

> Historical experience is generally the starting point for developing expectations about the future. Expectations based on historical experience should be modified to reflect ways in which currently available information indicates that the future is reasonably expected to differ from the past. The appropriate weight to place on historical experience is a matter of judgment, based on relevant facts and circumstances.

What is critical about this statement, as it deals with vesting, option exercise, and volatility, is that it fully recognizes the importance of judgment—as long as it is reasonable and supportable.

VALUATION METHODOLOGY FOR STOCK OPTIONS

The actual valuation of a stock option, using the BSM model, is easy and straightforward, at least for what we can call plain vanilla options. Given values for the variables discussed previously, one can find a Black-Scholes calculator on the Internet, insert the values, and obtain the FV in no more than two seconds. A representative model can be found (as of late 2005) at:

www.numa.com/derivs/ref/calculat/option/calc-opa.htm

However, relying on a no-charge Internet site that may or may not be available next time you want to perform the calculation really represents poor internal control.

Some companies have written their own option valuation program, using Excel and inserting the BSM formula, which is readily available. We do not recommend this approach because commercially available software has an order of magnitude more flexibility. Such software can handle virtually any option feature that a consultant could dream up, is in effect guaranteed to be stable and auditable, and will certainly comply with any internal control requirements of Sarbanes-Oxley.

We have utilized FinTools® software (*www.fintools.com*), developed and supported by Montgomery Investment Technology, and found it to be very worthwhile at an almost nominal cost. The advantage of using such canned software is that the developers have already handled virtually every type of imaginable option; in addition, the program is totally stable. Option theory can be complex, and the formulas are sometimes difficult to follow, much less to program in Excel. Utilizing software that your audit firm has obtained and is familiar with will provide a degree of comfort that is well worth the small expenditure.

The FASB, while expressing support in SFAS 123R for the "lattice model," in contrast to BSM, certainly permits use of the latter, while encouraging the former. It then goes on to state that as financial theory develops in the field of option valuation, companies should be prepared to utilize whatever valuation method provides the best and most supportable methodology available at the time. As an example, use of the lattice option valuation model requires detailed assumptions about expected volatility at different points in time, different exercise patterns depending on the future stock price, and different patterns of price change over the ten-year time horizon.

In addition to the BSM and lattice models, many practitioners recommend use of the Monte Carlos simulation approach. This effectively generates a series of random numbers, which in turn project different assumed outcomes. By running the simulation for, say, 100,000 times, one can obtain a probability distribution that most valuation experts believe can be used for financial reporting. Going back to the discussion on software, few companies have the in-house resources to develop software that can run 100,000 iterations in less than two minutes. The Monte Carlo simulation is a powerful tool that when used properly will support valuation of options for financial reporting.

In summary, we strongly recommend that companies required to utilize SFAS 123R obtain commercially available software. This is not the place to try do-it-yourself valuation. Leave the software to the experts and concentrate management time on the supportability of the assumptions, something that cannot be outsourced.

DEVELOPING SUPPORTABLE ASSUMPTIONS
FOR THE VALUATION

The design of an optimum stock compensation plan is certainly outside the scope of this book, much less the author's expertise. We start with the assumption that the plan's outlines have been determined by management and approved by the firm's Board and shareholders. At that point it is necessary for the financial staff to develop reasonable and supportable assumptions basically about (1) the future expected volatility of the stock and (2) the exercise pattern expected for the option grantees. These two factors most affect the option value(s). How much the valuation will change, based on changes in these two variables, can be tested very quickly on commercial software such as FinTools®.

In SFAS 123R, the FASB suggests that the starting point for *estimating future volatility* is past volatility that actually occurred historically. The calculation of past volatility has been automated by FinTools, using historical prices of stocks shown in Yahoo® Finance. From the Fin-Tools menu, one accesses the historical prices and FinTools automatically calculates the actual volatility. A word of caution is necessary: The volatility calculation is only as valid as is the accuracy of the data on Yahoo. Even one wrong data point on Yahoo can dramatically affect the final calculation. So, for example, if the database incorrectly recorded a stock split, or missed a decimal point on one day's entry, the historical volatility calculation will be thrown off to a far greater degree than one would intuitively believe.

The FASB suggests that if you are going to value options with an expected life of six years, that you take the previous six years' history. In other words, you go back as far as you are looking forward. A six-year forward horizon requires obtaining six years of history. On the surface this makes sense because a six-year projection should be based on more than the most recent six days or even six months. So, if you are going to rely on this number, it would repay the effort to at least scan the Yahoo data points for the six-year period for reasonableness.

But how likely is the future to reflect the past? If one were looking back six years from 2006, one would pick up the sizable fluctuations in stock prices in the early years of the century. Now maybe those same fluctuations will repeat in the future, at some point, but if they do not, if the future does not mirror the past, it is likely that you will be overstating the option values, and hence the answer overstates reported expense.

A second approach to estimating volatility is to calculate the *implied volatility* of currently outstanding options. Publicly traded options are available for literally thousands of companies. Almost all large companies, and many small companies, can go directly to current quotes for outstanding options and calculate the volatility investors are currently expecting. This implied volatility takes the same variables as the option pricing model, but substitutes the current price and solves for the volatility. What is interesting is to see that even implied volatilities can be uncertain. If a company has options that expire for six different future periods (say one month out to one year), and each option expiration date has seven or eight different strike prices, then the volatility is going to differ among the various permutations and combinations of exercise price and expiration date. Exhibit 12.1 shows the implied volatility matrix for one company, Progressive Corp., on one day. The implied volatilities range from 17% to 23%, or a factor of almost one-third. A one-third change in the volatility assumption is going to affect an option calculation, albeit by less than one-third of the total value.

When we look at historical volatilities in Exhibit 12.2 (also for Progressive), we see why it is necessary to use judgment in deriving the amount to be used as the expected future variable. Exhibit 12.2 shows that if you use a ten-year perspective, you would have to utilize 33% volatility, whereas a four-year time horizon would require only a 21% volatility. Looking at each year by itself, we see a range from 17% to 56%. These are large changes. Would it make sense to use 56% volatility for pricing this year's options if they had a six-year time horizon? That happens to be the point in time with the highest volatility during the entire 11-year time frame. However, the most recent 17% volatility might not be considered totally representative inasmuch as it is the absolute lowest amount over the entire time frame.

Exhibit 12.1 Implied Volatility Matrix

Company:	Progressive Corp.	
Symbol:	PGR	
Underlying Price:	100.05	
Date:	21-Sep-05	
Time:	2:41:00 PM (ET)	

Model:	99.5 Binomial
Dividend Amount:	0.03
Ex-Dividend Date:	07-Dec-05
Days to Dividend:	77
Dividend Period:	91

Implied Volatility Averages

Overall:	19.40%
Calls:	19.69%
Puts:	19.11%
Long-Dated:	19.40%

Implied Volatility Matrix

Expiration	Calls				Puts			
	21-Oct-05	18-Nov-05	17-Feb-06	19-May-06	21-Oct-05	18-Nov-05	17-Feb-06	19-May-06
Days	30	58	149	240	30	58	149	240
In-the-Money	22.99%	21.73%	21.14%	20.79%	16.79%	16.83%	17.81%	18.18%
Near-the-Money	19.30%	18.88%	19.61%	19.69%	18.96%	18.41%	19.13%	19.04%
Out-of-the-Money	17.69%	17.32%	18.38%	18.72%	22.52%	21.14%	20.45%	20.01%
Average	19.99%	19.31%	19.71%	19.73%	19.42%	18.79%	19.13%	19.08%

Source of Data

Stock and Option Prices:	www.cboe.com
Interest Rates:	www.bloomberg.com
Dividend Info:	www.esignal.com

Updates may be required to IVM contingent upon changes in the source data format.

Implied volatility calculations are provided by Montgomery Investment Technology, Inc. based on the information provided by the CBOE, eSignal and Bloomberg.

The calculations are for informational purposes only, and are not intended for trading and valuation purposes. Verification of the data validity is incumbent upon the user. Montgomery Investment Technology, Inc. shall not be liable for any errors in the content, or for any actions taken in reliance thereon.

Source: Used with permission. Copyright © Montgomery Investment Technology, Inc.

Exhibit 12.2   Historical Volatility Matrix

Company	Progressive Corp.
Symbol	PGR
Data Type	Adjusted Close
Data Frequency	52 Weekly
Target Date	19-Sep-05
EWMA Weight	0.999

Historical Volatility Matrix

Start Date	End Date	Annual	Time	Horizon	EWMA
19-Sep-04	19-Sep-05	16.92%	1	16.92%	16.70%
19-Sep-03	19-Sep-04	19.03%	2	17.96%	17.81%
19-Sep-02	19-Sep-03	25.04%	3	20.54%	19.83%
19-Sep-01	19-Sep-02	21.29%	4	20.69%	20.09%
19-Sep-00	19-Sep-01	45.81%	5	27.96%	24.50%
19-Sep-99	19-Sep-00	55.70%	6	34.13%	28.36%
19-Sep-98	19-Sep-99	44.04%	7	36.00%	29.63%
19-Sep-97	19-Sep-98	28.40%	8	35.09%	29.57%
19-Sep-96	19-Sep-97	29.95%	9	34.57%	29.58%
19-Sep-95	19-Sep-96	21.52%	10	33.47%	29.40%
19-Sep-94	19-Sep-95	21.85%	11	32.58%	29.27%

Source of Data

Stock Prices: *finance.yahoo.com*

Updates may be required to the HVM contingent upon changes in the source data format.

Historical volatility calculations are provided by Montgomery Investment Technology, Inc. based on the information provided by Yahoo! Inc. and Commodity Systems, Inc. (CSI). The calculations are for informational purposes only, and are not intended for trading and valuation purposes. Verification of the data validity is incumbent upon the user.

Montgomery Investment Technology, Inc. shall not be liable for any errors in the content, or for any actions taken in reliance thereon.

Source: Used with permission. Copyright © Montgomery Investment Technology, Inc.

The point is that the choice of expected volatility really requires top management input and should not be left to either a lower-level company employee or even to an independent valuation specialist. In this case, to modify a familiar aphorism, "the choice of a volatility estimate is too important to leave to the appraiser." Some companies that are publicly traded and all privately held companies cannot look to outstanding traded options for calculating implied or historical volatility. There is a solution.

It is possible to identify *other* publicly traded firms, in the same industry or with similar economic characteristics, that do have outstanding publicly traded options. It is not only feasible to use these "comps," but it would actually be desirable in some cases. The publicly traded options of these comps represent the consensus estimate of all market participants; in other words, exactly what the FASB is looking for.

Even a calculation of implied volatilities for one month to one year (up to $2\frac{1}{2}$ years for so-called LEAPS—long-term options) is going to be a shorter period than is needed for most ESO calculations. Realistically, the choice of an implied volatility (one estimate for BSM, and perhaps multiple estimates for lattice model and Monte Carlo simulations) is going to be a matter of judgment. The judgment will involve looking at history, looking at implied volatilities, and then deciding whether the future will look similar to the past or different from the past.

An assumption essentially to disregard historical volatilities will require fairly strong reasoning to demonstrate just what happened in the past that is not likely to be repeated. This assumes that historical volatilities are high and the company wishes to use a lower estimate. Without coming up with a definitive list of such factors, just as an example, if the firm had been involved in a merger, and stock prices tend to be more volatile in such a situation, one could reasonably argue that there is a low probability of a merger in the future. If there were one, then the options might be modified because it would be a different company. Once again, it is our experience that reasonable assumptions will be accepted by auditors and the SEC, whereas unreasonable assumptions chosen to arrive at a certain answer are not going to be accepted easily.

Estimating expected life involves the same use of past and anticipated future results. Many companies may not have kept detailed records of exactly which option grantee has exercised his or her options when and at what the then-current price was. This information, however, is critical in supporting an estimate of the expected life of the option. Remember that while options are often granted with a ten-year expiration, experience suggests that by and large they are exercised far earlier.

Reasons for this might include one's personal financial situation (think college tuition), gift or estate taxes, or a plan to leave the company before the ten-year period.

The FASB recognizes this tendency, and in fact encourages companies to utilize an appropriate exercise assumption. Using a ten-year life for an option, when on balance they will have an average outstanding life of six years, would significantly overvalue the options. The FASB permits, even urges, companies to develop supportable expected lives.

One comment must be made at this point. There are obviously several differences between ESOs and publicly traded options: (1) the term, 10 years versus $2\frac{1}{2}$ years; (2) they are lost if the employee leaves before the vesting period; and (3) ESOs are not marketable. They can be held by the employee and exercised upon completion of the vesting period. The options cannot be sold, traded, or otherwise exchanged for value. In short, they are nonmarketable.

It is a fundamental principle of valuation theory that an asset with a limited market is worth less than one with a fully open and competitive market. An asset with no market may be worth very little, unless there is a chance that the limitation(s) will be removed at some point in the future; an example would be an environmentally sensitive land parcel that can not be rezoned for alternative use until it is cleaned up. If the environmental problems are remediated, then the land can have value, particularly after a rezoning.

The reason for bringing up land, in a discussion of ESOs, is that during the vesting period the options essentially have zero value to the participant, other than the *potential* for future value. The employee has to keep working through the vesting period, *and* the price of the stock has to increase over the exercise price. From the perspective of the company, which is what the FASB took in SFAS 123R, the option is an expense to the shareholders; that expense is ratably charged to profit and loss (P&L) over the vesting period based on the initial grant-date valuation.

Again, looking at the option from the perspective of the executive who received it, such an ESO is worth markedly less than a freely traded option. Even after the vesting period expires, and option theory says the option has value because of the time value of money, holders only have one choice—to exercise the option or not. If they exercise, they lose the remaining time value of the option. If they do not exercise, they risk having the market price of the stock decline.

The one thing they can *not* do is sell the option, at its then-current theoretical value, to a third-party investor. Options quoted on the Internet or by a broker such as Merrill Lynch can be sold at a moment's notice and the then-current value captured. An employee holding a similar option (expiration date and exercise price) can only sit on the sidelines and watch the market move.

When we value ESOs for individuals, say for estate tax or for gift to a Family Limited Partnership, we definitely consider this lack of marketability in determining the tax attributes of the transaction. For ESOs, from the issuing company's perspective, this lack of marketability is assumed to be irrelevant because of the FASB's "generosity" in letting options be valued on the expected exercise date rather than at the end of the option period, say ten years. The FASB argues in its Statement that allowing this shorter time period reflects the real FV, but we disagree. The real exercise period is calculated based on expectations about actual behavior, supported usually by past experience. If we are already valuing the option based on an accurate estimate of when it will actually be exercised, where is the allowance for the lack of marketability to the participant? There is none.

The answer to this conundrum is simple. Any ESO is going to have less value to the grantee than it creates expense to the company. Because financial statements are prepared by, and relate to, the company, the FASB's position is understandable. Most holders of options, however, look at the value of options from their personal financial position. It is absolutely clear that an ESO, with its many restrictions, is worth less to an individual than is the amount of expense that the company reflects on its books.

CONCLUSION

Employee Stock Options have value to employees, and their granting by a company triggers expense. SFAS 123R requires calculation of the option value, and a charge to P&L of that value over the vesting period of the employee.

There are six variables utilized in virtually all approved and accepted option pricing models. Four of them are straightforward and depend solely on the plan design and the date the options are granted. Two variables, however, must be estimated by management, and the values assigned for those two variables will significantly affect the value(s) developed by any of the option pricing models. These variables are the expected volatility of the stock price in the future and the anticipated period before the options are actually exercised. The lower the expected volatility and the shorter the time frame, the lower will be the values assigned to the options.

While the FASB provides some guidelines to management in estimating these two variables, we cannot stress too much the necessity for top-management involvement in this part of the valuation process. A change in the nominal amounts for the two variables, both in the same direction, could easily double, or halve, the option expense.

We strongly recommend the use of a commercial option pricing system, one that can perform what-if exercises and can test alternative valuation models. As discussed in the next chapter on auditing of valuations by independent auditors, and review of their work by the SEC and PCAOB, it behooves management to devote sufficient time and resources to options to ensure that everything done is totally supportable.

ENDNOTES

1. We cannot conceivably cover all of the variations in option grants and restrictions. There are consulting firms that specialize in designing option programs for companies; essentially no two plans are identical. The valuation issues of these unique elements are beyond the scope of this chapter. They are all susceptible to estimation and hence valuation.
2. In this chapter we are deliberately excluding consideration of the taxation, and tax consequences, of ESOs. There are two types, qualified and nonqualified, with different tax treatments. Readers should discuss tax issues of ESO with a qualified tax professional.
3. SFAS 123R Financial Accounting Standards Board, Norwalk, CT 2004, p. 281.

CHAPTER 13

Auditing of Valuation Reports and Selecting an Appraiser

B efore the passage of the Sarbanes-Oxley Act (S-Ox), valuation reports, particularly for use in financial statements, were reviewed by auditors. Their procedures were similar to those used to verify virtually everything else they looked at. The purpose was to develop a professional opinion that the clients' financial statements properly reflected the underlying economics and were prepared in accordance with Generally Accepted Accounting Principles (GAAP).

When S-Ox was adopted, it made two significant changes in terms of valuation. First, of interest to independent valuation firms, S-Ox absolutely prohibited auditors from developing valuation information for their audit clients. At one stroke this opened up a lot of new business for valuation firms. The following true anecdote, which is totally accurate, will reveal the depth of the problem that independent valuation specialists had been facing:

> A large publicly traded company had made a major purchase as a business combination and required a valuation, as discussed throughout this book. The valuation firm called on the prospective client, for whom it had previously performed valuation assignments. Discussion with the Chief Financial Officer elicited all the information necessary to prepare a thorough proposal. The pricing on the proposal was competitive because the valuation firm at that moment needed additional work to keep its professional staff busy.
>
> *(continues)*

About a week later, the CFO called with the bad news that the company had awarded the valuation assignment to its auditing firm, this being prior to S-Ox. We asked what had happened since we had been optimistic about our chances. Fortunately, we were dealing with an individual who told it like it is. He said that the auditing firm had submitted a proposal that had a higher fee than ours. When informed of that, the audit partner told the CFO, "We will match their fee, and if you give us the assignment the audit will go a lot easier." In those days it would have taken a very strong CFO to turn down an offer that couldn't be refused, so he accepted and gave us the bad news.

Our CEO at the time called up the auditing firm's CEO and relayed the story. The immediate response was, "We would never do anything like that." But our firm asked him to check and see if our story was correct. Two weeks later, the auditing firm CEO called back and sheepishly admitted that "Yes, it did happen that way, but it will never happen again!"

About two months later, at a different office of the same Big 4 auditing firm, the identical situation arose. By that point we had simply resigned ourselves to the fact that the major accounting firms were now major competitors, so we just carried on and fought every single opportunity one at a time.

However, not willing to give up without one further struggle, we made an effort and obtained a meeting with one of the five Securities and Exchange Commission (SEC) commissioners. We relayed the then-current competitive condition and the fact that the auditors were auditing their own valuation work. I will never forget this Commissioner's response: "It's probably wrong, but there is nothing we at the SEC can do [this was prior to Enron, WorldCom, etc.]. One of these days this practice may backfire on an accounting firm, they will be taken to court, and then will have to reconsider the conflict of interest in performing a valuation and then auditing their own work."

The Commissioner's comment came before Enron sank Arthur Andersen, and without going into details, one could make a good case that the heart of Enron's problems revolved around its use of Fair Value (FV) accounting on derivatives. In fact, it appears that Andersen either helped with those valuations or never challenged Enron's unreasonable assumptions supposedly supporting the valuation of derivatives that were 20 years out into the future.

Subsequent to the meeting with the SEC mentioned previously, and before the collapse of Enron, the American Institute of Certified Public Accountants (AICPA) set up a group that it called the Independence Standards Board (ISB), made up of the heads of most of the then Big 5, plus a couple of outside neutral members. We attended the meetings of the ISB and were even more discouraged about precluding the obvious conflict of interest in having someone audit their own work. The author remarked at the time to more than one colleague, "The words 'conflict of interest' do not appear in the vocabulary of any Big 5 audit partner."

The ISB seemed to be going down the path of business as usual, permitting audit firms to perform valuation work for their audit clients when something started to change. Lo and behold, the ISB staff came up with a draft Standard that explicitly would have precluded the inherent conflict of auditors auditing their own valuation work. We in the independent valuation side of the business were ecstatic that change was about to happen. In fact, the ISB issued a draft Standard, and it appeared there were going to be enough votes to get it approved. Out of the blue, the then SEC commissioners decided that maybe the SEC should be involved in this issue rather than the AICPA, which was the professional lobbying group for the public accounting profession. So, just as the new Standard was about to be put into effect, it was totally suspended. Independent appraisers were downcast again.

But then the SEC decided to hold public hearings on the subject.

Among those testifying was the author, and the heads of the major accounting firms, including the CEO of Andersen, who later took the fall for the Enron debacle. With almost a unanimous voice, the accounting firms defended their involvement

(continues)

in consulting (including valuation) for their audit clients. As one, they each stated "We can do a *better* job of auditing because by consulting with them we get to know their business better!" During the course of the hearings, an academic pointed out his study showed that auditing firms performed consulting work (including valuation) for perhaps 25% of their audit clients.

The next Big 5 partner to testify before the very imposing bank of commissioners sitting up on the dais, with the testifiers down below looking up, was, if memory serves, from Andersen. In any event, after presenting the litany about how consulting helped the audit process, one of the commissioners gently asked, "Well, if you consult with 25% of your clients and can do a better job of auditing with them, what does that say about your audits of the other 75%? You mean you can't do as good a job?" That was the end of the "consulting helps auditing" argument!

The SEC did issue pronouncements dealing with auditors performing certain consulting assignments for audit clients, but the impression many observers had that rather than abiding by the spirit of the rules, many auditors chose to take the Commission's words literally and parse every clause. So, while independent valuation specialists were better off than before, there was still major competition from audit firms for work with their clients.

BE CAREFUL WHAT YOU ASK FOR!

Very shortly after the SEC had issued regulations dealing with auditor independence, the dam broke on corporate malfeasance. The scandals with Enron, Adelphia, WorldCom, HealthSouth, and the others were so dramatic, and so costly to employees and shareholders, that Congress acted. The result was Sarbanes-Oxley, and many in the valuation profession wonder if the cure has now been worse than the disease.

First, and helpful, was that the SEC's strictures against conflict of interest (i.e., that auditors cannot perform valuation work for their audit clients) were enshrined into statute. It is crystal clear that for an audit firm to provide FV information for incorporation into the client's financial statements, statements that the auditor will opine on, is illegal. That message has come through loud and clear to audit firms of all size. Without exception, auditors have toed the line on conflicts involving determination of FV for their audit clients.

The price that we all are paying, and all includes valuation specialists, auditors, and SEC registrant companies, is that the Public Company Accounting Oversight Board (PCAOB) has come into existence. The PCAOB has a legislated mandate to ensure that auditors are following the spirit and letter of independence and that the auditors are truly scrutinizing representations made by management. Auditors are now truly independent and have the PCAOB looking over their shoulders all the time to ensure this happens 100% of the time. Furthermore, companies are required to have complex and elaborate internal control systems that they must certify they have. And to top it off, the audit firms have to certify that management's representations about their internal control are correct. The only way to do this, to provide assurance, is to perform a lot more audit work than they ever did in the past.

Because audit firms charge by the hour for every individual engaged on an assignment, a 40% increase in man-hours translates into a proportionate 40% increase in audit fees. Companies must pay this audit fee or face not being in compliance with S-OX, which is a legal obligation if the company's stock is publicly traded or it has publicly held debt outstanding.

The result? Auditors are putting in more time and companies are paying more. Are financial statements any better? Are there fewer horror cases? Each reader will have to make that judgment, but as this book is being written (October 2005), the business press is full of news about a $430 million problem at a brokerage firm, Refco. "Where were the auditors? How could this have happened?" These phrases are already coming from the mouths of politicians. Readers should keep in mind that the SEC got its start in the 1930s because of horror cases like Ivar Kreuger and McKesson & Robbins. With all the laws, all the regulations, all the internal control systems, and all the testing of those systems in the last 70 years, people are still cheating and trying to hide that cheating.

Now let's put the S-Ox requirements into the perspective of this book. Appraisal techniques and methodology have not changed. We are doing the same kind of valuations with the same tools and the same assumptions that have been used for the last 25 or more years. S-Ox could not, and did not, change how appraisers do their jobs. As noted earlier in the book, there are three approaches to value (i.e., cost, income, and market), and those approaches were used in 1935, in 1955, in 1975, in 1995, and they are still being used in 2005. Neither Congress nor the SEC can develop anything new in terms of how to determine FV for financial reporting.

What has changed is the scrutiny that auditors are placing on the valuation reports prepared by appraisers. Before about 2002, auditors did review appraisal reports prepared by other than their own firms. Often the review was rather cursory, particularly if the report had been prepared and signed by a larger, well-known, and well-regarded firm of valuation professionals.

Later in the chapter we discuss how companies can choose and auditors recommend a valuation firm for a specific assignment. Here let it be said that there are literally thousands of individuals who print up business cards proclaiming they are appraisers or valuation specialists. Other than for certain real estate appraisals, where one must be licensed by a state, there are no prohibitions against anyone calling themselves an appraiser. Consequently, over the course of years, auditors see valuation reports from many different sources. The consensus is that there is a very wide range of expertise.

As a self-serving generalization, the large national valuation firms do very good work, and a number of smaller firms are also fully qualified. That leaves many small appraisal practitioners who may not have the experience or background to perform up to the standards required by the SEC for registrants. Thus any review of a valuation report first involves a determination by the auditor as to who is doing the work and what are their qualifications and background. Before S-Ox, after seeing who had done the valuation, if necessary the auditor would actually review the work in detail.

What changed with S-Ox is that the auditors for the Big 4, who audit the vast majority of larger publicly traded registrants, are now reviewing *every* appraisal report in detail irrespective of who did the work. Lest the reader think this is a trivial exercise, there are now numerous situations where the audit firm bills its clients more for reviewing someone else's appraisal than the valuation firm billed in the first place! Put a different way, the cost of valuations, subsequent to S-Ox, has in many cases more than doubled.

Just as physicians are accused of ordering "unnecessary" tests just to protect themselves against a possible lawsuit, so many appraisers are doing more work for the initial assignment than they ever did before. Readers must understand that this additional work effort, both for the initial report and for the subsequent audit review, does *not* produce any better or different answers. The values are the same. Only the *cost* of obtaining those values has gone up. Why has this happened? The favorable answer is that with the PCAOB looking over their shoulder to assure the highest possible quality audits, auditors are being extra-careful and asking their client to justify every assertion. These assertions include determinations of FV, whether originally made by a valuation consultant or developed internally by the client. So the audit profession justifies its extra billable time by explaining that it is required by S-Ox.

A less favorable answer as to why valuation costs have gone up, what might be called the cynical interpretation, is directly related to billable time. Auditors, like most consultants, keep close track of their time. Personal performance is measured by the amount of billable time to be charged to clients. Thus each individual on the consulting firm's professional staff is motivated, and incentivised through pay and bonus, to charge just as much as possible to clients.

Recall that when S-Ox came into effect, audit firms could no longer perform valuation work for audit clients. Furthermore, because the audit firms had never perceived there was a conflict of interest, they had aggressively been seeking, and winning, valuation assignments from audit clients. The valuation practices of the major audit firms were substantial, and in fact larger than all but one of the independent appraisal companies. Inasmuch as a very large percentage of the work performed by the valuation practice of the audit firms was related to audit client work, the S-Ox ban really affected the major accounting firms, at least with respect to the valuation staff. All of a sudden the work was not coming in over the transom; in fact, it was not coming in at all because for the most part Big 5 valuation practices had little, if any, business development (read sales) resources. After all, the audit partners had been telling the CFOs and controllers it was best to use their own firm to do the work, had given the name and phone number of the valuation consultants in their firm to the client, and the audit firms' valuation practitioners merely had to answer the phone. It was nice work if you could get it.

All of a sudden the accounting firms' valuation practices, with very large professional staffs, were faced with a substantial drop in volume. Keep in mind that there was just as much valuation work to be performed as before, it was just that all valuation work was now up for grabs, and the Big 5 were no longer perceived as preferred providers. Several of the accounting firms spun off their consulting practices, including valuation, into independent entities. Other firms retained their valuation practice but were forced to downsize. In the latter case, it turned out that two major firms developed reciprocal relationships, whereby Firm A recommended to their clients that they use Firm B's appraisers; in exchange, Firm B's audit partners recommended their clients use Firm A's appraisers. Even so, within a short period following implementation of S-Ox, there were about twice as many valuation firms as there had been before, now all going after the same business. There was more work (less tied to audit firms' own valuation practice) and more competitors.

Then the proverbial light bulb suddenly turned on. The major audit firms had an epiphany. Under the watchful eye of the PCAOB, and in full accordance with S-Ox's requirements, the auditors and their valuation professionals came to a marvelous conclusion. They realized the solution to reduced sales expectations was going to be that they had to review the work content of any and every valuation report relied upon by the audit client.

AUDITOR REVIEW OF VALUATION REPORTS

As indicated previously, we have now reached the situation, ridiculous as it may seem, where the same valuation requirement is being met twofold. The independent valuation firm performs the work for the client, and then the auditor's valuation staff, in the guise of review, effectively does the work over again. Who pays for this double effort? The client firm whose financial statements require FV information and whose statements must have the "seal of approval" conferred by the audit certificate. If the auditor refuses to certify the statements without redoing the valuation, what can the client do?

At one level, in the short term at least, a company is at the mercy of its accounting firm. Because most companies are usually pushing the SEC deadline for filing quarterly and annual statements, if an audit firm says two weeks before the deadline, "Sorry, we have to redo the valuation," there is little the company can say but "Okay, do it."

At the next level, however, the company hires the audit firm, not the other way around. If an audit firm is charging too much, particularly by performing what are perceived to be unnecessary tests, the ultimate sanction is to change auditors. Certainly there is a middle ground, which is usually the first attempt, and that is to have a frank discussion with the audit partner, laying out the client's unhappiness.

With reference to auditing of a specific valuation report, for example for an allocation of purchase price, we have found that one way to cut down on review and hence costs is to have a preliminary meeting with the client, the auditor, and the valuation firm. Some auditors do not want to do this, arguing that they would lose their independence by participating in such a discussion. We respond that we, as valuation specialists, are not asking the audit firm what to do or how to do it. Rather, we are telling them what we will do and how we will do it. Then we ask them if they have any difficulty with our approach. Usually they will tell us, "The approach looks fine, but we will have to wait and see the results."

Discussing with the auditor in advance just what we are going to do and how we are going to do it solves one problem, but leaves a second issue unresolved. What is resolved, and what could arise if this step is *not* undertaken, is a comment by the auditor after the valuation work has been completed, "Why didn't you think of this?" The "this" can be anything—ranging from the use of specific comparables to the choice of a discount rate to the financial projections. The more detailed is the initial workplan discussed with the client and the auditor, the fewer are such issues likely to be raised at the end. Keep in mind if an appraiser has to go back and redo something, or do something new not included in the original scope of work, that there is now extra nonproductive time to get out the working papers and get up to speed on the specific question that has to be answered.

Laying out a detailed workplan with the client and auditor is the best preventive medicine we know. However, it does not solve all the potential problems. As will be discussed in the next section of this chapter, *every* valuation involves professional judgment. A review appraiser working for an audit firm, if he wants to challenge a valuation report, can *always* find something to question. And some of the items challenged cannot be proved by the appraiser because it was, and remains, a matter of professional judgment.

Such conflicts between an independent valuation specialist and an audit firm's review appraiser *should not be allowed to escalate*. This means that at the first sign of a major disagreement between two valuation specialists, the client should be brought into the discussion. The client is going to be paying for the time of each of the two professionals to argue with each other. Often the difference of opinion is simply a matter of professional judgment. For example, the first appraiser thinks a 14% discount rate is appropriate while the auditor reviewing the report says, "No, I think 16% is a better discount rate." Neither is right and probably neither is wrong.

The client must ultimately choose one of the two assumptions and prepare its financial statements accordingly. Keep in mind that financial statements are *always* the responsibility of the company, not of the appraiser *or* the auditor. The client has to say, "I am going to use the independent appraiser's 14% assumption. Period." Then the auditor can, in theory, say that it will not sign the opinion. In practice this rarely happens because it is as hard for the audit firm's valuation specialist to prove his 16% discount rate is correct any more than the independent appraiser can prove his 14% rate is correct. When a difference of opinion is just that, opinion, it is unlikely that an auditor can refuse to sign an opinion. At least we have only seen it happen once.

We had a case where the auditor of a Fortune 500 firm was so recalcitrant on the assumptions going into the valuation related to a specific accounting issue that the client, forced to accept the auditor's assumptions, changed audit firms the next year. The fight over the valuation was, literally, the reason for making the change because the client thought the auditors were wrong and unreasonable. Fortunately, this is a fairly infrequent occurrence. In the next section we look at why it is so likely that an aggressive auditor, either trying to score a point or to run up billable hours, can always challenge what appear to be quite reasonable valuation assumptions.

EVERY APPRAISAL HAS AT LEAST ONE KEY ASSUMPTION

As stated in the Preface, valuation is an art, not a science. There are no formulas, no computers, and no rules of thumb that will provide FV information. The appraiser given a valuation assignment will draw on standard definitions of value, determine the correct premise of value (i.e., value for continued use or value for sale), research the relevant market, and apply the appropriate valuation methodologies. The latter, valuation methodologies (i.e., cost, income, and market), in turn require assumptions about past and future events. Past events have to be analyzed to adjust for unusual and nonrecurring events. In turn this adjusted historical information becomes the starting point for evaluating future events. Finally, in evaluating the future, one can take an optimistic perspective, a pessimistic perspective, or try to be totally neutral.

With all these factors that have to be considered, it is no wonder that after an appraiser has determined his own best estimate of FV, that someone else (an auditor) can come along and challenge any or all of the above factors. We saw that in the case of a divorce, two appraisers can and will come to diametrically opposite conclusions, based on their respective outlooks for the business's potential growth and profitability.

The best possible valuation report will show where the appraiser obtained his information and will provide support for all the key assumptions. While appraisal reports do not usually provide footnote support, as does a typical academic study, nonetheless the appraiser ought, whenever possible, to validate all of the statements and assumptions.

As the British say, "at the end of the day," there will *always* be at least one (and often more) key assumptions that are based solely on the professional judgment of the appraiser. Not only is this to be expected, but it represents the essence of professional judgment. Let's look at two other examples of professional judgment.

Assume a victim of an auto accident goes to a plaintiff's attorney and is told, "I think you have a good case, I will take it on for 40% of the judgment. I believe we can win $200,000." Does this mean the jury will decide in favor of the plaintiff and award exactly $200,000? Of course not; the attorney was providing his client with his best professional judgment, but there was no guarantee, no certainty of outcome. Could a different attorney, say the defendant's, come to an opposite conclusion? Probably yes, and he would tell his insurance company client, "I think we can prevail. There are some weaknesses in the plaintiff's case." Can either of those statements be *audited* by a skeptical observer? No, because in each case the attorneys were utilizing professional judgment.

Assume this time that a wife brings her 60-year-old husband to the emergency ward because the man is complaining of severe pain in the belly. After reviewing lab tests and possibly an X-ray, the physician tells the wife, "I think your husband has appendicitis and we should operate. I will call the surgeon and schedule the operation." The couple can either agree with the doctor or ask for a second opinion. A second doctor may examine the man, look at the films and lab results, and say, "Well, it could be appendicitis, but I think it is just severe indigestion, caused by an infection and I recommend rest and antibiotics." Can the wife prove either physician is correct? Yes, she can authorize the operation and that will tell. However, an unnecessary operation can have severe negative consequences. Of course by waiting, the appendix may rupture, causing even more problems. In this medical example, as in the legal example, qualified professionals come to opposite conclusions. The third party who has to make a decision is really going to be torn as to which way to go. In each situation someone has to make a decision and live with the consequences.

Now let's get back to the valuation profession. In a business combination, an appraiser may say, "I think the customer relationship has little value because competitors are constantly undercutting the price, and this is a price-sensitive market." The appraiser therefore puts a low value on that particular intangible. Then an auditor comes along with a checklist prepared by his national office, which in turn is based on an AICPA *Toolkit for Auditors* that deals with auditing FV measurements and disclosures. The audit firm's checklist says that customer relationships have to be measured in such and such a way. In this case the original independent valuation specialist did not utilize the approach called for in the checklist because in his professional judgment specific factors suggested a different approach was preferable.

Lest the reader think the example is hypothetical, it is not. Just as with the legal and medical examples, different professionals come to different answers. In the case of the valuation dealing with the business combination, it is easy to see how the appraiser and the auditor can spend a lot of time, and time is money, arguing the issue(s). All the while, two separate meters are ticking for the mutual client.

The author has never seen an appraisal report that does not contain at least one critical assumption, an assumption that cannot be proved. Put a different way, someone can *always* challenge the value indication contained in any appraisal report. The auditor will never be able to prove he is right and the appraiser is wrong; similarly, the appraiser cannot prove he is right and the auditor is wrong. This section was headed "every appraisal report has one key assumption"; that statement is 100% accurate, and the unfortunate corollary is that any auditor can always challenge an appraisal report, and by doing so he commits the client to paying in some cases significant additional professional fees.

There is no perfect solution for this conundrum, but experience suggests that there are opportunities to minimize the cost of any professional disagreement. The first, discussed previously, is for the client's valuation professional to discuss in a mutual meeting with the auditor what is going to be done, why it will be done that way, and what key assumptions will be utilized. While not requiring the auditor to sign off in advance, this communication at least puts the auditor on notice, and he cannot come back later and say, "I disagree with your approach and assumptions."

The second step a company can take is to instruct its appraiser to respond only to written inquiries from the audit firm. Too often an auditor will call up the appraiser, ask some questions, and in effect open the gates to challenges on any and every aspect of the report. Had the inquiries been written, this would have the effect of focusing the auditor's thought process on the truly important issue(s) and not go chasing down some "bunny trails." Putting questions in writing simplifies the appraiser's time and effort in responding.

The third and final step that must be taken if there is still a disagreement, and hopefully before both sides have dug in their heels, is to have the client, the company whose statements are being prepared, obtain the arguments on either side, and then the client must make a decision. Usually the issue of contention between the appraiser and the auditor is totally immaterial to the overall financial statements, albeit it may be material to the valuation.

Assuming the impact of adopting one side or the other does not affect materiality, as discussed by the SEC in its Staff Accounting Bulletins, then the client simply prepares its financial statements. The company has to let the auditor make his own judgment on the overall fairness of the financials. It will be highly unlikely the audit firm will withhold its signature over a disagreement between two equally competent professionals who happen to disagree.

Lawyers disagree and cases go to court. Physicians disagree and the patient goes into surgery or not. Appraisers disagree and the financial statements may differ by a penny a share. In the overall scheme of things, differences about FV rarely rise to the level of true materiality. Having said that, it does appear that many of the problems at Enron were caused by faulty valuations, but in that situation the company did the valuations and the auditors (Arthur Andersen) did *not* challenge the assumptions when they should have. With that and possibly a few other unusual situations, we come to our conclusion: *Valuations required by GAAP do not influence the actual operations or true profitability of the company.*

We now change the subject for a final word on selecting an appraiser.

HOW TO CHOOSE AN APPRAISER

The reader should always keep in mind that no law or regulation requires that an appraiser be hired to determine the FV of any asset or liability. While by law companies must have their statements certified by an independent accountant (auditor), there is no corresponding requirement for valuations. Companies can perform their own valuations, and as long as their auditor agrees with the answer, the issue is closed. This flows from the fact that financial statements are those of management; even if the company hires a valuation specialist, the final numbers appearing in the balance sheet and income statement are still management's responsibility. Management is entitled to rely on an appraiser, but as we saw earlier, an auditor can and probably will challenge a valuation specialist.

In most situations auditors will not insist on an outside valuation specialist as long as the FV information is immaterial. In testing for impairment of goodwill, for example, if the FV of a reporting unit is estimated by management at $100 million, and the book value is $40 million, there would be no possible goodwill impairment. Why should the company hire an appraiser to come up with a more precise valuation of the reporting unit? The true FV would have to be below $40 million, and it is highly unlikely that someone on the company's financial staff could be so far wrong. Alternatively, if management estimates the FV of the reporting unit at $45 million, it would take only a small error in the estimate to require going to Phase 2 of the impairment procedure. In that case an auditor might well ask the company to obtain an independent valuation of the reporting unit. Management has an incentive not to report an impairment charge, and the auditor wants assurance that overly optimistic assumptions are not being made simply to preclude a possible impairment.

Our experience, and that of most other appraisers, is that managements by and large are fully capable of performing simple valuations. Even complex valuations can and should be performed by the company as long as the answer is going to be immaterial no matter how it comes out. This, however, leaves a lot of valuation work for independent valuation specialists, and we estimate there is currently over $1 billion of work performed annually by appraisers and appraisal firms. As FV becomes increasingly common in financial reporting, the need for appraisers to develop and support the values is only going to increase. So, the question is how should management select an appraiser or an appraisal firm? The easy answer, but *not* one we are necessarily proposing, is to contact the author!

Our experience suggests that perhaps 20% to 30% of the time, we are called in by a client and asked to do the work on a noncompetitive basis. This usually happens when we have done prior work for that client and they have been satisfied. The remaining 70% to 80% of the time, companies will solicit proposals from two or more valuation firms.

OBTAINING AND EVALUATING PROPOSALS FOR VALUATION

Having been on the receiving end of innumerable Requests for Proposals (RFPs), we have some fairly strong ideas on the subject. The following information ideally should be in every RFP:

- Asset(s) or liability(ies) to be valued, including the scope of the work
- Valuation date
- Due date for the report, including any early date for preliminary indications of value

- Description of the information currently available from the client

In turn, an ideal reply from a valuation firm, in responding to an RFP, would include:

- Commitment that the work can be performed by the firm and that the due date can be met

- An indication of the firm's experience and expertise in the type of valuation required

- A listing of the key professionals who would be assigned to the engagement, with their professional experience

- A brief summary of the valuation approach(es) proposed to be utilized by the appraisal firm

- A fairly detailed summary of how the valuation firm will value each asset category (i.e., land, buildings, machinery and equipment, intangibles)

- The proposed fee

We discuss each of these points from the perspective of a CFO who will make a choice among respondents to the RFP.

In today's environment, valuation service firms can usually provide preliminary indications of value within two to three weeks. There is a substantial difference between such a preliminary value indication and a completed valuation report. Nonetheless, competent and experienced firms, and their professional staff, have had sufficient experience in all types of valuations that close approximations can be developed rapidly. These value indications cannot be audited, but in terms of management judgment, and choice of a course of action, such preliminary values will turn out to be highly reliable. Thus if the client is interested in a rapid response, this should be included in the RFP. A responsive valuation firm should indicate what time commitment it can meet.

Clients are always interested in the experience that a valuation firm or a specific professional appraiser has had. There is an assumption that if the appraiser has valued three auto dealers that he should be able to value another dealership. That assumption is true. However, the converse is not true. Just because an appraiser has *not* valued a comparable firm does not indicate whether he can do the work. The fact is that an experienced valuation consultant should be able to value almost any type of property. This does not mean you should hire a real estate appraiser to evaluate machinery and equipment or a financial appraiser to value real estate.

There are four major areas of specialization in valuation:

1. Fine arts, antiques, and jewelry
2. Real estate
3. Machinery and equipment
4. Financial, including intangibles, business enterprise values, and closely held securities

We disregard the first area because the valuation requirements for corporations rarely include fine arts, antiques, and jewelry. Where needed, one must go to specialists in these areas, such as Sotheby's and Christie's.

With regard to the remaining three categories, an appraisal firm should have in-house expertise in all three. Some firms do not actually have, for example, real estate appraisers on staff, and they subcontract any real estate assignments. In our judgment, coordinating the work of valuation specialists is difficult enough; trying to manage the work effort and quality control of more than one firm presents some real difficulties. It is not that such problems cannot be overcome; it simply is more work and carries some risk to the client.

Our recommendation is to look at the overall experience of an appraisal firm; experience in the client's specific industry should at most be considered a plus, but not a necessity. The author has to acknowledge that in a competitive situation where we have had substantial industry experience, we mention this and tell the prospective client that it is really important. Such comments, however, should be considered puffery and not given undue weight.

These words will undoubtedly come back to haunt the author and his firm at some time in the future, but being totally candid about it, as a prospective client I would rather hire an appraiser with 15 years' experience overall, and no direct experience in my industry, than a three-year veteran whose entire practice has been solely in my industry. No two appraisals are the same. An experienced appraiser builds on his background and utilizes that background in every new situation. It simply is not possible in three years to see the wide variety of assignments those 15 years do provide. There is very little personnel turnover in the valuation profession because the work is so varied and intellectually challenging. You cannot obtain 15 years' experience in three years.

With respect to the professionals who will staff the engagement, every firm will provide resumes or CVs of the individuals who will be assigned. Frankly, it would be difficult for a corporate financial manager to evaluate the resumes of Mr. X from firm A in comparison to Ms. Y from firm B. Nonetheless, valuation firms are required to and do provide such resumes. Our only suggestion is that more overall experience on the part of the individuals proposed to staff the assignment is better than less experience.

In our list of required responses, we stated the valuation firm should provide: "A brief summary of the valuation approach(es) proposed to be utilized by the appraisal firm." What we mean here gets to the heart of the philosophy of the valuation firm in terms of how much work will be performed. Many clients, trying to keep costs down, will request only what we refer to as a desktop appraisal. This means that the appraiser will not see or inspect the assets and will determine the values solely from information supplied by the client. This approach may or may not comply with the Uniform Standards of Professional Appraisal Practice (USPAP) that govern the professional execution by firms that subscribe to the industry-wide standards. Such a desktop valuation will certainly be less expensive.

A different approach to valuation has come to our attention at times, particularly when dealing with the IRS. Some valuation firms will provide only minimum support for their valuation, saying in effect "If the IRS questions this, then we will do the rest of the work." Other firms have a philosophy of doing the work in total the first time. The trouble for the client is in comparing and evaluating quotes from two firms with such diametrically opposite approaches to professional execution. Up front the first firm will have a lower fee, while in total the cost may be twice as high—but only if the IRS challenges that aspect of the firm's tax return. This is why we suggest that clients insist on a clear understanding of what work will be performed and how much support will be available in the working papers.

Given the fact that many, if not most, valuations for financial reporting are being scrutinized by the company's auditors, it is more difficult for any valuation firm to take shortcuts. A good rule of thumb should be if a client receives two or more proposals and one is more than 20%

different, questions should be asked about the proposed scope of work. In other words, if the fee difference is *less than 20%,* it means one firm wants the work more than another; it is willing to operate on lower margins, possibly because it has unbilled staff it wants to put to work on billable engagements.

If the fee quotes are greater than 20% apart, the work effort in most circumstances is *not* comparable. Most valuation firms have the same basic economics in terms of technology, travel expense, staff compensation, rent, and other expense elements. Some firms prefer less work at higher margins, whereas other firms prefer more work at lower margins. Our ±20% differential captures this margin difference. Above or below that, the proposals have to be dealing with different anticipated work effort.

Other than the specific fee quoted, our last recommendation was for the valuation firm to specify in some detail the methodology it proposes to use. Two examples will suffice. If there are multiple locations, say 100 service stations or fast-food restaurants, how many locations will be visited and how will the appraiser value the locations not visited? If it is a valuation for a possible impairment of goodwill, will the appraiser use a Discounted Cash Flow (DCF) analysis of the client's projections, or will the appraiser develop his own projections? Will the appraiser also value the reporting unit on the basis of publicly traded comparable firms, or will he rely solely on the DCF approach. We are not saying that one approach is correct and the other is incorrect. What we are suggesting is that the client should ask this type of question if the proposal does not clearly delineate what the appraiser proposes to do.

Finally, we come to the all-important fee. Some valuation firms will quote a firm all-inclusive fee including out-of-pocket expenses. Others will quote a fee *estimate,* plus out-of-pocket expenses as incurred. Still other firms will say, "here are our billing rates per hour or per day, and we will charge you for whatever time is spent"—in effect a "trust us" approach. We make no recommendations as to which of these fee methods is best; what we do urge is for the client to make a true apples-to-apples comparison. In case of doubt or confusion, any prospective client should feel free to ask for clarification by the valuation firm of its billing policies and, if necessary, ask for a change to put all proposals on a fully equivalent basis.

CONCLUSION

It is up to a company to control the audit process on any FV requirements. This is not to say that companies should try to prevent auditors
from reviewing information prepared by independent valuation consultants. What is necessary is to realize that different appraisers may utilize
different approaches, different methodologies, or different assumptions.
Many review appraisers insist that any valuation be done using *their*
approach, methodology, and assumption. The effect is that the client ends
up paying twice for an answer that does not change.

We recommend in a business combination allocation that the company and its auditor sit down with the appraiser at the start of an
engagement. They should reach agreement, laying out in as much detail
as possible, just *what* will be done, *how* it will be done, and *why* it is
being done that way. This will not preclude the auditor from reviewing
the final determination of values by the independent appraiser. It hopefully will preclude interminable, and costly, disagreements that are totally
non-value-added.

With respect to selecting an appraiser, we lay out several issues that
should be considered by the company, and discuss how prospective
clients should review proposals from one or more valuation specialists.
The choice of an appraiser is just as important, and can have the same
consequences, as the selection of an independent auditor.

Index

A

Accounting Principles Board (APB) 16,
   business combinations, 163
Accounting Research Bulletin (ARB)
   43, 264–266
Accounting rules and principles
   bright lines, 130
   conservatism, 48, 49, 69, 264
   development of and reliance on
     rules, 163, 164
   matching revenue and expenses,
     48–51, 69
   mergers and acquisitions, prior rules,
     4
   and use of FV in financial reporting,
     47, 48
Accounts receivable, 3, 4
   valuation of, 277–281
American Institute of Certified Public
   Accountants (AICPA)
   calculation of IPR&D, 247
   Independence Standards Board (ISB),
     305
   Practice Aid on IPR&D, 247, 248
   steps, 248–261
American Society of Appraisers
   cost approach for assets, 214
   economic obsolescence defined,
     221
   functional obsolescence defined, 217,
     218
Amortization of intangible assets, 161,
   162, 203, 206
   definite life, 6
   goodwill, 9, 20, 21, 119, 120, 141,
     185, 245, 247
   indefinite life, 7, 9

   noncompetition agreements, 141
   tax treatment, 20, 21, 119, 120
Appraisals
   accuracy, 42–45
   assumptions. *See* Assumptions
   desktop, 320
   differing results from different
     appraisers, 35–38, 45, 46
   differing values, 32–35
   evaluating report, 38–42
   origin of, 45, 207
   point estimate versus range of values,
     46, 61
   purpose of, 30–35, 210, 211
   reports. *See* Reports
   uses of valuation information, 45
Appraisers. *See also* Reports
   areas of specialization, 319
   auditors, working with, 311, 312
   confidentiality agreements, 27
   differing results from different
     appraisers, 35–38, 45, 46
   experience, 90–92, 94, 318–320
   fees, 92, 93, 321
   independence, 260
   integrity of, 32, 33, 43, 44
   judgment required, 45, 76, 105, 106,
     189, 190
   Machinery and Equipment
     specialists, 212, 215, 319
   not required, 71
   professional standards, 44
   qualifications and expertise, 308
   Requests for Proposals, obtaining
     and evaluating, 317–321
   role of, 3, 29
   selecting, 90–93, 316, 317